Arrogance

Arrogance as a specific constellation of affect, fantasy, and behavior has received little attention in psychoanalysis. This is striking in light of the enormous amount of literature accumulated on the related phenomenon of narcissism. Rectifying this omission, the book in your hands addresses arrogance from multiple perspectives. Among the vantage points employed are psychoanalysis, evolutionary psychology, cross-cultural anthropology, fiction, as well as clinical work with children and adults. The result is a harmonious gestalt of insight that is bound to enhance the clinician's attunement to the covert anguish of those afflicted with arrogance.

Salman Akhtar, MD, is Professor of Psychiatry at Jefferson Medical College and a Training and Supervising Analyst at the Psychoanalytic Center of Philadelphia.

Ann Smolen, PhD, is a Training and Supervising Analyst at the Psychoanalytic Center of Philadelphia.

Arrogance

Developmental, Cultural, and Clinical Realms

Salman Akhtar and Ann Smolen

Routledge
Taylor & Francis Group

LONDON AND NEW YORK

First published 2018
by Routledge
2 Park Square, Milton Park, Abingdon, Oxon OX14 4RN

and by Routledge
711 Third Avenue, New York, NY 10017

Routledge is an imprint of the Taylor & Francis Group, an informa
business

Chapter 10 has been previously published under the title
"Humility" in the *American Journal of Psychoanalysis* 78: 1–27, 2018.
It is being reprinted here with the editor's and the publisher's
permission.

British Library Cataloguing-in-Publication Data
A catalogue record for this book is available from the British
Library

Library of Congress Cataloging-in-Publication Data
A catalog record has been requested for this book

ISBN: 978-1-78220-666-8 (pbk)
ISBN: 978-0-42942-968-2 (ebk)

Typeset in Times New Roman
by Apex CoVantage, LLC

To
Müge Alkan
&
Ted Hicks
Not only because they lack arrogance . . .

Contents

Acknowledgements

We are deeply grateful to the distinguished colleagues who contributed to this volume. We appreciate their effort, their sacrifice of time, and their patience with our requirements, reminders, and requests for revisions. We are thankful to Dr. Steven Gordon for some important bibliographic assistance, and to Ms. Jan Wright for her skillful help in preparing the manuscript of this book, and to Oliver Rathbone and Kate Pearce for their unerring support of this project throughout various phases of publication.

Salman Akhtar & Ann Smolen

About the Editor and Contributors

Salman Akhtar, MD, is professor of psychiatry at Jefferson Medical College and a training and supervising analyst at the Psychoanalytic Center of Philadelphia. He has served on the editorial boards of the *International Journal of Psychoanalysis*, the *Journal of the American Psychoanalytic Association*, and the *Psychoanalytic Quarterly*. His more than 300 publications include eighty-two books, of which the following eighteen are solo-authored: *Broken Structures* (1992), *Quest for Answers* (1995), *Inner Torment* (1999), *Immigration and Identity* (1999), *New Clinical Realms* (2003), *Objects of Our Desire* (2005), *Regarding Others* (2007), *Turning Points in Dynamic Psychotherapy* (2009), *The Damaged Core* (2009), *Comprehensive Dictionary of Psychoanalysis* (2009), *Immigration and Acculturation* (2011), *Matters of Life and Death* (2011), *The Book of Emotions* (2012), *Psychoanalytic Listening* (2013), *Good Stuff* (2013), *Sources of Suffering* (2014), *No Holds Barred* (2016), and *A Web of Sorrow* (2017). Dr. Akhtar has delivered many prestigious invited lectures including a plenary address at the 2nd International Congress of the International Society for the Study of Personality Disorders in Oslo, Norway (1991), an invited plenary paper at the 2nd International Margaret S. Mahler Symposium in Cologne, Germany (1993), an invited plenary paper at the Rencontre Franco-Americaine de Psychanalyse meeting in Paris, France (1994), a keynote address at the 43rd IPA Congress in Rio de Janeiro, Brazil (2005), the plenary address at the 150th Freud Birthday Celebration sponsored by the Dutch Psychoanalytic Society and the Embassy of Austria in Leiden, Holland (2006), and the inaugural address at the first IPA-Asia Congress in Beijing, China (2010). Dr. Akhtar is the recipient of numerous awards including the American Psychoanalytic Association's Edith Sabshin Award (2000), Columbia University's Robert Liebert Award for Distinguished Contributions to Applied Psychoanalysis (2004), the American Psychiatric Association's Kun Po Soo Award (2004) and Irma Bland Award for being the Outstanding Teacher of Psychiatric Residents in the country (2005). He received the highly prestigious Sigourney Award (2012) for distinguished contributions to psychoanalysis. In 2013, he gave the commencement address at graduation ceremonies of the Smith College School of Social Work in Northampton, MA. Dr. Akhtar's books have been translated in many languages, including German, Italian, Korean, Romanian, Serbian, Spanish, and Turkish. A true Renaissance man, Dr. Akhtar has served as the film review editor for the *International Journal of Psychoanalysis*, and is currently serving as the book review editor for the *International Journal of Applied Psychoanalytic Studies*. He has published nine collections of poetry and serves as a scholar-in-residence at the Inter-Act Theatre Company in Philadelphia.

Kathryn Ann Baselice, MD, graduated from the University of Virginia School of Medicine in 2017. She received a bachelor's degree in psychology from Johns Hopkins University in 2012, where she was elected to the Phi Beta Kappa Honor Society and chosen as the captain of her cross country team. While attending Johns Hopkins University, she interned for the forensic psychiatrist, Dr. Fred Berlin, and worked with sex offenders in Baltimore, Maryland. Between her university education and entering medical school, she worked as a mental health counselor at a program that specialized in patients with developmental disabilities and comorbid psychiatric diagnoses. Her academic interests include evolutionary psychology, postpartum psychosis, the insanity defense, and the broader field of forensic psychiatry. She is currently completing her psychiatry residency at New York University, and plans to pursue a career in academic forensic psychiatry.

Jerome S. Blackman, MD, DFAPA, FIPA, FACPsa is clinical professor of psychiatry at Eastern Virginia Medical School, Norfolk, VA; training and supervising analyst with the Contemporary Freudian Society in Washington, DC; and a past Designated Sexual Abuse Treatment Resource for the State of Louisiana. He has been visiting lecturer at Beijing University, Fu Dan Medical University (Shanghai), and Zhe Jiang Medical School in Hangzhou, China. The Psychiatry Teaching Award at Naval Medical Center, Portsmouth, VA was named in his honor in 1992. He is the author of *101 Defenses: How the Mind Shields Itself* (2003), *Get the Diagnosis Right: Assessment and Treatment Selection for Mental Disorders* (2010), and *The Therapist's Answer Book: Solutions to 101 Tricky Problems in Psychotherapy* (2013). The first of these books has been translated into Romanian, Chinese, and Turkish.

Nilofer Kaul, PhD, is a Delhi-based training analyst. She is also an associate professor of English at Hansraj College in Delhi University, and part of a supervision group of the Delhi Chapter of Psychoanalysis. Her doctorate work was on "Masks and mirrors: configurations of narcissism in women's short stories" (2012). She has since then written on bisexuality – presented at IPSO, Istanbul, 2013; child sexuality – "Afterwords" in *Dark Room* (ed. Pankaj Butalia); on "Separation" (at the Second International Psychoanalytic Conference in Fortis, Delhi); "Myth, Misogyny, Matricide" (ed. Anup Dhar et al., in press); on homosexuality – "Morphology of the Closet" in the *Psychoanalytic Review*, 2015 (ed. Salman Akhtar); on "The Rehearsed Language of Unconscious" (a paper presented at the International conference in Mumbai, 2016), and has written "On Strangeness" (forthcoming in *Div/Review*). She has contributed a chapter to *Regret: Developmental, Cultural, and Clinical Aspects*, edited by Salman Akhtar (Karnac, 2017).

Kathleen Ross, PhD, LCSW, is a faculty member of the Psychoanalytic Center of Philadelphia, where she teaches candidates and serves as chair of the Curriculum Committee of the Adult Psychoanalytic Program, in addition to holding numerous other leadership positions. She is a therapist and supervisor at the Therapy Center of Philadelphia, a nonprofit agency serving women and transgender communities. From 2010–2013, Dr. Ross served as cochair of the highly selective Fellowship Program of the American Psychoanalytic Association. Dr. Ross holds a PhD from Yale University in Spanish language and literature. Prior to becoming a psychoanalyst and clinical social worker, she had a long career in academia, most recently as professor of Spanish at New York University, a position she left in 2009. While at NYU she also served as chair of the Department of Spanish and Portuguese. In her academic life she specialized in the fields of colonial Latin America and literary translation, and as a visiting scholar has taught translation theory and practice at the University of Pennsylvania to graduate students in Romance languages. She has published numerous translations of narrative and poetry from Spanish, including Domingo Faustino Sarmiento's classic *Facundo: Civilization and Barbarism* (University of California Press, 2004), and Jesus Diaz's *The Initials of the Earth* (Duke University Press, 2006). Dr. Ross maintains a private practice of psychotherapy and psychoanalysis in Center City, Philadelphia, PA.

Apurva Shah, MD, is a child and adolescent psychiatrist, currently working at Kaiser Permanente in Lancaster, California. After finishing his medical school in Ahmedabad, India, he moved to New York City where he did his residency and fellowship training at the Albert Einstein College of Medicine. He became a candidate at the New York Psychoanalytic Institute, but left it to move back to India. In Ahmedabad, he started a not-for-profit company, Antarnad, for teaching psychoanalysis and training psychoanalytic psychotherapists. Under his patronage, Antarnad has thrived and he teaches and supervises there on his annual visits and via Skype. Now in Southern California, he is a professional affiliate member and the co-coordinator of the Film and Mind Series at the New Center for Psychoanalysis. In his presentations and publications, he focuses on the intersection of psychoanalysis and culture, often through the analysis of movies.

Dhwani Shah, MD, is a clinical associate faculty member in the Department of Psychiatry at the University of Pennsylvania, School of Medicine and an attending staff psychiatrist at Princeton University's Counseling and Psychological Services. He did his residency in psychiatry at the University of Pennsylvania,

School of Medicine, where he also served as chief resident. Later, he completed a fellowship in treatment of resistant mood disorders at the same institution, and then trained at the Psychoanalytic Center of Philadelphia. He is the recipient of several awards, including the University of Pennsylvania's PENN Pearls Teaching Award for Excellence in Clinical Medical Education, the University of Pennsylvania Residency Education's Psychodynamic Psychotherapy Award, and the Laughlin Merit Award for professional achievement. He has published papers on diverse topics, including neuroscience, mood disorders, and psychotherapy. Dr. Shah has also addressed the experiences of hopelessness, jealousy, and arrogance in the realm of countertransference. He maintains a private practice of psychiatry, psychotherapy, and psychoanalysis in Princeton, NJ.

Susan P. Sherkow, MD is the founder and director of the not-for-profit Sherkow Center for Child Development and Autism Disorder. She is a training and supervising analyst at the Berkshire Psychoanalytic Institute and a supervising analyst and instructor in the Child and Adolescent Division of the New York Psychoanalytic Institute, as well as on the faculties of Mount Sinai College of Medicine and Albert Einstein College of Medicine. Dr. Sherkow's scientific publications have appeared in the *Journal of the American Psychoanalytic Association*, *Psychoanalytic Study of the Child*, and *Psychoanalytic Inquiry* on the topics of autism spectrum disorder, primal scene, intergenerational transmission of eating disorders, the diagnosis of sexual abuse in young children, Watched Play, and psychoanalytic treatment of children under five. She is coauthor of *Autism Spectrum Disorder: Perspectives from Psychoanalysis and Neuroscience* (Jason Aronson, 2014), and has presented and published extensively on the application of psychoanalytic developmental theory to the treatment of children, adolescents, and adults with ASD, including a TEDx Talk on the developmental model of ASD. Dr. Sherkow received the Ritvo Prize from the Yale Child Study Center in 2010 for excellence in the field of child psychoanalysis.

Ann Smolen, PhD, is a training and supervising analyst in child, adolescent, and adult psychoanalysis at the Psychoanalytic Center of Philadelphia. Dr. Smolen has won several; national awards for her clinical work, which she has presented both nationally and internationally. Dr. Smolen is the 2016–2017 recipient of the Helen Meyers Traveling Psychoanalytic Scholar Award. Dr. Smolen has published several articles including 'Boys Only! No Mothers Allowed' published in *The International Journal of Psychoanalysis* and translated into three languages. Dr. Smolen has published several chapters in edited books. In addition, Dr. Smolen is the author of two books; *Mothering Without a Home: Representations of Attachments Behaviors in Homeless Mothers and Children* (Aronson, 2013), and *Six Children: The Spectrum of Child Psychopathology and Its Treatment* (Karnac, 2015). She maintains a private practice in child, adolescent, and adult psychotherapy and psychoanalysis in Ardmore, PA.

J. Anderson Thomson, Jr., MD, is a psychiatrist in Charlottesville, Virginia. He received his BA from Duke University (1970), his MD from the University of Virginia (1974), and did his adult psychiatry training at the University of Virginia (1974–77). His private practice is oriented toward individual psychoanalytic psychotherapy, forensic psychiatry, and medication consultation. He was the assistant director of the Center for the Study of Mind and Human Interaction at the University of Virginia, which involved interdisciplinary intervention and research in large group ethnic and political conflict, primarily in the former Soviet Union. He is a staff psychiatrist for Counseling and Psychological Services at the University of Virginia Student Health Services. He serves on the clinical faculty at the Institute of Law, Psychiatry, and Public Policy at the University of Virginia. He has publications on narcissistic personality disorder, evolutionary theories of depression, antidepressants, criminal behavior, the function of serotonin, post-traumatic stress disorder, religion, suicide terrorism, and the psychology of racism. In 2010, his work with Paul Andrews, "Depression's Upside," on an evolutionary theory of depression, was featured in *Scientific American Mind* and in *The New York Times Magazine*. He coauthored *Facing Bipolar: The Young Adult's Guide to Dealing with Bipolar Disorder* (2010) and authored *Why We Believe in God(s): A Concise Introduction to the Science of Faith* (2011), which has been translated into Spanish, German, Italian, Polish, Turkish, and Urdu. His current research interest is evolutionary psychology and its application to religious belief, well-being, resilience, suicide, the insanity defense, and psychiatric illnesses. Since 2006, he has had the privilege of serving as a trustee of the Richard Dawkins Foundation for Reason and Science.

Introduction

Unlike narcissism, which has received a huge amount of attention from psychoanalysts, the character trait of arrogance has largely been ignored. Perhaps the potentially pejorative connotations of the word discourage a dispassionate discourse on the topic. Lack of clarity about what affects and behaviors are subsumed under the rubric of "arrogance" might also cause intellectual laziness. Countertransference reactions to encountering arrogance in the clinical situation further the attitude of distaste towards thinking about arrogance. To wit, the lack of literature on arrogance might also reflect the unconscious resistance of psychoanalysts to acknowledge and account for vulnerability to arrogance on their own part and on the part of their profession at large.

Our book aims to fill this lacuna in psychoanalytic literature. It is comprised of essays by ten distinguished scholars who address the complex affect of arrogance from diverse theoretical, cultural, and clinical perspectives. The first section of the book is devoted to the evolutionary and developmental substrate of arrogance and to its vicissitudes over the human life span. The second section of the book deals with cultural and cross-cultural aspects of arrogance. The final section addresses the clinical issues pertinent to this realm. Utilizing illustrative clinical vignettes, the contributors to this section elucidate the nuanced relationship of arrogance to aloneness, the problems posed by arrogance in the analyst, and the technical handling of arrogance in adult patients and in working with children and families. The inclusion of a chapter length discussion on the phenomenon exactly opposite to arrogance, namely humility, adds further flux to the discourse and opens up a new realm of clinical attunement and praxis. The result is harmonious gestalt of enhanced understanding of an under-investigated emotion of profound intrapsychic and interpersonal significance:

Prologue

Chapter 1

The realm of arrogance

Salman Akhtar

Nearly two decades ago, some ten or twelve psychoanalysts were having a post-meeting glass of wine and sharing the sort of trivia and gossip that they generally claim to detest. That New York evening, a senior and well-known analyst who had recently attended a paper presentation by me, declared that I was "very arrogant." Unbeknown to him, one of the analysts engaged in this bonhomie was my friend and stood up in defense of me. "What exactly do you mean when you say that Salman is arrogant?" asked my friend of the old man. The latter responded by pointing out the effervescence, theatrical element, poetry, and spontaneity in the manner of my talking and to the fact that I never read from a written text or even refer to notes while delivering a paper. My friend took it all in and then said, "Look, that is his style. Don't you know that he comes from some six to seven generations of great Urdu poets and it is their tradition to recite poetry by heart for hours? And, a bunch of his family is in Bollywood. So it is not surprising that he speaks like a poet and an actor. Please try to look beyond such stylistic matters. See that his papers always contain a thorough review of preexisting literature on the topic and incorporate insights from non-psychoanalytic sources as well. Even in informal conversations, Salman generously acknowledges his peers' contributions and never fails to thank those who mentored, taught, and helped him. That is hardly arrogance, wouldn't you say?"

My purpose in recounting this story is to highlight the complex nature of the phenomenon we call "arrogance." Does it reside, like beauty, in the eye of the beholder? If so, can calling someone "arrogant" serve as a defense against envy and personal feelings of inferiority? Is arrogance a deeply anchored character trait? Is it always discernible via overt behavior or can it be masked by powerful defenses against its expression? Returning to envy for a moment, one can also raise the question whether envy of others gives rise to defensive arrogance in oneself or one's arrogance stirs up reactive envy in others? In an effort to address these and related other issues, I will begin with descriptive features of arrogance and then move on to the psychoanalytic literature on the topic. Following this, I will make some sociocultural comments and elucidate the technical problems posed by arrogance, that of both the patient and the analyst. I will conclude with a few summarizing remarks and by indicating areas that need further scrutiny and investigation.

Definition and manifestations

The word "arrogance" first appeared in the English language around the four-teenth century and is derived from the Latin word *arrogans*. Its dictionary definition refers to "a feeling or impression or superiority manifested in an overbearing manner of presumptuous claims" (Mish, 1998, p. 64). "Arrogant," "arrogantly," and even "arrogate" and "arrogation" are words related to "arro-gance." Synonyms of "arrogance" include "disdain," "haughtiness," "loftiness," "superbity," and "superciliousness." And then there are words related to arro-gance including "conceit" and "smugness." " 'Conceit" does refer to excessive estimation of one's virtue but is used in other senses as well such as being fanci-ful or deploying a strained metaphor (ibid., p. 238). "Smugness" implies undue self-satisfaction but also means being "scrupulously clean, neat, or correct" (ibid., p. 1110). Thus both "conceit" and "smugness" do not exactly replicate "arrogance."

"Arrogance" focuses specifically upon (i) an attitude of superiority that is exag-gerated and undeserved, (ii) a lack of self-questioning, and (iii) a tendency to look down upon others. Arrogance involves making false claims about one's knowl-edge and skills, and, in the process, losing genuine contact with both oneself and others. In essence, arrogance is a mask that misrepresents the subject to both itself and its objects. It is boastful. It has a hard texture that repudiates one's "softer" and more humane sides. It wishes to stab the onlooker with a shining knife of hostility. The following daily life snippets illustrate the operation of arrogance in the interpersonal matrix.

A middle-aged couple is renovating the bathroom attached to their bedroom. All goes well till they have to find a six foot by three foot mirror to hang over the newly installed vanity. They have difficulty finding a suitable mirror of that size. One day, the husband, looking through various catalogues, finds a "floor mirror" that not only fits the size but matches the vanity's color to a tee. He happily shows the ad to his wife, hoping that the next minute they will be on the phone ordering the mirror to be delivered to their home. The wife, however, surprises him by declaring that "floor mirrors" are meant to be kept vertical and cannot be hung horizontally. She adds, "That's why these mirrors are called 'floor mirrors.'" She seems absolutely certain of this. The husband is shocked and, noting her certainty, feels a bit confused. Something does not fit well with him, however. He decides to call the shop that is selling the mirror. He asks the person who responds to the phone call if the mirror they have advertised can be hung horizontally on the wall. The salesperson says, "Of course, it can be hung that way." The husband, while relieved, wants to know more. "Then why are they called 'floor mirrors'?" he asks. The sales-person explains that the designation arose during the Depression era when many people lost their homes and, moving to smaller quarters, realized that the mirrors they had brought from their larger rooms were not suitable for the new, smaller, living quarters. So, they simply stood them up against the walls.

The later serendipitous discovery that women could check their hemlines, their shoes, etc. better in a mirror leaning against the wall fixated the term "floor mirror" in colloquial vocabulary. It had nothing to do with whether they could be hung horizontally or not.

The wife's certainty that "floor mirrors" could not be hung on a wall was thus a manifestation of arrogance. She took her thought, based on little factual knowledge, to be an indisputable truth. Her narcissism was boundless and so was her envy-laden sadism towards her husband. This was a case of arrogance, plain and simple. The same is true of the following claim made by a general practitioner of medicine in a large city of the United States.

Two physicians in their early sixties are talking. They have known each other for many, many years. One is a full-time professor and academician with a distinguished career of research and publications. The other is a wealthy private practitioner with a broad clientele of medically ill patients. Soon the topic of retirement comes up. The professor asks the busy doctor, "How long do you plan to continue working like this? And, if you give up your practice, what would you do?" The practitioner responds with complete equanimity and confidence: "You know, I have thought about it. What I am planning to do is this. After three or four years, I will close my practice and then I will become the chairman of the local medical school's Department of Medicine and lead a quiet, academic life." The professor is shocked and cannot resist objecting, "You can't become the chairman of an academic department just like that! The medical school you are talking about is very prestigious and would want someone with a long academic career behind them." Even this does not satisfy the professor. He adds, "Besides, how do you know that the chairmanship will be open right when you want it?" The private practitioner dismisses all the professor's queries with a shrug of his shoulders and says, "Look, I will give them a couple of million dollars and they will make me the chairman of internal medicine. This is how these things work, you know."

The sad commentary about the financial corruptibility of our institutions implicit here notwithstanding, the smugness of the private practitioner and his disdain for academia (and of his academically devoted friend) speaks of his arrogance. But how and why people become this way and what allows them to make such preposterous claims (e.g., "floor mirrors" cannot be hung horizontally, someone who has never written a paper can become the department chair in a medical school)? To answer such questions, we turn to psychoanalysis.

Psychoanalytic contributions

While "narcissism" has accrued a large body of psychoanalytic writings, the same is not true of "arrogance." The reason for this is unclear though the potentially pejorative connotations of the term might have played some role in such inattention.

What little literature does exist can be divided into four categories: (i) Freud's views, (ii) elaborations and additions by his early followers, (iii) Bion's perspective, and (iv) the contributions of more recent psychoanalysts.

Freud's views

The word "arrogance" appears only eleven times in the entire corpus of Freud's scientific writings (Guttman, Jones, & Parrish, 1980, p. 374). While most of its usages are colloquial, some do deserve mention since they reveal the depth of Freud's thought and the all-encompassing range of his observations. The first comes from his monograph, *Totem and Taboo* (1912–13): "Children show no trace of the arrogance which urges adult civilized men to draw a hard and fast line between their nature and that of other animals" (pp. 126–127). Freud repeated this observation on many subsequent occasions (1916, p. 209; 1917, p. 140; 1939a, p. 100). His use of the expression "other animals" (instead of "animals") in the sentence cited above left little doubt that Freud regarded, in a psychic sense, man to be an animal and to have a profound intrinsic kinship with animals. The significance of this observation becomes evident when we consider that he felt that the process of becoming 'civilized' inherently leaves a significant residue of discontent (1930a) and all psychopathology indicates a threatened breakthrough of "animal nature" via the pleasure principle (1905d, 1915c, 1926d). Moreover, his acknowledgement of the fundamental kinship between man and animals opens up new vistas for understanding the man-animal fusion in art and in the mythological iconography of certain religions. It lays bare the "arrogant" and presumptuous foundations of the Judeo-Christian and Islamic disdain at the animal deities of Hindus, for instance.

Freud also talked about the "arrogance of consciousness" (1910a, p. 39), which often looks upon dreams with contempt, and about the "arrogance of the well-to-do" (1930a, p. 113) which can hurt their less fortunate peers. Ironically, since he was immensely proud of his Jewish heritage, Freud explicitly wondered as to ". . . where did this tiny and powerless nation find the arrogance to declare itself the favorite child of the great Lord?" (1939a, p. 65).

In the clinical context, it comes as a surprise that the word "arrogance" does not appear even once in Freud's paper on narcissism (1914c). The single clinical mention of arrogance, curiously, is found in regards to the patient's attitude about the door between the waiting room and the office proper. Freud (1916–17b) concluded that the patient who leaves this door open as he enters the clinical chamber is implicitly declaring, "Ah, so there's no one here and no one's likely to come while I'm here" (pp. 247–248). Freud went on to say that such a patient is "ill-mannered and deserves an unfriendly reception" (p. 247), and should be asked to go back and close the door. Freud added that such a patient "would behave equally impolitely and disrespectfully if his arrogance was not given a sharp reprimand at the very beginning" (p. 248). The merits of this recommendation and the authoritarian bent of clinical practice that underlies it might be found questionable today but deciphering nonverbal communications of the patient has, over time, become an integral part of psychoanalytic technique.

All in all, Freud's comments on arrogance were mostly colloquial, *en passant*, and non-metapsychological, even though some of them did have the potential for further beneficial elaboration.

Elaborations and additions by his early followers

Like Freud, his early followers said little about arrogance. Some scattered remarks do exist, however. The following are perhaps the most pertinent ones.

- Reich (1933) portrayed "phallic-narcissistic character" as energetic, promiscuous, and "reacting to any offense to his vanity by arrogance, cold disdain, marked ill-humor, or down-right aggression" (p. 218).
- Fairbairn (1940) regarded three characteristics to be of central significance to the schizoid group of individuals: "(1) an attitude of omnipotence, (2) an attitude of isolation and detachment, and (3) a preoccupation with inner reality" (p. 6). He emphasized that often these attitudes were marked by defenses. "Thus the attitude of omnipotence may be conscious or unconscious in any degree. It may also be localized within certain spheres of operation. It may be over-compensated and concealed under a superficial attitude of inferiority of humility" (pp. 6–7). While the word "arrogance" does not appear here, it is quite likely that Fairbairn's "omnipotence" represents what I am calling "arrogance" in this contribution; his contrasting "omnipotence" with "humility" lends support to such an assertion.
- Fenichel (1945) noted that "[M]any persons who manifest more or less arrogant behavior are actually fighting against becoming aware of their deep inferiority feelings; other persons who despise themselves for their insignificance are covering up for a deep-seated arrogant attitude" (p. 473).
- Horney (1947) declared that emotional maturity has two essential ingredients: "the capacity to see others and situations outside ourselves in their stark reality *and* the capacity to assume full responsibility for ourselves. Neurosis, in contrast, makes us self-absorbed and our perceptions misty" (p. 85, italics in the original). She added that "[O]n top of our insecurity we build a lofty edifice of arrogance which makes us believe that we are the only ones to be fair, intelligent, to understand and solve absolutely everything. In order to protect the vulnerable pride which goes with such arrogance, we see the mote in another's eyes and fail to see the beam in ours" (p. 85).
- Melanie Klein (1963) did not employ the word "arrogance" and opted for the Greek *hubris*. This attitude, according to her, subsumed "the wish to triumph over everybody else, hate, the wish to destroy others, to humiliate them, and the pleasure in their destruction because they have been envied" (p. 280). It arose from a frustrating infancy and was at first directed at the mother. With the unfolding of oedipal and latency phases, and their attendant competitiveness and ambition, father and siblings also become the target of *hubris*. The unconscious guilt that accompanied these developments was usually covered

up by denial. Later on, adult life successes "confirmed" the right to hubris and led to "a hardening and deterioration of character" (p. 282).

A common theme among these observations is their attention towards the defensive function of arrogance. All the analysts cited above regard arrogance as shielding the individual against psychic vulnerability and fragile self-esteem. This gives rise to the question whether arrogance is defensive only in its adult-life function or in its very origin as well. Two models of ontogenesis exist. One is advocated by Kohut (1971) who sees a heightened need for acclaim as a fixation on a preexisting, childhood grandiose self that was not renounced because it was not adequately mirrored by parents. The other is favoured by Kernberg (1975) who sees pathological narcissism as an abhorrent development in the face of severe and chronic frustrations with important love objects of childhood. Kohut's model necessitates viewing a patient's arrogance as an exaggeration of a developmental *need* whereas Kernberg's model dictates regarding a patient's arrogance as an aggressive wish that seeks to undo inferiority and envy. These contemporary perspectives contain unmistakable echoes of the early Freud-Ferenczi controversy, and somewhat later, Balint-Klein schism (for details, see Akhtar, 1988, 2002; Haynal, 1988).

Kohut's and Kernberg's models do not exhaust the possible pathogenic pathways to the character trait of arrogance, however. Sustained over-indulgence and undue pampering of the child can also deplete his or her motivation to advance towards reciprocity, responsibility, and even reality itself. Profound seduction of the child during the oedipal phase two can preclude the "forward projection of narcissism" (Chasseguet-Smirgel, 1984, p. 74)[1] necessary for feeling humble, idealizing elders, and entering into the temporal order of life. An arrogant and pervasive character then evolves which, at its deepest core, harbors feelings of inauthenticity and unconscious guilt.

Bion's perspective

Bion (1958) stated that a triad of "curiosity, arrogance, and stupidity" is often evident in the associations of some patients. Most of the time it appears in a scattered fashion (i.e., with its three elements separated from each other). Bion suggested that when this triad makes its appearance, the analyst must take it as evidence that he is dealing with a "psychological disaster" (p. 144). He declared that "Where life instincts predominate, pride becomes self-respect, where death instincts predominate, pride becomes arrogance" (p. 144). Using the Oedipus myth to illustrate his ideas, Bion stated that the main problem in this Greek tragedy does not involve incestuous sexuality but the relentless and arrogant (and ultimately, stupid)

---

1   Often such children are cocky, insolent, and disrespectful of generational boundaries. This malady should not be confused with the "pretend-mode" (Target & Fonagy, 1996) playful grandiosity of some latency-age children. I am reminded here of eight-year-old John Miller, the son of a junior colleague, who merrily declared to his family: "I am awesome!"

curiosity that led the prince to lay bare his own crime. In the same vein, the patient displaying this triad – curiosity, arrogance, and stupidity – shows undue inquisitiveness towards the analyst while arrogantly considering the analyst stupid and equally arrogantly disregarding the potentially harmful impact of such curiosity upon his analysis. I will return to this point in the technical section of this contribution. Here, it will suffice to note that Bion regarded the genesis of this triad to be in his patient's disastrous relationship with an early object (most likely the mother) who rejected and denied his infantile use of projective identification as communication. This led to the establishment of a primitive injunction in the mind against links with objects (see also Bion, 1959) and a bifurcation of curiosity into its heightened and exaggerated form on the one hand and its arrogant and stupid misuse on the other.

The work of more recent analysts

Four contributors stand out here: Cushman (2005), Kernberg (2007), Weber (2006), and Zimmer (2013). I will only refer to the descriptive, ontogenetic, and philosophical aspects of their work in this subsection and return to its technical implications later. Cushman (2005) enters the psychoanalytic discourse on arrogance from a novel perspective. He takes Martin Heidegger's (1953a, 1953b, 1954) ontological hermeneutics and Michel Foucault's (1985, 1986) postmodernism as a starting point and asserts the former's perspective suffers from "monocultural arrogance" (p. 399) and the latter's perspective from extreme relativism. Cushman suggests that we, as contemporary psychotherapists, need to ground our clinical practices in a historicity that lacks Heidegger's solipsism and Foucault's avoidance of the moral. He advocates that therapists avoid both "the monologic rigidity of the right" (p. 415) and "the left's moral phobia and unquestioning valorization of powerlessness" (p. 415), and that they cultivate respect for the other while being mindful of the sociopolitical impact of their praxis.

Weber (2006) represents the burgeoning consilience of Buddhism with psychoanalysis (Coltart, 1996; Epstein, 1995; Hoffer, 2015; Rubin, 2005). She sees arrogance as an unfortunate, though common, outcome of the doubt that we – all of us – feel in our encounter with life. Weber sees both self-doubt and arrogance as states of mind that result from emotional attachment. It is by letting go of such "self-cherishing" (p. 218) and surrendering to the life force itself that one overcomes the anguish of doubt and the euphoria of arrogance. Weber recommends two pathways to accomplish this: (i) compassionate motivation, that is, seeking betterment not only for oneself but for the sake of all sentient beings, including animals and plants, and (ii) cultivation of humility which connects the self to others and the world-at-large.

Distinct from Weber's charitable vision is Kernberg's (1975, 1984, 1992, 2007) delineation of arrogance associated with pathological narcissism.[2] According

---

2 Individuals with paranoid personality disorder also manifest arrogance (Akhtar, 1990; Shapiro, 1965) and might do so with even greater ferocity than those diagnosed with narcissistic personality

to him, such patients manifest excessive self-centeredness, avoidance of realities that challenge their inflated self-image, inordinate envy, greed, exploitative behavior towards others, remarkable lack of empathy, an underlying self-state of boredom and emptiness which propels them to seek excitement via sexual promiscuity or substance abuse. The symptom of "pervasive arrogance." (Kernberg, 2007, p. 515):

> . . . may dominate in patients who, while recognizing that they have significant difficulties or symptoms, obtain unconscious secondary gain of illness by demonstrating the incompetence of the mental health professions and their inability to alleviate such symptoms. They become super-experts in the field of their suffering, diligently research the internet, check out therapists for their background and orientation, compare their merits and shortcomings, and present themselves for treatment "to give the therapist a chance," but consistently obtain an unconscious degree of satisfaction in defeating the helping professions. The pervasive arrogance may be rationalized by the patient in terms of cultural or ideological features, as when a female patient rejects all male therapists because "they do not understand women," while berating her female therapist for being submissive to men's rules, including those governing the therapeutic relationship.
>
> (pp. 515, 516)

Finally, we have Zimmer's (2013) paper titled, "Arrogance and surprise in the psychoanalytic process." Zimmer distinguishes the "hubristic arrogance" described by Bion (1958) from what he terms "contemptuous arrogance." The former centers upon inflation of self and the latter upon devaluation of others. Both are ways of dealing with the pain of not knowing, the former through omniscience and the later through idealization of the quest for knowledge. According to Zimmer, both forms of arrogance are discernible in the clinical situation where assumption of superior knowledge on the part of one member of the dyad is accompanied by projection of ignorance upon the other.

Synthesis

Putting together the four sets of psychoanalytic observations mentioned above leads to the following conclusions: (i) arrogance has been addressed under this very designation by some contributors (Freud, 1910a, 1912–13; Horney, 1947; Reich, 1933) and under other labels such as "omnipotence" (Fairbairn, 1940), "hubris" (Klein, 1963), and "pathological narcissism" (Kernberg, 1975, 2007) by others; (ii) arrogance has been noted to exist on an overt level as disdain,

---

disorder. However, owing to the rarity with which paranoid persons seek help, the literature on their arrogance is sparse.

overconfidence, and haughtiness (Kernberg, 1975; Reich, 1933), and on a covert level as defensive modesty and pseudo-humility (Fenichel, 1945); (iii) arrogance is seen as having defensive functions against feelings of inferiority and envy (Fenichel, 1945; Klein, 1963) as well as discharge functions of sadism and turning tables on envied others by causing them envy of one's supremely confident attitude (Kernberg, 2007; Klein, 1963); (iv) arrogance distorts both the self-experience (by repudiating its shame-laden aspects) and object relationships (by forceful projection of disowned parts of self into them); (v) arrogance usually arises from a background of un-mirrored childhood "grandiosity" (Kohut, 1971) and severe "oral frustrations" (Fairbairn, 1940; Kernberg, 1975; Klein, 1963) but can also be the consequence of undue indulgence and seduction leading to a sense of oedipal triumph (Chasseguet-Smirgel, 1984), and, finally (vi) arrogance, like any other psychic phenomenon, is subject to the principle of "over-determination" (Freud, 1895d) and "multiple function" (Waelder, 1936). A summary of this sort should prepare clinicians to discern, experience, interpret, and reconstruct the patient's arrogance from many different vantage points during the course of an analysis. Before delving into such "technical" matters, however, allow me to take a brief foray into the sociocultural dimensions of the topic at hand.

Sociocultural aspects

Since man is a "biopsychosocial" animal, it is hardly conceivable that his character traits would not have contributions from all three sources: constitutional, hard-wired proclivities; formative interactions with early caretakers; and, the values upheld or decried by the sociocultural surround he grows up in. So far in this contribution, I have addressed only the psychological variables in the genesis and manifestations of arrogance. About the constitutional givens, we know little though infants do vary, from early on, in the extent of their self-confidence and self-assertion (Thomas & Chess, 1984) and as early as 1908c, Freud commented upon the child who "in consequence of his unyielding constitution, can not fall in with suppression of instincts" (p. 187). While the mere existence of overconfidence is not sufficient for the later development of "arrogance," it may indeed provide the fertile soil for the pathogenic seed of defensive ego-inflation to blossom. Such a constitutional tendency is then "shaped" by severe childhood frustrations in the direction of arrogance.

This brings us to the third of the "biopsychosocial" triad, the sociocultural variable in the genesis, manifestation, and sustenance of arrogance. This realm is large and its investigation warrants a major anthropological undertaking. Lacking the needed expertise, I restrict myself to three basic questions here: (i) Is the contemporary culture more prone to arrogance than the eras gone by? (ii) Is the West more prone to arrogance than the East?, and, (iii) Is the possession of "specialness" (e.g., beauty, talent, money, power) more conducive to developing arrogance? Allow me now to take up one of these questions at a time.

Does contemporary culture fuel arrogance?

The response one frequently encounters to this question is a resounding "Yes!" Of course, one needs to discount the inevitable modicum of nostalgia for a bygone – and, often idealized – era in all such proclamations. Nonetheless, there are important arguments to ponder here. Ranging from the weighty critique of modernity by the American historian, Christopher Lasch (1979) through the exaltation of collective wisdom by the organizational consultant Alan Briskin (2009) to the lament of today's cultural decline by the Nobel laureate, Mario Vargas Llosa (2015), one repeatedly comes across the assertion that something has changed, that finer values have been eclipsed by rampant self-promotion, and that we now live in a "culture devastated by frivolity" (Llosa, 2015, p. 18). The pervasive decline of religion has unmoored the masses from their trustworthy and often sole guide for an ethical conscience and humility. The sidelining of an intellectual elite has led to vulgarization of literature and smugness among those who even care to read books these days. And, the marginalization of the future in a world devoid of hope (most people believe nowadays that their parents had a better world and that their children will inherit a worse world) has the effect of sucking people into the regressive vortex of hedonism. Even the near-disappearance of dress codes has impeded the transition from a shallow and childish casualness in attire to a psychosocial stature-appropriate way of dressing. Working in unison, all these variables preclude respect for the passage of time, damage the institutions of filial and intellectual hierarchy, and weaken the desire to cooperate with fellow human beings. Instead, they promote hurry, self-centeredness, ambition, greed, and arrogance.

Are Westerners more prone to arrogance than the people of the East?

Stereotypical views of Eastern people would have us believe that they are far more modest and humble than ordinary Americans who are self-assured and even a bit arrogant. But what is the data to support such representations? Psychoanalysis is averse to large-group generalizations but a few analysts do offer some pertinent observations. For instance, Roland (1988, 2011), who has worked with Indian and Japanese patients in their respective countries as well as in the United States, has noted these individuals' "familial self," a psychic structure with less firmness of self-boundaries than are common in the West. Such self remains forever in close emotional contact with relatives (e.g., parents, siblings)[3] and retains a constant

---

3 In Japan, the need for *amae* (emotional refueling experience – see Doi, 1962; Freeman, 1997) extends to departed parents and grandparents. They continue to be experienced as being alive and

need for their approval. As a result, self-effacement, interdependence, and humility acquire a greater adaptive value than self-assertion, autonomy, and pride.

My own clinical and social experience prompts me to assert that Indians continue to be far more respectful and humble towards their elders (e.g., parents, teachers) than do Americans in general. This is especially evident in the realm of pedagogy with the mentor-apprentice model being explicitly hierarchical in India and agreeably egalitarian in the United States (Akhtar, 2011). The resulting impact of this upon the humility-arrogance dialectic is that in the West, the student begins as "arrogant" and over time evolves into a "humble" teacher whereas in the East, the student starts as "humble" and over time evolves into an "arrogant" teacher (see Chapter 11 for more details on this). This opens up the possibility that the East-West difference resides not so much in the actual prevalence of arrogance as in its chronological consolidation (youth in the West, older age in the East) and its psycho-structural location (ego in the West, superego in the East). Vis-à-vis the latter point, my earlier observation (Akhtar, 1992, p. 63) that Green's (1986) "moral narcissism" might be a more frequent presentation of narcissistic personality in Eastern cultures is quite pertinent. Additional light on such cross-cultural differences between the prevalence of humility and arrogance is shed by empirical studies of "national culture," social behavior, and, to wit, body postures.

In a series of studies spanning four decades and including subjects from more than seventy countries, the esteemed Dutch sociologist, Geert Hofstede (Hofstede, 1984, 2001; Hofstede & Hofstede, 2010) investigated the patterns of modal national character. They used six dimensions: power distance, individualism, masculinity vs. femininity, uncertainty avoidance, long-term orientation, and indulgence. Sifting through this enormous and multivariate data is no easy task. Suffice it to say that two of their findings pertain to our discussion of arrogance: (i) people in societies with high degree of power distance (e.g., Russia) accept a hierarchical order; authority figures there lean towards arrogance and subordinates manifest humility; in societies with lesser power distance (e.g., USA), authorities and subordinates have more egalitarian exchanges; (ii) societies with greater "masculinity" scores breed assertiveness, self-centeredness, heroism, and a "tough" business approach, whereas societies with greater "femininity" scores breed cooperation, sympathy for the weak, modesty, and a "tender" business approach.

Somewhat greater clarity is offered by a general population survey of Thai and American citizens by Fieg and Mortlock (1989). These researchers found that while Thais, like their American counterparts, uphold self-reliance, their individualism exists within an ethos of group harmony in which the type of aggressive self-assertion typical of American individualism would not be accepted. Fascinatingly, in this study, both Thais and Americans derided the traits of pomposity

---

one continues to "interact" with them periodically. "There is no stark, impenetrable wall to divide the living from the dead. The dead still linger, offering comfort and counsel to the living" (Kristof, 1996, p. 1).

and arrogance and yet there were variations in their leanings towards the poles of humility and overconfidence. Thai students had higher scores for humility and American students for overconfidence.

A third study comes from the perspective of anthropological posturology. Kudoh and Matsumoto (1985), studying the ways in which Japanese and American college students sit, stand, walk, and interact with others, found that the former's physicality often bears the stamp of a vertical (hierarchical, respectful) socialization, whereas the latter's physicality expresses a horizontal (lateral, collegial) socialization. The extrapolation of this finding to the modesty-assertion and humility-arrogance polarities is tempting but requires a little too much of a heuristic leap. However, when pooled with all other data provided above, the study adds weight to the East-West differential in prevalence of humility and arrogance.

What if one is truly special?

Mirza Asad-Ullah Khan Ghalib (1797–1869), commonly known as only Ghalib, and, according to the Oxford University scholar, Ralph Russell, "one of the greatest poets South Asia has ever produced" (2000, p. 8), once wrote:

> *Baazecha-e-atfal hai duniya mere aagey*
> *Hota hai shub-o-roz tamasha mere aagey.* (1841, p. 112)
> [This world is but a kindergarten that I behold
> And continually in front of me, a child's play does unfold.][4]

And, the eminent American poet, Walt Whitman (1819–1892) merrily declared: "I am vast/ I contain multitudes" (1855, p. 4). Most of us shrug off a poet's self-congratulatory foray with an amused chuckle.[5] But what is the basis of our charitable stance? Could it be that great poets – and creative artists in general – belong to the category of individuals who "compel our interest by the narcissistic consistency with which they manage to keep away from their ego anything that would diminish it?" (Freud, 1914c, p. 89). Could the fascinating effect of such narcissism (Olden, 1941) be due to the fact that it offers us vicarious indulgence in the infantile omnipotence that lurks in the basements of our own psyches? Equally plausible is the explanation that witnessing outstanding talent (regardless

---

4 My amateurish translation does not do justice to the sonorous majesty of Ghalib's verse. The fact is that poetry does not travel well across languages and its translation, even in experienced hands, always leaves a residue of failed communication. This is because poetry deploys words not only for their denotive value but also for their connotative significance, kindling potential, and prosodic qualities.

5 Having grown up as a child and adolescent with many great poets of my language, I have all sorts of memories of individuals whose arrogance often crossed over from the realm of verse to the realm of actual behavior. Firaq Gorakhpuri (1896–1982) was the most impressive example of such interpersonal excess.

of whether it is in art, science, or athletics) mobilizes humility and thus permits a forgiving attitude towards the great one's arrogance.

But must an individual who possesses great talent become arrogant? Is he or she entitled to self-exaltation? And, the same question can be raised about the stunningly beautiful, the majestically powerful, and the astoundingly wealthy. Does the popular aphorism that power corrupts and absolute power corrupts absolutely apply to all such situations? Perhaps. However, a quick recovery from succumbing to the dictum's seductive influence occurs with the recall of men and women of great achievement and success who forever remained humble. Numerous examples can be given but I will restrict myself to the following: Rumi (1207–1273), Emily Dickinson (1830–1886), Gandhi (1869–1948), Helen Keller (1880–1968), Mother Teresa (1910–1997), Charlie Parker (1920–1955), Jimmy Carter (1924–present), Martin Luther King, Jr. (1929–1968), Neil Armstrong (1930–2012), Warren Buffet (1930–present), Dalai Lama (1935–present), and Pope Francis (1936–present). Admittedly, random and subject to my biases, this list reflects a wide band of psychosocial praxis: politics, poetry, spirituality, space travel, resilience, finance, and music. This goes to show that success, achievement, wealth, and power do not necessarily translate into arrogance. Closer to home, in the United States, the sharply different locations along the humility-arrogance spectrum of ex-Presidents Jimmy Carter and George W. Bush and of wealthy businessmen Warren Buffet and Donald Trump give further testimony to the mutual independence of power and arrogance. This very fact that given the "opportunity" or "luck," some people become arrogant and others humble brings us full circle back to the etiologic role played by individual psychological backgrounds in which each personality gets moulded. We re-enter the psychodynamic and clinical realm.

Technical implications

It is well known that arrogance can seep into the affective matrix of the clinical dyad. However, so far, the focus of the clinical literature on this topic has been on the patient's arrogance. Little attention has been paid to the analyst's arrogance and its deleterious impact upon the clinical process. In an attempt to rectify this error, I will divide my comments upon the technical handling of arrogance into separate sections on analyst's arrogance and patient's arrogance.

Analyst's arrogance

To begin with, we must acknowledge that the field of psychoanalysis has displayed some arrogance from its very inception. This has manifested in (i) the assumption that its phallocentric and Eurocentric conceptualization of personality development was universally valid, (ii) the disdain of "culturalists" like Karen Horney, Erich Fromm, and Herbert Marcuse, (iii) the creation of a solipsistic vocabulary, (iv) the imposition of Freudian metapsychology upon other disciplines in the form of "psychoanalytic anthropology" (Akhtar, 2013a), (v) the denial of "colonial" and "post-colonial" transferences (Akhtar, 2011) in the analyses of patients from erstwhile colonized nations, and (vi) the fossilized import of technical principles evolved in early twentieth-century Vienna to the clinical situation faced over a hundred years later in markedly different cultural settings.

The belief many psychoanalysts held that analysis was the "best treatment" for all emotional difficulties, that it could cure psychoses and addictions, and that other mental health professionals were somehow "beneath" them also revealed the arrogance endemic to the psychoanalytic profession. Its isolationist stance was also evident in the fact that a very small ethnic minority, namely Jews, constituted the overwhelming majority of this profession's membership (at least in the United States) and that one could come across declarations such as "Much analytic theory may have been built on Jewish cultural inner beliefs and psychoanalysis lends itself particularly to the Jewish patient" (Schechter, 1997, p. 193). Moreover, few analytic papers cited works of general psychology, sociology, or heaven forbid, Eastern philosophy or literature; this gave still more testimony to the discipline's conceptual arrogance.

Fortunately things are changing now. "Psychoanalytic anthropology" is giving way to an "anthropological psychoanalysis" (for details, see Akhtar, 2013a). The language of psychoanalysis is losing its exalted and magical aura. Diversity of thought is allowed to a greater extent than before. More Christians, Hindus, Muslims, Sikhs, and Parsis are entering the profession and meaningful exchange is occurring with our Far Eastern colleagues in China, Japan, and South Korea. Such advances are having the salutary impact of thawing the icy arrogance of early psychoanalysis. There were always exceptional individuals and exceptional perspectives even from the very inception of analysis but now one notices a renewed fervor of empathy with others, greater tolerance of conceptual diversity, and much more openness to accommodate insights from other disciplines such as neurophysiology, large group psychology, etc.

The legacy of arrogance nonetheless raises its ugly head in the form of doctrinaire allegiance to a particular theoretical "school" which, in turn, is compounded by idiosyncratic factors in the analyst's character and phase-specific (e.g., very experienced, renowned, aging analysts) exacerbations of narcissism. Regardless of its etiology, arrogance in the analyst can have a devastating impact on his clinical work. This can take myriad forms but the following are it most commonly encountered manifestations.

- Arrogance in the analyst, evidenced by the conviction that *everything* is psychically determined, can make him overlook random and chance occurrences which, at times, regulate patients' affects and utterances. Under such circumstances, analytic work turns paranoid, magical, and un-anchored in reality (Werman, 1979).
- Arrogance in the analyst, manifesting as a belief that one particular theoretical model (e.g., Freudian, Kleinian, Winnicottian, relationalist) should always

guide his listening, can provide him with a prepackaged and formulaic understanding. This robs him of the grasp of diverse, nuanced, and contradictory
aspects of the patient's communication (Akhtar, 2013b; Hedges, 1983). Rigid
commitment to a theory can make the analyst deaf.

- Arrogance in the analyst also has a harmful effect upon the development
  and consolidation of a "therapeutic alliance" (Zetzel, 1956), also known
  as "working alliance" (Greenson, 1965) and "helping alliance" (Thoma &
  Kachele, 1994). If the analyst makes pronouncements and declarations, the
  patient feels deprived of his desire and capacity to collaborate. The risk of
  false compliance on the part of the patient is magnified in such situations.
- Arrogance in the analyst can make him misconstrue a patient's realistic
  annoyance as a manifestation of negative transference. This, in turn, can preclude his offering an apology to the patient when it is truly needed (see Goldberg, 1987, for details on this matter).
- Arrogance in the analyst can lead him to explicitly or implicitly encourage
  the patient to keep what is transpiring between them secret from others. Such
  "hyperconfidentiality" (Celenza, 2007), often precedes and/or accompanies
  boundary violations on the analyst's part.
- Arrogance in the analyst can inhibit his capacity to seek supervisory input
  and/or peer consultation and thus deprive him of the opportunity to resolve
  the puzzlements and countertransference blocks in handling difficult cases.

The foregoing points make it abundantly clear that the analyst's arrogance can
play havoc in the clinical situation and might lead to serious boundary violations.
Consultation with colleagues and return to personal treatment constitute helpful
measures in such circumstances.

Patient's arrogance

The appearance of the patient's arrogance in the clinical situation, either as a generalized character trait or as a specific form of transference, has been noted long
before the publication of Bion's 1958 seminal paper on the topic and its current
rediscovery by North American analysts (e.g., Zimmer, 2013). As early as 1945,
Ivimey commented upon "the problem of arrogance as transference" (p. 10). She
observed that such arrogance was often associated with dishonesty and sadism.
The triad vitiates the true purpose of the patient's communications and seeks to
corrupt the essentially ethical nature of psychoanalytic treatment. Ivimey emphasized that the patient's false claims about his faculties and status, and his dishonesty and cheating must be actively drawn into focus. She acknowledged that the
analyst's efforts are bound to meet with severe resistance at such times. According
to her,

> Immorality in the broader sense, as exemplified by arrogance, intellectual
> and spiritual cheating, lying stealing, [and] cruelty, is a matter about which

we have enormous sensitiveness and shame, compared to the feeling we have about inhibitions and other disorders in sex life. Where it is a predominating tendency, or a strong and conspicuous part of the character, we find frequently terrific conflict, enormously strong defences, and formidable resistances.

(p.11)

Ivimey recommended that the analyst working with such patients has to avoid the extremes of strict neutrality and interpretive overactivity while retaining "the capacity to move about freely, psychologically speaking, in his relationship with the patient."

(p. 13)

Another important early contribution was that of Rappaport (1956) who noted that there is a kind of patient who seeks to reverse the analytic situation: "Instead of trying to change for the sake of the analyst, he expects the analyst to change out of love for the patient" (p. 516). Such a patient tries to control and enslave the analyst. Rappaport went on to state that:

Patients who in childhood sensed that they were expected to accomplish tasks not for their own benefit but for the narcissistic gains of a parent, will in treatment also act as if their cooperation would serve not their own needs, but the needs of the therapist. They will display an arrogant behavior based on the megalomanic delusion that the analyst ought to be grateful. They will persist in teasing him with only a trickle of free associations or with regular silent intervals between each communication, and other so-called habits of a negativistic character. Such a patient must not gain the impression that he is able to frustrate the analyst. He must be told that the hour is his and that he can do whatever he wants with it, but that he will not profit from his antagonistic attitude though he will survive it and, – certainly, – the analyst will too. The analyst must not react with anger to the patient's provocative behavior. Should the analyst become exasperated he will lose self-control and dignity. He thus allows the patient to feel that he has the power to make the parent angry and to triumph over him. The analyst must not give in to the patient's desire to provoke him to repeat interpretations in stronger and stronger form, but must completely disregard it. The only way to continue the analysis and still avoid giving the patient erotic gratification is by scarcity of interpretations.

(pp. 525–526)

Rappaport cautioned against therapeutic zeal and interpretive overactivity with such patients and felt that inclinations of this sort arise from the retaliatory increase in the analyst's narcissism.

The next important contribution was that of Bion (1958). Since I have already highlighted the descriptive aspects of his paper on arrogance, only the technical aspects of it need elaboration here. Bion emphasized that curiosity accompanies arrogance and stupidity, ". . . the very act of analysing the patient makes the patient an accessory in precipitating regression and turning the analysis into a piece of acting out" (p. 144). What is to be done then? Bion suggests that the analyst has to grasp the fact that the arrogant patient is desperately trying to communicate via projective identification, a developmental necessity of which he was deprived during childhood. Analytic insistence on verbal communication is therefore felt as an assault by the patient. Talking of his own work with such a patient, Bion said that once he became aware of the patient's preferred (and needed) mode of communication, there emerged in his mind:

> . . . a variety of procedures which were felt to ensure emotionally rewarding experiences such as, to mention two, the ability to put bad feelings in me and leave them there long enough for them to be modified by their sojourn in my psyche, and the ability to put good parts of himself into me, thereby feeling that he was dealing with an ideal object as a result. Associated with these experiences was a sense of being in contact with me, which I am inclined to believe is a primitive form of communication that provides a foundation on which, ultimately, verbal communication depends.
>
> (p. 146)

Echoes of these early contributions can be heard in recent writings on handling arrogant patients. Zimmer (2013) extends Bion's (1958) triad of arrogance, stupidity, and curiosity by adding a fourth element to it: surprise. He notes that insights gained from analytic work can alter the patient's adaptive strategies and affect transference, causing surprise to the analyst. And, the analyst's deepening contact with the patient's inner world might result in his making newer interpretations, causing surprise to the patient. At such moments, the risk of either or both members of the clinical dyad retreating into "arrogant self-satisfaction [and] ensconcing him- or herself in an internal relationship with what is known" (p. 393) is great and must be avoided.

Kernberg (2007) advocates a tactful confrontation and systematic analysis of the defensive function on analysis in the transference. Unlike others writing on this topic, he suggests that the analyst should warn the patient at the very outset that, given his emotional disposition, there is a risk that the treatment will end prematurely due to the devaluation of the therapist and his techniques.

> Typically, the patient fears, by projective identification, that the therapist has a depreciatory disposition toward the patient, and that therefore, if the patient's superiority is challenged or destroyed, he will be subjected to humiliating devaluation by the therapist. Because the unconscious identification of the patient with a grandiose parental object is often at the bottom of this characterological disposition (and an important component of the pathological grandiose self), it is very helpful, from early on, to interpret this identification whenever possible. This identification with a grandiose and sadistic

object seems on the surface to bolster the patient's self-esteem by protecting his sense of superiority and grandiosity; at bottom, however, the patient is submitting to an internalized object that stands against any real involvement in a relationship that might be helpful, an object profoundly hostile to the dependent and true relational needs of the patient.

(p. 518)

Kernberg seems well aware that, in some patients, arrogance is hidden under a superficial cloak of masochism. The temptation to "reinforce the positive and avoid the negative transference" (Klein, 1957, p. 225), to adopt "a supportive attitude in an effort to reassure the patient that he is not so bad" (Kernberg, 2007, p. 519), and to retaliate with countertransference sarcasm is great with such patients. All this needs to be avoided. And, even though the risk of a "negative therapeutic reaction" (Freud, 1923b), looms large, consistent and firm interpretation of the patient's "arrogant masochism" is the only sensible path to take. Some leeway for oscillating between affirmative and interpretive intervention (Killingmo, 1989) should, however, be retained since the patient's suffering, even if self-induced and harboring sadistic aims, is genuine.

Two further points of technique deserve mention. The *first point* pertains to the analyst's allowing himself the possibility to regard the patient's arrogance as a sign of hope. Here keeping Winnicott's (1956) "antisocial tendency" and Casement's (1991) "unconscious hope" papers in mind should prove to be of help to the analyst. Essentially, both discourses point out that outrageousness (including arrogance) is the patient's way of seeking redress for an early emotional deprivation.[6] The *second point* pertains to the fact that arrogance as a clinical, transactional phenomenon is not restricted to "sicker," narcissistic patients. In subtler forms, defensive arrogance can also be encountered while working with healthier patients. Many such patients received little interest from their parents and some were sadistically mocked by their older siblings, causing them to withdraw inwards and tightly guard their weakened authenticity. They do not like surprises in the clinical situation, respond to the analyst's intervention with the conditional "yes, but" response, and do a lot of "self-analysis" outside and during the clinical hours. Joseph's (1988) observations and technical recommendations are perhaps our best guide under such circumstances.

The patient talks in an adult way, but relates to the analyst only as an equal or near-equal disciple. Sometimes he relates more as a slightly superior ally who tries to help the analyst in his work, with suggestions or minor corrections to personal history. If one observes carefully one begins to feel that one is talking to this ally *about* a patient – but never talking *to* the patient. The "patient" part of the patient seems to remain split-off and it is this part which

6 Weber's (2006) technical stance, though more implicit than explicated in her paper, leans in this direction.

seems more immediately to need help, to be more infant-like, more dependent and vulnerable.

(pp. 76–77)

Joseph suggests that the analyst should remain mindful of this split, clarify the activities of the two parts of the patient, point out the acting out of the "perverse" adult part of the patient, and interpret the fact that the patient has deposited his frightened and help-seeking parts in the analyst. The analyst's focus must remain upon "the process being acted out, rather than about the content of whatever may have been under discussion before" (p. 82).

Concluding remarks

In this contribution, I have provided a wide-ranging survey of descriptive and psychoanalytic perspectives on the topic of arrogance. I have noted its genesis in severe and sustained frustrations during early childhood and, occasionally, in luxuriating overindulgence. I have also pointed out its overt and covert forms, its defensive and discharge functions, and its serving as an unfortunate, if manic, barrier to deeper contact with oneself and others. After a brief foray into sociocultural matters, I have returned to the clinical realm and elucidated the complex matters of psychoanalytic technique in dealing with patients with marked and pervasive arrogance.

One matter that has remained unaddressed pertains to gender. In other words, are men and women equally prone to arrogance or is one more given to arrogance than the other? And, a related question is whether the difference, if any, is quantitative or qualitative? Averse to generalizations, psychoanalysis provides few answers to such questions. Empirical studies from the disciplines of general psychology and business management turn out to be more helpful. Chamorro-Premuzic (2013), reporting in the highly respected *Harvard Business Review*, for instance, notes that his normative data (which includes thousands of business managers from across all industries and forty countries) shows that men are consistently more manipulative and arrogant than women. Even more impressive is the research by Grijalva et al. (2015) who sifted through 355 journal articles, dissertations, monographs, and technical manuals spanning thirty-one years and involving 475,000 subjects in order to ascertain gender differences along three dimensions: (i) leadership/authority, (ii) entitlement/arrogance, and (iii) generosity/exhibition. These University of Buffalo School of Management-based researchers found that men consistently scored higher on the first two variables. In other words, while vanity-based wishes to show off occurred equally in men and women, men displayed far greater hunger for authority and power; they were more arrogant than women.

Informed and impressed, we return to the clinical realm and acknowledge that the incidence of narcissistic personality disorder is greater in men (Reich, 1933). Could this reflect a diagnostic bias whereby more men are labeled "narcissistic" and more women "borderline" even when they have similar psychological

constellations? Or, could the heightened narcissism of men reflect some fundamental constitutional element, some sociocultural "shaping" influence, or some
difference in their childhood separation-individuation process (Mahler, Pine, &
Bergman, 1975)? Could it be that most girls' shifting of their love from mother
to father lays down an experiential substrate of mourning which makes them
stronger to handle reality and not revert to arrogance? Altman (1977) has put this
most eloquently: "This renunciation prepares her for renunciation in the future in
a way that a boy is unable to match. The steadfastness of commitment [in love]
is, in this view, the renunciation of alternative possibilities and the future woman
has already made it in childhood. The boy has not, can not, and will not" (p. 48).
Altman's words shed light on why *men* might carry a greater core of arrogance in
their hearts than do women. But it is Bion's words that lay bare why *both men and
women* are vulnerable to self-inflation, undue self-reliance, and self-absorption.
Talking to an analysand during a clinical hour, Bion remarked that the hardships
of the patient's childhood were so difficult that he was "reduced to becoming
omnipotent!" (cited in Grotstein, 2007, p. 29).

Part I

Developmental realm

Chapter 2

An evolutionary hypothesis on arrogance

Kathryn Ann Baselice and J. Anderson Thomson, Jr.

Arrogance wins. Look no further than the 2016 U.S. presidential election. The winner, Donald J. Trump, now the forty-fifth president of the United States, is a supremely arrogant man. Why is he that way? Why is anyone arrogant? What is arrogance, and how did it become a common feature of human nature, especially male human nature? Why are we distressed by it, yet arrogance flourishes?

We will argue that arrogance is a product of women's preferences in a mate. During our long evolutionary history, those women who chose men who could acquire and commit resources to them and their offspring left more descendants. Men are a long breeding experiment by women.[1] Men were shaped by the women whose choices let some of them pass muster and gain sexual access. Since the traits that mark a man's ability to acquire resources and hold those resources into the future are indirect, it opened the door for men to deceive women about their abilities, and ultimately to self-deceive and exaggerate even more effectively about their resource generation and holding potential. Women chose men with high resource-holding potential as well as men who deceived and self-deceived about their capacities, and we are left with the human phenomenon of arrogance. Arrogance also allowed men to intimidate stronger rivals and secure allies and followers, which further enhanced their reproductive success. The capacity for arrogance must have emerged early, because there has been enough time for detection and dislike of arrogance to evolve and cultural rituals to contain it.

We will begin our argument with a definition of arrogance and then build our hypothesis of arrogance's origins with reviews of natural selection, human evolution, evolutionary psychology, sexual selection, parental investment theory, self-deception, and the evidence of arrogance's success in humans and other animals.

---

1 "Re: quip about men being a vast breeding experiment run by females – it was a memo circulating around Harvard back in the late seventies. I cannot take credit for it. Could be any of a number of people who said it first – Robert Trivers or John Hartung seem the likeliest, but Irv DeVore delighted in repeating it. I happen to think the quip needs a caveat: assuming female autonomy and unconstrained choices (i.e. in species with langur-like infanticide by usurping males, males are actually canceling the last 'choice' a mother made) while in highly patriarchal human societies, patrilineal preferences constrain female choices, etc. Still, given what Patty Gowaty calls 'free female choice', it's a cute idea" (Sarah Hrdy, personal communication, February 13, 2017).

Arrogance is applied to the sense of superiority that comes from someone who claims, or arrogates, more consideration or importance than is warranted. Arrogance is an attitude of superiority manifested in an overbearing manner or in presumptuous claims or assumptions. The word "arrogance" derives from "arrogate," which means to claim or seize without justification, or to make undue claims to having. Arrogate comes from the Latin, *arragatus*, past participle of the verb *arrogare*, which means to appropriate. The Latin verb in turn comes from the prefix *ad* ("to" or "towards") and the verb, *rogare*, ("to ask"). "Arrogate" is similar to the more familiar "arrogant," and there is a relationship between the two words. Arrogant comes from the Latin *arrogans*, the present participle of *arrogare*. Arrogant is applied to that sense of superiority that comes from someone claiming, or arrogating, more consideration than is due to that person's position, dignity, or power. Arrogance has two parts: overconfidence and an air of superiority. Arrogance is often accompanied by contempt for presumed inferiors.

A brief review of evolution

Evolutionary theory was born in 1837 after a five year circumnavigation voyage taken by the young Charles Darwin (1809–1882) on *HMS Beagle*.[2] Three months after his return to England in 1836 Darwin gave his collection of birds from the Galapagos Islands to John Gould, the bird expert of the London Zoological Society. Gould reported that three of the four specimens of Galapagos mockingbirds were distinct species, new to ornithology, and different from all known mockingbirds. Gould also concluded that Darwin's collection contained thirteen or possibly fourteen species of unusual finches, all so closely related that Gould put them in a single group. Twenty-five of the twenty-six species Gould judged to be new to ornithology and unique to the Galapagos Islands. Darwin realized that if Gould was correct, the long believed, immutable, God-built barrier between species had been broken. Gradual evolution through geographical isolation was the only workable explanation (Sulloway, 2009). "Seeing this gradation and diversity of structure in one small, intimately related group of birds, one might really fancy that from an original paucity of birds in the archipelago, one species had been taken and modified for different ends" (Darwin, 1845, p. 380).

In the spring of 1837 Charles Darwin began to search for a mechanism that could explain this evolutionary change and the puzzle of the highly adaptive nature of each species to its environment. In September of 1838 he read Thomas Malthus's 1826 *Essay on the Principle of Population*. Malthus asserted that populations grow geometrically, the food supply is limited, and most offspring fail to survive, swept away by predators, famine, and disease. Darwin had finally discovered the mechanism. In the struggle for existence beneficial variations would be naturally selected, and they would confer increased survival and increased adaptive traits.

---

2 For a more thorough review of evolutionary theory, see Buss (2004, 2016) and Dawkins (1989, 2000).

It was a natural process similar to an animal breeder's choice of desired traits in the animals he selected to mate. Darwin also had an unexploded bombshell. He had a natural explanation for complex adaptations, the design features of nature, with no need to invoke a god or an intelligent designer.

At age twenty-nine, Charles Darwin had the most important insight ever to occur to a human mind (Dennett, 2009). He gave us the only workable explanation we have for the design and variety of all life on earth, and the only workable explanation we have for the design and architecture of the human mind. Yet, for fear of the likely firestorm with the idea's publication and his deeply religious wife's reaction, Charles Darwin sat on the idea for two decades. In 1858 an obscure naturalist, Alfred Russel Wallace, sent him a manuscript that contained the same idea, also derived from reading Malthus's essay. Only then did Charles Darwin take frantic steps to publish his great idea.

His remarkable theory was published in 1859 in his seminal work *On the Origin of Species by Means of Natural Selection, or the Preservation of Favoured Races in the Struggle for Life*. This book was groundbreaking. It challenged the theory of special creation, known now as Intelligent Design, and everything people thought they knew about the human race (Sulloway, 2006).

What Darwin discovered was that a species' environment plays a role in shaping characteristics of that species over time. Individuals within a species who have characteristics that are best suited for the particular environment or challenges they encounter on a day-to-day basis will not only survive but will thrive. In contrast, those individuals whose traits are less able to provide them with the necessities of life will not only struggle to survive but will often fail to reproduce. Over thousands of generations, the more desirable traits, passed on from successful ancestors between generations, slowly become the norm. The less desirable traits, which led to daily struggle and failure for the ancestor who possessed them, died with those unsuccessful ancestors.

Darwin died without knowing the biologic mechanism by which these traits were passed from parent to offspring. It was not until the discovery of the nature and function of DNA and genes, and the merger of this new knowledge with natural selection, that humans fully understood how evolution works. This merger has been deemed the Modern Synthesis. It is because of this Modern Synthesis that we continue our discussion about evolutionary theory with DNA.

It is important to remember that DNA and genes are extremely complex in both structure and function. For the purpose of our argument, however, a simple overview of basic mechanisms will suffice. DNA or deoxyribonucleic acid is composed of two strands of nucleotides wound together in a double helix. The nucleotides are labeled A, C, G, and T based on their structure. DNA is the blueprint of life. In the nucleus of all of our cells, sections of DNA called genes are transcribed into RNA. This RNA is transferred to another portion of the cell and is translated into proteins.

Aside from making proteins, DNA replicates. This process involves many troubleshooting mechanisms, and errors seldom occur. But, DNA replication remains an imperfect process. Errors do occur, like an A placed in the strand instead of a G. This usually occurs in DNA regions called "non-coding" regions, or areas of DNA that are not translated into proteins. These errors go unnoticed. However, errors sometimes occur in coding regions, areas of DNA that are transcribed and translated into proteins. Because of this error, the structure and function of this protein may or may not be altered. Sometimes this has deadly consequences. Sometimes it improves proteins, whether their job is to channel molecules, to signal other cells, or perhaps to turn "on" and "off" areas of the DNA itself.

Why do we review the details about DNA and imperfect replication? Though the proteins that derive from DNA are small, they can cause specific changes in that individual's behavior, appearance, or abilities, especially when changes occur in numerous interconnected proteins over time. In the case of humans, that person might be a faster runner, might be stronger, or might be better able to perceive the emotions of friends and neighbors. Overall, he or she may be better suited for the environment, both physical and social, and the pressures that those environments present. These traits remain with the individual and may be passed on to that person's offspring who will gain the same benefit, repeating the cycle for thousands of generations to come.

Evolutionary psychology

We want to return to Darwin for a moment. It is crucial that one appreciate the dislocating sweep of Darwin's achievement. Tooby (2002) states:

> The discovery of natural selection, the austere logic of reproducing systems, was only Darwin's first step. He used this new logic to span three seemingly unbridgeable metaphysical chasms. He showed how selection united the nonliving and the living, the nonhuman and the human, and the physical and the mental into a single fabric of intelligible material causation. If one could accept the price, the prize was a principled explanation for the history and design of all life. Unacceptably, this included the architecture of the human mind, all that now remained of the soul: our cherished mental life was a naturally selected product of organized matter, just one downstream consequence of the uncaring immensities of time and chance. The mind with its moral sense was taken out of the authoritative domain of clerics and philosophers. For Darwin, the responsibility for its investigation would be in the hands of evolutionary psychologists, of which he was the first.
>
> ("The Greatest Englishman Since Newton,"
> *New York Times Book Review*, October 6, 2002)

We will continue in this tradition. We will provide an idea about arrogance's origins that may unsettle the reader and disturb what he or she thinks might be pathological about arrogance and its place in human psychology. Let us first turn to modern evolutionary psychology.

The fibers that make our thoughts, emotions, and behaviors began to slowly emerge as humans did, approximately five to seven million years ago when hominids first split from our closest ancestor, known as the last common ancestor of humans, bonobos, and chimpanzees. Our own species, *Homo sapiens*, is a relative latecomer among the hominids, appearing approximately 300,000 years ago.

Our brains are designed to grasp the timescales of our own lifetimes: seconds, minutes, hours, days, and years (Dawkins, 1998). We start to stumble at the prospect of comprehending larger timescales and fall when we attempt to grasp the eons of evolution, even human evolution. It is hard to truly comprehend, but here is one thought experiment: Imagine that each hour is 100,000 years. We will take a day as representative of 2.4 million years. At midnight our genus *Homo* appears in Africa. At dawn some leave Africa for the first time. By lunchtime some have reached present-day Europe. At dinnertime our most immediate ancestor, *Homo heidelbergensis* emerges in Africa. Some of them migrate to Europe and become the Neanderthals. Anatomically modern humans emerge in Africa from the remaining *heidelbergensis* population about 9 PM at night. Fully modern humans, our species, emerge about 11:20 PM. It is not until six minutes before midnight, 11:54 PM, that we start to settle into early agriculture communities in the Near East. For all that time, from midnight until almost midnight the following evening, we lived in small, kin-based hunter-gatherer bands in Africa. All seven billion people on the planet today arose from a small number of those hunter-gatherers in Africa. That is the physical and social environment that shaped all of us.

The disappearance of the rainforests around this time forced us to adopt the African plains as our home (Walter, 2013). On these plains, the threat of predation and starvation was ever present. Early humans found that cooperative group living provided better protection and access to resources than single living. Those who were predisposed to group living and navigating the social environment flourished, while those who chose solitary lives perished. Thus rudimentary societies emerged.

The social and physical environments that shaped the human race can be viewed as a lifelong camping trip with extended family and relatives, with limited resources and an unending concern for safety (Cosmides & Tooby, 1992, 2013). Because evolution requires tiny changes in DNA over innumerable replication cycles, and because it is often more than one alteration that leads to a beneficial trait, it takes tens of thousands of years for adaptations to form. Therefore, we must look to those early hunter-gatherer societies on the savannahs of Africa when examining how our current traits are adaptive. Those early years are referred to as our "environment of evolutionary adaptedness" or EEA (Bowlby, 1969).

> . . . the only relevant criterion by which to consider the natural adaptation of any particular part of present-day man's behavioral equipment is the degree to which and the way in which it might contribute to population survival in man's primeval environment.
>
> (p. 59)

And as Cosmides and Tooby (2013) point out, the behaviors, cognition, and emotions that made sense in our EEA often fail to fit in our ever-changing world. In fact, our environment has changed so much that what was once an advantage to our ancestors can seem downright maladaptive today. Murder could mean survival tens of thousands of years ago, while today it carries a sentence of life in prison or execution. Evolutionary psychology seeks to examine human cognitions, behaviors, and emotions in the context of this EEA.

Because everything about humans, from the way we act to the way we look, has evolved to aid our ability to navigate and reproduce in the EEA, understanding these factors requires that we analyze how they aided our survival and reproductive success in the past. This includes everything from mate choice to personality features. If personality traits such as arrogance served a purpose in at least a small subset of situations encountered by our ancestors, it would have afforded those who possessed it with reproductive success, propagating the feature through generations upon generations of individuals. With this in mind, we now consider the factors that make one reproductively successful.

Sexual selection and mate choice

Sexual relationships and mate choice are vital to understanding the evolution of all traits, including arrogance. They puzzled Darwin and seemed at odds with his theory of natural selection (Buss, 2004). He was so perplexed, that he created a separate theory, which he deemed "sexual selection." This theory was first proposed in Darwin's *On the Origin of Species* and was later refined in his 1871 publication, *The Descent of Man*. As in much of evolutionary theory, the theory of sexual selection is complex, and we will take a basic view of it, with a focus on two key aspects – intersexual competition and intrasexual competition (for a full discussion see Buss, 2004; Dawkins, 1986, 1989).

Intrasexual selection occurs within one gender of a species. In humans, men compete against other men to attract a woman and vice versa. We will focus on male intrasexual competition because it is a building block of arrogance. In some animal species, the competition is physical, such as lions fighting to control a pride of lionesses. The winner gains access to the territory and the females that make up the pride. In humans the competition is often more subtle (although remnants of such instincts to literally fight over the opposite sex can be seen in drunken bar fights wherever young males gather). If a male possesses more traits that a woman wants or can outcompete his male counterpart, then he will be able to reproduce. In reproducing, he will pass on these desirable traits to his male offspring. Furthermore, the female will pass on a preference for those traits to her female offspring. Over thousands of generations this trait in males and preference for it in females will replicate and spread throughout a species. Those traits possessed by the loser of intrasexual competition will fail to replicate and will disappear from the gene pool.

Intersexual selection looks at what one gender of a species desires in the other. A frequently cited example is the peacock. It often surprises people to learn that the more decorated gender of this species is the male. A peahen is quite drab by comparison. Females prefer males with large, bright plumage as this is correlated with male health – a good immune system and low parasite load. These males are selected by females for copulation and reproduction. Over time the genes that allowed bright and robust plumage would have been passed down more frequently, as males who possessed these genes were chosen more often by females. Males with dull feathers would not have been as successful at mating and, over time, the genes for dull feathers would have slowly disappeared from the gene pool.

It is important to remember that if a certain organism is better suited for its environment, it will likely survive and prosper. The mere fact that an individual survives longer and spends less time struggling to navigate the environment means that that individual will likely be more successful in procreating. The better the traits that an individual possesses, the more likely he is to find a mate and procreate. The more offspring an individual has, the more those genes are replicated in the next generation. And as traits are passed within those genes, presumably the next generation will have equal reproductive success. This leads to a preference, a selection, for those traits and their corresponding genes.

Keep in mind that much of sexual selection occurs at an unconscious level. Most of us do not walk into a potential sexual encounter weighing the pros and cons of a mate. Our instincts, our hormones, our basic human nature does it for us. These mechanisms are in place because, over the hundreds of thousands of years of human history, they have improved the chances of success for those who possess them, and are therefore possessed by more individuals with each successive generation.

Parental investment theory

One key aspect of our modern understanding of the differences in the sexes is parental investment, a concept introduced by Robert Trivers (1972). Parental investment (PI) is defined as the investment in an offspring to increase its survival at the expense of one's ability to invest in other offspring, both current and future. The sex with the greater PI will be the limiting resource of reproduction. The sex with the greater PI will be smaller and choosier about who he or she mates with. The sex with the lesser PI will be larger, more aggressive, and will compete fiercely with members of its own sex for access to the sex with the greater PI. In the human species the female has the greater PI. However, there are other species in the animal kingdom in which males have the greater PI, and all the behavioral differences hold true.

Let's consider humans. A male's genetic contribution to reproduction is a sperm and two and a half minutes, while the female's contribution is an egg and much more. Men produce billions of sperm over the course of their lifetime, while a woman only produces a finite number of eggs. Men have the advantage of walking away from a reproductive encounter relatively unchanged. They can go about their daily lives much the same as they had done before, free to impregnate other women and provide as much or as little support to their offspring as they choose.

Unfortunately, women hardly have it as easy. In addition to the production of a nutrient rich egg, women also bear the burden of the expensive construction of a placenta, the energetic demands of gestation of a fetus for nine months, and the production of breast milk and lactation for years with each infant. They cannot conceive another baby in those nine months and indeed for a time after giving birth. They must endure the hazards of childbirth. They also must care for the infant once he is born, no easy task over the course of evolutionary history, where predators, human and animal, and starvation were constant facts of life. Even if a man were to stay and provide resources and protection for a woman, the basic physiologic investment is exponentially greater for a woman than it is for a man.

What does this differential parental investment mean? It means that women benefit more by being selective about their sexual partners. They can have less offspring, which means they need to choose the best fathers for their offspring that they can. A man who was healthier, wealthier, wiser, stronger, better looking, and more symmetrical, would have been more desirable to a woman than a man who was ill, poor, dumb, weak, ugly, and less symmetrical. The better genes a man could provide for the offspring, the better chance that offspring would thrive and attract mates, allowing those genes to be copied from one generation to the next.

Women who chose men who were willing to stick around and care for them and their babies after they were born fared better than those who did not, which provided enough evolutionary pressure to select for traits where women could accurately gauge how committed a man was. It also provided pressure for women to choose men who had the tools to both protect and provide resources for her and her baby – strength and athleticism, physical resources, status in the social hierarchy, and intelligence. The female offspring of women who selectively pursued these traits in a mate not only did better in the long run, they inherited DNA that allowed them to make similar choices. And the male offspring of men who were stronger, able to acquire more resources, and better at navigating the social hierarchy were equally successful as their fathers, both in their daily lives and in their reproductive success. Most important, the men who were better able to broadcast to potential mates that they either had these features or could gain them in the future had more reproductive success. As we will see, this benefit may also be afforded to arrogant individuals who exaggerate their own abilities.

"Show me the money!" That was the constant refrain of the Cuba Gooding character, the football wide receiver, to his agent in the movie *Jerry McGuire* (1996). For ancestral women, in harsh and dangerous environments, when they selected a man to mate with it had to be, "Show me the resources, the ones you have now and the ones you can provide in the future." The problem for ancestral women was that the markers for resources, resource acquisition capacity, resource holding potential, and resource commitment to her were difficult to discern. She had to rely on indirect measures: strength, status, his allies, intelligence, kindness, and diligence. Women had to view men as current and future success objects.

Social status is a universal cue to the control of resources. They flow at the top of the social hierarchy and dribble out at the bottom. A man who was "eligible" was one whose resources were not committed, or completely committed, to another woman. The men women mated with had to possess traits that gave the man a chance for the sustained acquisition of resources in a harsh and dangerous world. Looks alone failed to cut it.

Self-deception

It is important to highlight a fundamental difference between two sets of confident individuals. An individual may be confident about abilities and resources that he or she actually has. For instance, the renowned boxer, Muhammad Ali (1942–2016) often boasted about his strength and ability in the boxing ring. When he was a young fighter, he was seen as arrogant. As everyone knows, Muhammad Ali had the goods to back up his words. "I am the greatest. I said that even before I knew I was" (*USA Today, Sport,* June 3, 2016). On the other hand, an individual may also be confident about abilities and resources that he or she fails to possess. An example here may be Donald Trump, who boasted about his linguistic prowess with his claim, "I know words. I have the best words" (South Carolina campaign rally, December 2015). While we will return to the evolutionary benefit of the first group in later sections, it is this second group that requires special consideration.

Think about a time when you told a blatant lie. The most salient examples may be from our childhood, when we tell a parent that we did not steal a cookie or blame a transgression on a sibling. Some among us may have more recent or serious examples, such as lying to a spouse about a love affair or lying to a supervisor about a work-related mistake. It is easy to recall the physical and mental discomfort that accompanied the lie. Lying requires concentration and control. It is no easy task.

Polygraph machines rely largely on that before-mentioned physical discomfort, or physiological changes associated with deception. These physical changes are largely uncontrollable[3] and include increases in galvanic skin conductance (due to increased sweat production), and increases in heart rate and in blood pressure. We may have seen the physical manifestations of these changes in a particularly nervous liar – the flushing of the face, the quivering of the voice, etc. And, then there are more subtle cues to lying behavior. Increases in periorbital temperature have been observed (Pavlidis, Eberhardt, & Levine, 2002) as have increases in voice pitch (Streeter, Krauss, Geller, Olson, & Apple, 1977; Trivers, 2011). Furthermore, the cognitive load imposed on the liar while in the act of lying can cause other subtle behaviors such as a decrease in blink rate and inability to suppress minor unconscious movements, such as twitching (Trivers, 2011).

Cognitive load can often lead to interesting phenomena. For instance, a spontaneous denial is often an assertion. One theory that supports this is the "ironic

---

3 Although it should be noted that certain individuals may not have these particular responses when consciously lying, and polygraph machines are hardly considered credible evidence in a court of law.

process theory." In essence, our brains have two simultaneous processes, a conscious one to suppress the truth and an unconscious one that attempts to troubleshoot and check for errors in this process. Sometimes, especially when under heavy cognitive load, this process can produce errors that the unconscious mind fails to immediately correct. This may lead to blurting out information (such as admissions of culpability or a word that an experimenter tells you not to think about) that the conscious brain is attempting to suppress since it is that very piece of information that the cognitive mind is examining at that moment (Wegner, 2009). Clearly, lying is an imperfect art.

Evolution is an arms race. In this case, it pins the liars against the lie detectors. Liars over time have gotten better at lying, and those attempting to detect lies have gotten better at detecting them. Even subtle twitching and changes in voice may cause at least unconscious suspicion in a lie detector's mind. How could the liar one-up the lie detector, giving the liar the ultimate advantage?

The answer to this question was elegantly laid out by Robert Trivers in his 1976 foreword to the original edition of Richard Dawkins's (1976) *The Selfish Gene* and fully developed in the former's book, *The Folly of Fools* (2011). Trivers points out that the best way to lie is to believe the lie you are telling. In other words, the best liars engage in self-deception. This decreases the cognitive load on the deceiver and presents a particularly vexing problem for those they are attempting to deceive. How can one possibly tell if someone is lying when they are not, in fact, lying?

Trivers notes that one's brain is filled with mechanisms that allow for a distorted image of one's self. For instance, we tend to ignore information contrary to our opinions and beliefs, and place more emphasis on information that supports us. We externalize blame onto others and rarely look at our own contributions to problems. We rationalize behavior after the fact to avoid any self-blame or cognitive dissonance we may encounter. We even misremember events and conversations to bolster or to maintain the image we hold of our past self. The brain truly is a remarkably deceptive organ.

> How can the self deceive the self? Does that not require that the self knows what it does not know? This contradiction is easily sidestepped by defining the self as the conscious mind, so that self-deception occurs when the conscious mind is kept in the dark. True and false information may be simultaneously stored, only with the truth stored in the unconscious mind and falsehood in the conscious.

> (Trivers, 2011, p. 9)

The fact that our brains may be hardwired for self-deception speaks to its importance in our evolutionary history. It has taken much longer for scientists to even begin to understand the brain when compared to other organs, and it is this very complexity that may allow us to both assess the truth and simultaneously ignore it. Trivers even points out that the separation of our brain hemispheres may play a functional role in this deception. He notes that the right side of our brain may be "less conscious" than the left side. It is interesting for our purposes that the corpus callosum in women is generally larger than in men, meaning that there is likely a greater harmony in information sharing between the two hemispheres (Trivers, 2011).

As Trivers notes, self-confidence is no exception to self-deceit. Humans can inflate their own abilities in order to deceive others. Of course, he points out, there is a caveat to this. The self-deceit has a ceiling effect because it has to be believable to those on the receiving end of the lie.

Does the self-deception that leads to overconfidence work? One study found that overconfident individuals were judged as confident by potential partners reading their pages on a dating website (Murphy et al., 2015). Another study found that those who were overconfident about their abilities in a classroom setting were perceived by their peers as being more capable, regardless of actual abilities (Lamba & Nityananda, 2014). And, finally, another study found that, when motivated by monetary gain, participants displayed overconfidence despite objective knowledge of their performance. This led to increased scores from evaluators, although this was not the case for those who had been coached by a lie detection tutorial (Schwardmann & van der Weele, 2016).

One final note about this view of self-deception is that it is "offensive" (Trivers, 2011). Classically, we viewed self-deception as a defensive strategy, one that was pathological. The view of self-deception as an "offensive" strategy allows for a more realistic view of its potential to benefit the self-deceived. By extension, this would mean that arrogance is likewise an "offensive" strategy rather than a defensive one. It represents a personality characteristic that, in some cases, benefits those who possess it.

Arrogance and intrasexual competition

The world that our ancestors lived in was much different than our world is today. Our ancestors did not have the luxury of grocery stores, computers, money, or even houses. Life was a constant struggle. Resources were scarce, and mainly comprised of food and perhaps some rudimentary tools. The more resources a male was able to scrape together, the more desirable he would be to a potential female partner, and the more respect he gained in the small community in which he lived.

If our traits were selected for in such an environment, one question that remains is how such a seemingly off-putting personality trait as arrogance improved one's chance at garnering resources? Johnson and Fowler (2011) set out to answer this very question in a letter to *Nature* magazine. The researchers proposed a mathematical model that showed that, given a set of potential costs and benefits, overconfidence may lead to more success in certain situations, particularly when an opponent does not know the true abilities of the challenger. Specifically, they found that when the reward/cost ratio was just right, it benefited the individual to possess overconfidence about his own abilities and to project that overconfidence to potential opponents who would then struggle to know how much of the confidence they perceived was warranted.

Let's take, as the authors did, an example of a physical competition. Subject A comes into the competition the stronger and more formidable of the opponents. If Subject B challenges Subject A and the fight is allowed to proceed, he will likely lose. However, the resources Subject B wants – a mate, money, prestige – may be very valuable to Subject B and may be worth the fight. The good news for Subject B is that Subject A has never met Subject B and does not know all of Subject B's abilities. He must make an educated guess based on what information is available to him. He assumes that Subject B would not engage in a fight if he did not think he could win. So if Subject B comes into a contest with his chest puffed out and fists raised, confident in his ability to win, Subject A must take his confidence at face value and use it when considering his opponent. And sometimes, this overconfident display will be enough to make the stronger, more equipped opponent, Subject A, back down and retreat.

This is not to say that every overconfident individual can avoid having to "put up or shut up." Subject A may be perfectly confident in his abilities and challenge Subject B, in which case Subject B may incur a large cost or be forced to retreat. But, as mentioned previously, if the reward is high enough compared to the potential cost, it may benefit Subject B to play the game. Ultimately, though he will take some losses, he may win big along the way, which will lead to a net benefit for him in the evolutionary game. And if this strategy works, Subject B will pass that trait to his offspring, and so on and so forth, propagating the trait of overconfidence.

To illustrate this, let's use an example from the animal kingdom. Consider the genus *Uca* (the fiddler crab). When a male fiddler crab loses his brachychelous (original) claw due to predation or a fight with a rival, he regenerates a new leptochelous claw. To a human observer, the leptochelous claw is smoother, more slender, and lighter than its brachychelous counterpart when controlling for claw length (Backwell, Christy, Telford, Jennions, & Passmore, 2000; Reaney, Milner, Detto, & Backwell, 2008). It also possesses a weaker closing and pull-resisting force in relation to its size than the brachychelous claws (Backwell, Christy, Telford, Jennions, & Passmore, 2000; Lailvaux, Reaney, & Backwell, 2008). These characteristics are important for the fiddler crab, the former being important for combat and the latter important for defending one's territory from rivals looking to steal it.

Clearly, possessing a leptochelous claw could be disastrous for a fiddler crab. However, keep in mind that his rival cannot tell the difference between the two claws in quality (Reaney, Milner, Detto, & Backwell, 2008). Furthermore, although leptochelous claws are significantly weaker, they tend to be similar in size to the brachychelous claws they replace (Zimmer, 2008). And as claw size is supposed to demonstrate fighting ability, leptochelous claws represent a dishonest signal in male fiddler crabs (Lailvaux, Reaney, & Backwell, 2008).

Does this dishonest signal work? While one might expect leptochelous possessing crabs to be challenged more frequently due to their disadvantage, this is not the case (Reaney, Milner, Detto, & Backwell, 2008). Most important, this dishonest signal is often enough to deter rivals (Backwell, Christy, Telford, Jennions, & Passmore, 2000). Without this dishonest signaling, male fiddler crabs with regenerated claws would not stand a chance against their opponents. Clearly, such an overconfident display, without the strength to back it up, has evolved due to its ability to provide the maimed crab with an advantage in at least some situations.

How does this translate into the human world? Similar to our fiddler crab example, there is evidence that false conceit may ward off competitors. In one experiment where participants were monetarily rewarded by warding off potential opponents on a cognitive exam, male participants broadcasted higher confidence about their abilities when compared to experimental treatments in which warding off opponents was not beneficial. More important, this broadcast was effective in deterring their opponents from engaging in competition against them (Charness, Rustichini, & van de Ven, 2013).

Overconfidence is a common theme in many studies about financial decisions. Male overconfidence, in particular, is striking. Men trade stocks more than women, despite incurring decreases in returns, and this is more robust when comparing single men and women (Barber & Odean, 2001). Male executives are more overconfident and take more financial risks than their female counterparts (Huang & Kisgen, 2013). And male overconfidence contributes to more men entering into a competition for greater monetary compensation than women with equal abilities (Niederle & Vesterlund, 2006).

The difference between male and female overconfidence and the associated behaviors reflects evolutionary pressures. Males in our EEA have more to gain from resource allocation, which in our modern times equates to financial success (Trivers, 2011). This would allow them to attract better mates, provide more for their offspring, and gain higher social status, which affords them more protection and better access to preferable females. At times, an overconfident male who took risks in our EEA could have garnered more resources for himself, even if more often than not he failed. These instances of success would have allowed for greater reproductive success and therefore propagation of this trait. In other words: no risk, no reward.

Overconfidence has important implications in status and power acquisition. Overconfident individuals were found to use behavioral cues, such as speaking more, employing a confident tone, exhibiting a calm and relaxed demeanor, providing more information during group discussions, and answering questions first when working in a group (Anderson, Bryon, Moore, & Kennedy, 2012). Overconfident individuals were rated as more competent and deserving of higher status (deserving of respect, influential, leader in decision making) by their peers (ibid.). This is unsurprising, as the authors note: "A high level of unjustified confidence (i.e., overconfidence) should lead the individual to exhibit more competence cues, just as high levels of confidence does. In the eyes of the observer, it is difficult to differentiate justified from unjustified confidence" (p. 720).

Interestingly, this effect was not diminished after working with an individual for an extended period of time (ibid.). Those individuals who were overconfident were also seen as more competent and deserving of higher status than individuals who were accurate in self-assessment. Even when groups are confronted with objective results and see individuals as having been overconfident, overconfident individuals still have a net positive gain of social status (Kennedy, Anderson, & Moore, 2013). The results of these two studies demonstrate that overconfidence is not only overlooked by peers, it leads those peers to have more faith in one's leadership abilities and raises the status of the overconfident.

In fact, the United States was recently faced with the darker side of male overconfidence and its role in status acquisition. A controversial statement by our recently sworn-in commander-in-chief in 2005 provides an excellent illustration of this behavior.

> I better use some Tic Tacs just in case I start kissing her. You know, I'm automatically attracted to beautiful [women] – I just start kissing them. It's like a magnet. Just kiss. I don't even wait. And, when you are a star, they let you do it. You can do anything. . . . Grab'em by the pussy. You can do anything.
>
> (Donald J. Trump, recorded in 2005,
> transcript October 8, 2016, *New York Times*)

> "Well, if I was twenty years younger, and in my prime, I would let him touch my pussy . . . he is rich!"
>
> (Trump supporter, January 2017,
> Charlottesville, Virginia)

Donald Trump's 2005 arrogant claim that he was entitled to assault women with impunity and a female supporter's affirmation provide an unvarnished illustration of our formulation of the dynamics of arrogance.

What President Trump describes as "locker-room talk" can now be understood as an ancient strategy to elevate prestige and status among one's male peers. The admiration a careful observer will hear in Billy Bush's voice as he responds to this statement clearly demonstrates that Donald Trump has won Billy Bush's respect. Billy Bush demonstrates this again as the two emerge from the bus when Bush walks next to Trump and says, "It's hard to walk next to a guy like this." Bush derogates himself in comparison to the future president. In our EEA such an elevation of status and respect might have afforded the individual a better place on the social hierarchy. This would have given the individual access to preferable mates, power, and resources.

Clearly, overconfidence has a role to play in intrasexual competition in regards to status and resource allocation. But even more striking may be its ability to gain an advantage by lowering the pool of potential suitors. One study found that dating profiles that were rated high in confidence were also rated high in arrogance (Murphy et al., 2015). The authors posit that such displays, in person, would cause a rival to back off as the potential competition would seem too difficult. And indeed, follow-up studies confirmed that rivals who viewed the profiles of arrogant individuals were less inclined to challenge them for a desired partner.

One final note on overconfidence and competition: It appears that having objective data contrary to the person's overconfidence decreases the value of such displays. In fact, individuals present themselves more favorably in the presence of same-sex strangers versus same-sex friends (Tice, Butler, Muraven, & Stillwell, 1995). When subjects are unaware of an actor in a vignette's performance, self-enhancing actors had the most favorable overall impression and were seen as competent. However, accurate self-assessment was seen as more favorable when subjects were aware of how the actor had actually performed (Schlenker & Leary, 1982). It is best to save overconfident displays for individuals who do not know you well enough to call your bluff. Remember, in the competitive dating world, an attitude of superiority may defeat your rivals.

Male arrogance and the mating game

Almost every behavior and trait that human beings exhibit is for one purpose and one purpose only – to garner a better position in the mating game and successfully attract and keep a partner.[4] Each partner provides half of the genetic material that his or her offspring receives. It is in the best interest of each partner to find the best mate they can. The better a partner, the better genes a couple passes on to their little ones. And the better genes a little one has the better chance he has to navigate his social and physical environment and, in turn, produce offspring.

As we have seen, men and women are tremendously different in the ways they approach mating, and for good reason. Due to the differential in parental investment (Trivers, 1972), women have more to lose in a potential mating encounter, given the cost of carrying a baby to term and in raising it until it can fend for itself. Over time women benefited from selecting mates who were stronger, smarter, and better able to navigate the social hierarchy important for life on the savannahs of Africa. This would have meant that her offspring with that partner would also likely possess these qualities and be equally successful in attracting mates.

But there was another important consideration for women. Our EEA was harsh, and resources were scarce. Men did the hunting and provided the protection of the small clans in which people lived. A woman benefited from having a man who could garner resources, and as we have shown, arrogance could play a key role at times in a man's pursuit of resources, whether those resources be physical or less tangible, indirect resources such as status. This meant that he could provide for both her and her children.

A man need not necessarily possess resources and status when he meets a woman to be considered a good partner. Instead, women could look at whether or not he had potential to gain resources and prestige, an indirect marker of resource

---

4 One may wonder about arrogant hermits and stoic loners. Evolution works by simple majorities. If, on average, the majority of arrogant men out-reproduced other men in ancestral environments, those genes passed down the generations. Once the genes for arrogance developed, they remain in the gene pool regardless of the current possessors' other personality features, as long as they continue to contribute to the reproductive success of some of their current carriers.

potential, in the future. We see this trait in modern women: the desire for an educated man who is committed to his job and desires to climb the corporate ladder. Women, rarely, are attracted to men who lack ambition or goals. Those men will likely fail to secure resources needed for her children. A song made famous by Bobby Darin in 1967 illustrates the issue. "If I was a carpenter, and you were a lady, would you marry me anyway, would you have my baby?". For any reasonable ancestral woman the answer would be a resounding, "No." The knowledge of a woman's evolved bias is embedded in the song's question.

If you ask a woman what personality features she is attracted to, we can guarantee "arrogance" would not make her top three, five, or even ten. In fact, arrogance seems to be an off-putting trait in many situations, as we will discuss in a later section. How could it possibly aid in the mating game if it seems to be so unattractive?

First, let's consider what men and women desire in potential partners. Across all cultures men value physical attractiveness and youth above all other features (Buss, 1989). A man seeks youth as this feature indicates fertility (Buss, 2016). Men across cultures prefer neonatenous features, big eyes, and a small nose, as these features often indicate youthfulness and no children (Cunningham, Druen, & Barbee, 1997). Similarly, men desire women who have bigger breasts and slender bodies with a low waist-to-hip ratio, which signals youth, health, and fertility (Singh & Young, 1995). Other behavioral and physical indicators of fertility and health would have been good muscle tone, bouncy gait, high energy, lustrous hair, and smooth skin (Buss, 2011).

What do all of these features have in common? They are all objectively observable. A woman cannot be falsely arrogant about her physical appearance because potential mates can judge for themselves whether they find her attractive. Women gained little by such false arrogance. And, as we have seen, arrogance in the face of objective data to the contrary can be costly (Schlenker & Leary, 1982; Tice, Butler, Muraven, & Stillwell, 1995). In Tennessee Williams's (1947) play *A Streetcar Named Desire* Mitch is engaged to Blanche DuBois. He tells her he has only seen her at night and never in a well-lit room. Mitch turns on a bright light. Blanche recoils. She is older than she told him.

Unfortunately for women, male characteristics that are desirable and cues to resources and resource acquisition are indirect and less observable. Across cultures women value financial capacity, ambition, and industriousness (Buss, 1989). Women also value such features as intelligence, social status, strength, and physical prowess in addition to physical attractiveness (Buss, 2011). These are crucial clues to the ability to provide and protect. Features that women value in a man are difficult to discern just by looking at him. A man could be an exceptionally good hunter and well respected by his peers, but if a woman was unable to observe this for herself, what could she rely on to convince her that he had such abilities?

"Success hinges on providing signals that we will deliver what the partner we desire is seeking" (Buss, 2011, p. 151). This statement by Buss is the perfect argument for the evolution of arrogance. In our EEA there were no bank state-ments. There were no IQ tests. There were no advanced educational degrees. The tools that women had to judge a potential mate by were limited, both in regards to his current resources and abilities, and in those he may gain for himself in the future. What men and women did have was an ability to communicate. A man had the ability to puff out his chest, to talk about his past conquests, and to point out what he could offer. In short, he could brag. Some women may have been turned off by this display. Others may have been attracted to him in spite of it because they thought he still had the goods. They may have been rewarded by better protection, resources, and reproductive success, which in turn would create offspring equally attracted to such displays and equally likely to use such tactics to arrogantly display resources and potential. And in fact, arrogant displays are perceived by others as an effort to say that one is superior and has qualities that others lack (Hareli & Weiner, 2000).

However, because objective data to the contrary was rarely available, this left the door open for men to deceive and self-deceive about their current abilities, resources, status, and future potential. Some women may have waited until they were satisfied with objective proof in support of the man's claims. Others, likely the majority, would have taken the man at his word, rewarding this trait and allow-ing it to propagate generation after generation.

"Women distinguish false bravado from real self-confidence, and they find the genuine article more attractive" (Buss, 2011, p. 166). In order to deceive a woman, the bravado therefore cannot be false. This brings us back to the impor-tance of self-deception. Arrogance is a subjective truth and a factual lie. In order to better deceive potential mates, a man must have believed that he had abilities and resources far exceeding those that he actually possessed. The better the self-deception, the better the lie and the more likely he is to attract the female.

If arrogance is an adaptive strategy to attract potential mates, we would expect to see the types of things that men are arrogant about to reflect the types of fea-tures that a woman desires. The literature supports this. We have already dis-cussed overconfidence in the financial world, which allows men to take risks and gain resources, and allows them to be arrogant about future earning potential, something that women value greatly.

In general, thrill seeking and risky behaviors are seen more frequently in men when compared to women (Byrnes, Miller, & Schafer, 1999; Trivers, 2011). In one meta-analysis, these differences were more robustly seen in the categories of physical skills (when success was met with greater reward but failure came at a cost), intellectual risk taking (solving mathematical or spatial problems at the risk of "getting stuck" or exhibiting lack of skill), and risky experimentation (willingness to participate in experimentation that was described as potentially causing harm) (Byrnes, Miller, & Schafer, 1999). In our evolutionary past, those men willing to put themselves at risk could show off to potential mates, impress potential allies, and deter rivals. It would have allowed the risk takers to access more resources than the faint of heart. It is easy to see how this would have afforded a man an evolutionary advantage, making him a more desirable partner in the long run.

This overconfidence and willingness to take chances has a modern downside. One recent study found that patients of male internists had an increased thirty-day mortality and readmission rate when compared with patients of female internists (Tsugawa et al., 2016). As medical education is administered similarly to men and women, it stands to reason that these differences can be attributed to overconfidence.

Such displays of arrogance may have differential outcomes depending on the type of relationship one is seeking. Conceit and bravado are more effective for men pursuing short-term relationships (Buss, 2011). Men were judged to compete more effectively for short-term partners when they imparted resources immediately and when they promoted their dominance by implying that their rivals lacked dominance, status, or popularity (Schmitt & Buss, 1996). The reason that arrogant displays may work better for short-term mating is that such a time frame keeps the woman from the objective evidence to counter the arrogant display.

To demonstrate how the gathering of objective data may cause arrogant displays to fail, we will again call on our example from the animal kingdom, the fiddler crab. Male fiddler crab brachychelous claw size often correlates with the size of his territory. Males with the regenerated weaker claws often have smaller territories, as they usually back down from an initiated fight with a brachychelous-possessing male (Reaney, Milner, Detto, & Backwell, 2008). Leptochelous claws represent a dishonest signal, and females will still be attracted to it. Unfortunately, while regenerated males were visited more than those with their original claws, they copulated less. Once the female was able to objectively assess the burrow for herself, she often ended the encounter (ibid.). However, in another study, both brachychelous and leptochelous possessing crabs had the same level of success in attracting and copulating with their female counterparts (Backwell, Christy, Telford, Jennions, & Passmore, 2000). Even in the face of objective information, sometimes an "arrogant" display may still win the day.

Why we despise arrogance

In evolutionary theory there are no accidents, at least none that endure for hundreds of thousands of years. Arrogance may be one adaptive strategy to convey realistic reproductive potential and to gain resources and mates otherwise out of reach. But just as arrogance may have been adaptive, our distaste for arrogant individuals may also be an adaptive strategy.

It is no secret that we humans dislike arrogant individuals. Arrogance is seen as a negative personality trait, discussed by many as maladaptive, pathological, and immoral. Just as arrogance was propagated over evolutionary time, our distaste for arrogance was as well. Studies demonstrate that arrogance is viewed as a negative trait that can have an adverse impact on how one is perceived (Hareli & Weiner, 2000; Wosinska, Dabul, Whetstone-Dion, & Cialdini, 1996).

We see evidence of hatred of arrogance in literature. Vanity and pride are considered cardinal sins in the Bible. On the other hand, modesty is generally seen as a positive trait, or virtue (Ben-Ze'ev, 1993). Our children's stories are filled with arrogant individuals whose grotesque conceit is automatically seen as evil. Think of Gaston in the story, *Beauty and the Beast*. The women we see fawning over Gaston are portrayed as shallow, silly, and dumb. We instead hail Belle as the heroine we would like to emulate, as she is too smart to fall for Gaston and instead falls for the broken and socially outcast Beast. The Beast defeats Gaston, and Belle is better off for her choice in the long run, which tells us we need to heed the warning in the fairy tale: Do not fall for arrogance. Unfortunately, real life is filled with subtlety and nuance, and examples of arrogance are infrequently as ugly or apparent.

Evolution is an arms race. As we have demonstrated, overconfidence is an offensive strategy meant to gain males who possess it access to more resources and mates than they would have otherwise been capable of. Falling for an arrogant display would have imposed unique costs to men (as rivals in intrasexual competition) and to women (as potential mates in intersexual competition). To counter such costly harm arrogance detection and disgust for it evolved as a defensive strategy.

In order to see how such distaste for arrogance could have evolved, let us consider the benefits of such prejudices individually. For men, an arrogant rival poses a unique problem. It is hard to objectively evaluate that rival in the moment, and losing to this rival will often mean losing to a potential inferior. Resources and mates gained by an arrogant rival mean fewer resources and mates for others. This would have imposed great cost among men in our evolutionary past. In an effort to thwart the benefit that such arrogance could have brought this rival, men could have developed disgust towards arrogant displays and could have imposed a social cost on those men who displayed such arrogance. This would have reduced the net benefit of arrogant displays and may have prevented rivals from using them to gain valuable resources and mates.

An example of this can be found among the Kung San of the Kalahari Desert. Although we cannot observe our ancestors and their living conditions, we can see evidence of how they lived in the hunter-gatherer tribes that exist to this day. They are a window into deep time, into the environment that shaped who we are today. The living conditions and pressures experienced by the Kung San of the Kalahari Desert mimic what our ancestors would have experienced. Among the Kung San, we see evidence of hatred of arrogance. They have rituals to discourage arrogance among hunters. When a man has a successful kill, he must forego bringing the meat back himself, and must return to the settlement empty-handed. Another member of the tribe would then remark about the lack of kill, forcing the hunter to act humbly. A group goes out later that day or the next on the premise that perhaps an animal was hit by an arrow. The hunting party then seeks out the animal together. They scoff at the puny size of the kill and the waste of time it would be to drag it back to camp, further humbling the hunter. They then return to camp with the kill as a successful group. Such displays are intended to decrease arrogance among the men of the tribe (Lee, 2012).

For women, falling for an arrogant display would have sometimes led to mating with inferior individuals and loss of potential resources. Mating with a man who is overconfident about being able to protect and provide for her and her offspring would have been very costly to a woman in our EEA. For many, avoiding arrogant individuals meant avoiding this cost. A woman could have then used other factors when considering a potential mate, such as resources she could see or watching interactions between a potential suitor and other members of the group. Distaste for arrogance could have allowed her to avoid the lies of overconfidence, and may have benefited her in the long run, even at the cost of a potentially superior mate who used highly confident displays as an honest signal. Therefore, the reproductive success garnered by avoiding such displays would have allowed such distaste for arrogance to propagate for generations.

Concluding remarks

Arrogance pays big dividends. The evidence is overwhelming. But, we have an evolved distaste for arrogance, and that may lead us to underestimate arrogance's power, utility, and success. That evolved distaste may also lead us to see arrogance as pure psychopathology, a defect in human nature that arises from pre-oedipal problems or bumps in the later oedipal road, defects that can be treated or cured. Our hope is to remove those blinders. Arrogance evolved because it was successful in the only currency that shaped human beings, reproductive success. For ancestral women to survive and reproduce, for us to be here today to write and to read this chapter, those ancestral women had to secure mates who could provide and commit sustained reproductive resources in harsh, dangerous environments: food, shelter, protection, and healthy genes. The markers for those traits were largely invisible or indirect. Women had to make educated guesses. That left the door open for men to evolve the capacity to lie about those abilities, to the women and to themselves, in order to gain sexual access.

The psychology of arrogance, with its propensity for grandiosity, informs an obvious clinical entity, narcissistic personality disorder. If we are correct about arrogance's origins, the psychoanalytic formulations of narcissism and narcissistic personality disorder need revision. Inferiority and envy supposedly lurk beneath narcissism and contempt. Maybe not. Sometimes narcissism, narcissistic personalities, and the dark triad (narcissism, Machiavellianism, and psychopathy) may just be built with overconfidence and a genuinely held belief of superiority. Maybe what we see is all there is. At the same time, conceptual space must be left for a debate about complementarity of evolutionary and psychodynamic perspectives on arrogance.

We have laid out the argument for arrogance's innateness in human nature. Its causes are buried in deep history, our hunter-gatherer past, and Darwinian evolution. We have reviewed the evidence: the fact of natural selection, the fact of sexual selection, the evolutionary logic of self-deception, the fact of parental investment theory that shaped sex differences in all species, the cross species evidence, the cultural evidence, and the studies from psychological research. To reject this view of arrogance's nature, origins, and causes, with its sound theories and mountains of evidence, would be a bit arrogant.

Chapter 3

Arrogance of children and adolescents

Ann Smolen

It is not unusual to treat adults who demonstrate arrogance as a prominent personality trait. Most often these patients suffer with narcissistic personalities and are for the most part difficult patients, and may cause strong countertransference reactions in the analyst. In my experience as a child and adolescent analyst, arrogance is, for the most part, not a prominent feature in the majority of child and adolescent patients I see. Therefore when arrogance appears habitually, and as a commanding feature of the young child or adolescent, it is striking and disturbing. This chapter explores, through the treatment of three child patients (ages five, twelve, and fourteen) the development of arrogance as a prominent personality trait and defense.

The case of Bernard

Background information

Bernard, age fourteen, is the oldest of three siblings, and the only and highly revered son. His parents value and strongly emphasize academic achievement, and are extremely successful in their own high-status professions. Bernard's father is emotionally cold and aloof and his stressful job keeps him away from his family on business trips, sometimes for weeks at a time. Bernard's mother appears to be the emotional core of the family, but she suffers from moderate anxiety and depression, which has manifested in intrusive and controlling interactions with her son.

Bernard's history is surprisingly uneventful. His parent's financial successes have allowed Bernard every opportunity: the best schools, musical instrument lessons, sports, and a home with every amenity imaginable. He is a physically healthy adolescent, other than normal childhood illnesses over the years. Separations were always easy for him, and he is an exemplary student, exhibiting superior intelligence.

His mother described Bernard's early years wistfully as a sweet little boy with a wonderful sense of humor. So what went wrong? Why, now that Bernard was fourteen years old, was he sullen, belligerent, rude, and most of all arrogant? At age twelve, Bernard began spending most of his time alone in his room. Over the next two years, his behavior worsened as he refused to participate in family dinners and other family activities. He became disrespectful toward his parents, pouring the majority of his arrogant rage onto his mother, spitting out venomous verbiage. He seemed to enjoy name-calling, sneering the word "stupid" in daily interactions with his mother and sisters. In addition, Bernard's behavior toward his younger sisters was described by his mother as "deplorable and torturous," often resulting in the girls being reduced to tears.

Bernard's parents sought treatment because Bernard had confessed to a group of girls (his only friends at school) via text message that he was cutting himself and had suicidal thoughts. This information scared the girls and they reported it to the school counselor. It was suggested that he be seen by a strong male analyst, but after a few sessions, Bernard refused to see this analyst, citing that the analyst's office was too dark, dingy, and dirty. Bernard also refused to speak with the analyst, sitting mute, playing games on his phone, ignoring all efforts to engage in conversation. Bernard ended up in my office because I have a reputation of being open and friendly, thus it was thought by my colleague that I would be able to reach this silent, dour, and morose boy.

Meeting Bernard

He entered my office, eyes darting around seemingly taking in the surroundings to assess if my office was also dark, dingy, and dirty. I motioned to him where to sit and he proceeded to treat me in the same way he had treated my colleague. I found myself working very hard to connect with him and seemed to make some headway because at the end of the session, he told me how stupid his mother is and how much he hates her.

In the first weeks of our work, Bernard saw me as an advocate, and used me to get what he wanted from his mother. I was able to help his mother understand that an adolescent boy needs privacy (she now allowed him to close his bedroom door) and gain some autonomy (she began to let him venture out on his skateboard and bike). In retrospect, perhaps these parental interventions were a mistake because Bernard began to hate me as his arrogance overwhelmed both of us. He could not tolerate receiving anything nice or good from me, just as he could not accept anything good from his mother. I immediately became the overbearing intrusive mother in the transference to be hated and despised. I was hoping to develop a positive transference with Bernard knowing all too well what was to come, however only negative feelings persisted. When school began, he used his sessions to complete his homework. In one particular session, he needed colored pencils for a graph and asked if I had red and green pencils. I retrieved these pencils from my playroom and gave them to him. Bernard was unable to complete the assignment during his session so I offered him the pencils to take home. He could not accept my gift, broke and threw the pencils across the room and walked out.

The course of treatment

Each session was worse than the preceding one. Now that he had what he wanted from me – to get his way with his mother – he no longer had any use for me. Once again, he became mute and communicated his arrogant rage through physical acting-out behaviors. In every session, he would do one or several of the follow-ing: (1) break all of the light bulbs in my lamps by shaking the lamps; (2) cut up psychoanalytic brochures in my waiting room; (3) throw my newly upholstered chair across my office; (4) put his dirty shoes all over my newly upholstered fur-niture; (5) try to light a fire by playing with the lamp cord in the electrical outlet, making sparks; (6) throw glass marbles so hard against the wall in my playroom, shattering many; (7) bring food and eat in session, dropping crumbs and clean-ing his sticky fingers on the furniture. It goes without saying that I stopped all of these disruptive behaviors and attempted to translate his behaviors into words and attempted to understand the meaning behind the behaviors. I also sought consulta-tion in order to continue to try to reach this boy, but also to sort out my counter-transference. I was beginning to hate him as he hated me.

The day after the horrific terrorist attacks in Paris, Bernard began his session animated and uncharacteristically talkative. Earlier in the day his mother had left me a voice message despairingly describing how Bernard's treatment of his sisters had worsened and he was "terrorizing" the family. In his session, Bernard gave an oration emphatically declaring that the terrorists were not to be blamed for their murderous behaviors because they were indoctrinated: "That is how they were brought up to think, it isn't personal, it's their political beliefs." I won-dered aloud about the innocent people who were murdered and their families who were left behind to suffer in grief, and the senselessness of the terrorist acts. He again stated that none of that mattered because the terrorists were groomed to not care about individuals. They did what they did for the greater good. At that point, I remembered his mother's earlier message to me and I shared with Bernard that his mother felt he was terrorizing his family and she was extremely concerned about him. I asked him why he was acting like a terrorist, because surely that was not how he was being brought up. He got up and stormed out of my office.

This vignette is embarrassing to confess, as I certainly was not at my analytic best to say the least. Bernard was trying to tell me about himself in displace-ment and I was overcome by my countertransference and by my own dismay over what had transpired in Paris so was not able to meet him in his displacement. I could not stay in the "play," and Bernard could not tolerate the reality. Bernard's mother was alarmed that I had called her son a terrorist, but Bernard continued his therapy, attending all of his sessions. His acting out behaviors worsened. No matter how I attempted to explore his feelings that motivated these behaviors, Bernard remained silently destructive. However, his behavior at home dramati-cally improved. His mother reported that he was nicer to his sisters, had stopped degrading her, and was even asking her advice on his homework. He was spend-ing less time in his room alone and was now joining the family for meals and other family outings. Life at Bernard's home was far from perfect, but it was improved. Meanwhile in my office, I spent most of our sessions stopping Ber-nard from destroying my property. He replaced destroying my office with verbally degrading me, stating how stupid I am and how I could never be a help to him because of my low intelligence. I was now the cause of all of his problems. He claimed that if he no longer had to come see me all would be well. He had no memory of what had brought him into therapy in the first place, and could not tolerate any attempt at exploring the multiple meanings that were motivating his hostile, arrogant behaviors. When summer came, Bernard left treatment to travel through Europe with a teen group. He did not return in the fall.

The case of Chloe

Background information

When Chloe was twelve years old, her mother left the family precipitously. She divorced Chloe's father and moved to Indonesia to be with a man she had corresponded with via the internet. This came as a shock to Chloe, her little brother, and her father. Chloe's father was devastated as his life was turned upside down. During Chloe's first twelve years, he was rarely home, self-described as a workaholic. When he was home, he demanded near perfection from his children, often berating them when they brought home a B instead of an A on school work. Chloe's father did not know how to begin to fill-in for a mother who abandoned her children, as he did not even know how to be a loving father.

Meeting Chloe

Chloe elected to sit in my "adult" office, scoffing at the mere suggestion that she might find my playroom inviting. It has been my experience that twelve-year-old children tend to use both rooms, finding comfort in the ambiance of my playroom while trying on the feel of the adult room. Not Chloe. I got the impression that Chloe had forgotten how to play, or perhaps had not been played with for a very long time, if ever. My adult chair seemed to swallow-up this extremely thin, pale girl as she played solitaire on her phone, periodically stealing angry glances at me.

My efforts to engage her fell flat. She clearly did not want to talk about her mother and stated that it meant nothing to her; she had absolutely no feelings about her mother taking off across the world with a new boyfriend. "Her life has nothing to do with me. My life won't change. I don't know why everyone is making such a big deal about this." I heeded her warning that I must tread lightly, aware of how terribly painful her situation was.

Chloe's arrogance took the defensive form of being a "know-it-all." She insisted that she was always right, never needed to ask for help, and would creatively elaborate on the smallest crumb of truth until it became a very tall tale indeed. In the process, she caused her listener to feel stupid, foolish, and always wrong. Needless to say, Chloe had no friends. Her upscale private school was filled with girls who were not worth her time or energy. Chloe was a very lonely, sad child.

The course of treatment

For the first three years of treatment, Chloe's arrogance served as a protective shell. She barely spoke to me, always fiddling with her phone or iPod, occasionally making eye contact for only a second or two, but she came to every session and was never late. I was working with her father weekly, helping him to parent his bereft children as well as providing much-needed parent education on child and adolescent development. Most important, my presence seemed to be needed to help make this broken family whole. Even the nanny was allowed to come in for sessions. This father and family needed all the help he and they could get, and Chloe, in her soundless wrath, was grateful.

A change occurred at the end of our third year of treatment. By this time, Chloe had begun to trust me and would share problems about menstruation, her hair, her nails, what shoes to wear, a terrible teacher who graded her unfairly. I clearly was the stand-in, wished-for benevolent mother. Chloe's method of asking for help, however, was not straightforward. She approached her concern or worry by telling me the facts about a situation, stating emphatically that she was certain she was right and everyone else was wrong. If I offered to explore her worries from a different perspective or made a deeper interpretation pertaining to her own internal conflict, she instantly and with arrogant disdain, refused to entertain my offerings. I did not view our interactions as fighting one another or even disagreeing with each other. This was our dance. Chloe communicated to me (and the world) making use of her arrogance as a protective shield. In the moment, my words were discarded, as she attempted to belittle our work, and me, but she heard me, and slowly over time, began to integrate and make use of what I offered.

In our work as analysts, we hear about "ah ha moments" from our colleagues, or we read about such momentous moments in polished case studies, or perhaps we are lucky enough to have experienced such a moment in our own analyses. It seemed that Chloe did have an "ah ha" experience. Over the years, I wondered about all sorts of feelings Chloe may be having concerning her abandonment: sadness, missing feelings, frustration, and rage, even love for the mother who left her. As I stated earlier, she always dismissed my attempts at exploring her deeper hidden feelings; that was, until she became enraged with her mother and refused to visit with her when she came back into the country. This seemed to be Chloe's "ah ha moment." She found agency and power in her anger. The best part was she could share her sadness with me as she cried angry tears, and her arrogant defenses began to crack.

Over the next two years, Chloe blossomed. She developed a quick wit and was funny. She excelled in her sport and was valued by her team. She made a few friends and attended a prom at a boy's prep school nearby. She also worked hard and did well in school. Chloe began to forgive her mother to some extent, and began to visit with her, but always calling the shots, such as staying for one night only. Chloe chose to write her college essay about her experience of "growing herself up." When Chloe gets upset or narcissistically wounded, she resorts to arrogant defenses once again, but her recovery, over time, is much improved. As Chloe prepared to leave for college, I felt confident she would find her way.

The case of David

Background information

I nicknamed five-year-old David "my angriest little boy." He was a force to be reckoned with. His divorced parents brought him to me because they could no longer tolerate his outlandish behaviors. He kicked, screamed, hit, stole and hid his mother's belongings, broke household items, and shouted obscenities at both of his parents. His pediatrician claimed he was oppositional defiant, and suggested that soap be put in his mouth when he misbehaved. Needless to say, I was appalled at this labeling and suggestion of abusive punishment by a physician. His mother was convinced he would become a drug addict and be in jail by the time he was an adolescent.

In my meetings with David's parents, I was struck by their abysmal conduct toward one another. Both showed contemptuous behavior toward the other. When both parents were present, the sessions quickly dissolved into name calling by the father and David's mother melting into angry tears. It seemed more productive to meet with David's parents individually. Upon doing just that, I quickly became aware that neither parent was able to listen (especially David's mother), and both were in significant psychic pain. In addition, David's father demonstrated arrogant traits as a commanding feature of his personality. My earliest understanding of David's outlandish behaviors was that he needed to resort to annoying pranks (such as stealing and hiding his mother's cell phone), and rageful physical attacks on his parents' bodies in a desperate effort to be seen and heard. David's crude nasty language toward both his parents, but mostly his mother, was actually this little boy identifying with and mimicking his father.

Meeting David

I heard him coming from inside my office, behind double doors and two sound-numbing machines in my waiting room. It sounded as if someone was throwing large heavy objects against the hallway walls and then my waiting room walls. Within seconds, David, five years old, tiny for his age, had turned off the sound-numbing machines, changed the channel on the radio, and moved the time on my clock. Children's books that I keep in a basket were strewn across the room and he was hiding under the couch. He easily separated from his mother who gave me an exasperated look as if to say: "He is your problem now." David proceeded to continue his path of destruction in my office. I explained to David that I had few rules but there were two very important rules: (1) nobody is allowed to break my things on purpose; (2) nobody is allowed to hurt me. David continued to try to break my belongings and stated: "I don't care. I hate your things. I don't care about you or your things. I can do whatever I want to." Certainly, there was defiance in his actions and arrogance in his tone, but he was telling me how out of control he felt. I decided at that moment that even though it was exhausting for me and seemed like I was not helping him to control his feelings, I would allow him to make gigantic, huge messes in my playroom.

The course of treatment

In three sessions per week for over a year, David "stole" special objects that I keep in my adult office and hid them in my playroom. I would say: "Oh my, you have taken my very special china figurine and have hidden it so well that it will take me days to find it. I will have to spend so much time looking for it and all that time I will be thinking of you and remembering our time together." David would turn away from me in an effort to hide his smile. At first he smirked and laughed at me in a demeaning arrogant fashion as if to say: "You fool, I can make you do anything I want." Soon it evolved into a smile of genuine pleasure that I would spend time thinking of and remembering him. In every session, he would run into my office and immediately look for the object he had hidden to make sure I had kept my word and kept him in mind.

His play was chaotic: dumping baskets of Lego, baskets of small cars, baskets of army figures, baskets of whatever I had. I would interpret his messes, showing him I would do my best to understand his inner feelings of chaos and help him put words to his actions. He refused to help me clean up his mess, arrogantly claiming he sure didn't have to do that, because he didn't care how I felt ever! I would reply: "Wow, this sure is a big mess. You really want me to spend so much time thinking about you because it will take me a long time to clean this up after you go home and all that time I will be thinking about you and thinking about all these messy difficult feelings you are having."

During that first year, I met with David's mother weekly, and listened to her sad story as she cried. When David's mother began to feel heard and cared about by me, she gradually began to listen to what I had to offer about David and her parenting began to change. Over time, she came to understand that David was begging for time with her. My work with David's father was less productive as his arrogance was almost impossible for me to penetrate. But he too, over time, became a better parent and made use of some of my parenting advice.

Over the next two years, David's play became more contained and organized. He no longer needed to hide my belongings, and stealing and hiding his mother's things also stopped. Instead of punishing David's unacceptable behaviors, his mother began to provide limits and boundaries and validate the difficult feelings that were motivating the behaviors. In his sessions, when home life was challenging or he became anxious over schoolwork, he would once again regress to making huge messes, with one difference, he could tell me after making the mess what he was feeling, and best of all, he offered to clean it up, and we would do that together. I no longer thought of David as arrogant or as "my angriest little boy."

After a two-week vacation, David's mother emailed me the following statement from David: "I don't know how Dr. Ann does it. I think she must have magic because all we do is play and I feel better."

Discussion

Theoretical remarks

Elaborating on early Freud, where the child's omnipotence, regulated by the pleasure principle continues well into adolescence (Freud, 1914c, p. 91), Ferenczi (1913) developed his own stages of omnipotence. He began with the fetus, stating that there is unconditional omnipotence in the womb. Next came the infant/ preverbal baby who experiences magical hallucinatory omnipotence. Finally, the omnipotence of animistic thinking of the older toddler and preschool-age child. At this stage of omnipotence, magical thoughts and words infused with omnipotence are "validated by an adoring entourage of adults" (Novick & Novick, 2014, p. 442). Ferenczi's stages of omnipotence delineated the baby's connection to internal and outer reality. Ferenczi surmised: "All children live in the happy delusion of omnipotence, which at some time or other – even if only in the womb – they really partook of" (1913, p. 232). It was also thought that these stages could become fixation points for serious adult pathology.

Over the next several decades, child analysts such as Anna Freud (1936), Winnicott (1949), Bowlby (1969, 1973, 1980), Fraiberg (1959), and Mahler (1968), to name just a few, were influential in changing how we understand normal child development. Our psychoanalytic theories often dictate practice and unfortunately our theories do not evolve and transform fast enough to keep up with cultural and societal changes. It is imperative, when viewing arrogance as a prominent presenting trait in child patients, to also explore parenting through a historical lens. Over the last century, especially since the internet and social media explosion, parents were left confused as to how and when to set limits. In the early 1900s, ". . . children were afraid to lose their parent's love; by the end of the century, at least in the United States, it was parents who seemed afraid they would lose their children's love. Parents not only feared the neurotic consequences of repressing their children; even more, they feared loss and any reproach from their children if they set standards, made demands, or invoked any consequences of behavior" (Novick & Novick, 2014, p. 443). A majority of children, as a consequence of ineffectual parenting, no longer present with what analysts describe as "classical neurotic symptoms." Instead, we are seeing children who experience difficulties in regulation and often exhibit defiant and oppositional behaviors at home and at school. Parents complain that they feel powerless and cannot help their children attend to homework, behave at mealtime, and settle into bed at night. "In the popular view, psychoanalysis did not seem to offer anything useful; indeed, it seemed to have created a monster" (ibid., p. 443). Psychoanalytic theory postulates that the infant is born omnipotent and slowly and unwillingly accepts reality. The Novicks argue that omnipotence is not normal, but rather "[I]t is a defensive, compensatory belief, generated as a sometimes necessary response to the trauma of the failure of reality" (p. 444). In justification of their argument, the Novicks point out that the earliest relationship of the mother and her infant is not symbiotic, the anal phase of development is not just sadistic, the oedipal conflict is not always experienced as a trauma, latency is certainly not a time of repression, masochism, while pervasive, is not normal, and adolescence is not always experienced as a time of emotional instability. The Novicks are convinced that omnipotence is not a part of normal development; in fact they believe the complete opposite. In their view, the presence of omnipotence is a red flag and points to a pathological resolution to conflict. "Rather than the classical view that the failure of omnipotence forces the child to turn to reality, we suggest that it is the failure of reality that forces a child, at any point in development, to turn to closed-system OMNIPOTENT solutions, resulting in self-centered, entitled function" (p. 446).

More and more, child analysts are seeing children who are extremely anxious and out of control. Like Bernard, some of these children have been coddled and treated as "special." These children are entitled, grandiose, and arrogant. However, other children such as Chloe and David have a history of an absence of a good-enough, attuned mother and a modulating and organizing father.

Clinical remarks

All three children seemed to feel entitled "to be demanding and derogatory toward others" (Horney, 1945, p. 167). Of the three cases, Bernard demonstrated extreme arrogance. Unfortunately, his treatment ended prematurely and was not successful. In the weeks before Bernard left treatment he "appear[ed] to have no problems other than the existence of the analyst [her]self" (Bion, 1958, p. 144). Clearly, Bernard and his analyst "formed a frustrated couple" (ibid., p. 144). Freud (1915c), described arrogance as "in love with one's idealized image" (p. 138). Bernard was intellectually gifted, and was the favored and most admired child. He seemed unable to own up to or acknowledge his own limitations, and certainly could never admit that he had failed in anything, especially his inability to form friendships. Other children his age did not like him. He was often left out of social get-togethers. Once he reached puberty, Bernard became depressed with self-destructive urges and behaviors. The only way Bernard could figure out how to help himself feel better was to claim malicious victory over others by his demeaning and nasty thoughts and behaviors (Horney, 1950). However, clearly this tactic did not really work. It seemed to me that Bernard thought he was successful in fooling others into thinking he was superior to them, while in reality, Bernard was terrified that everyone would know the truth, and see that he possessed faults, and had limitations. He had to guard against this humiliation at all costs.

In my effort to develop a positive transference and to let Bernard know that I felt empathy for his pain, I fell into his trap where he used me as a means to an end. Once his mother took my advice and gave him more appropriate privacy and independence for a boy his age, he was done with me and had no further use for me. Bernard spent his sessions attempting to humiliate me and felt perfectly entitled to criticize and demean me. Bernard was not capable of insight, and heard everything I had to offer as a criticism, leaving a deep narcissistic wound. Bernard felt entitled "to the unabridged expression of his unfavorable observations and criticisms, but felt equally entitled never to be criticized himself" (ibid., p. 200).

Buried beneath Bernard's arrogant façade was an overwhelming distrust in others. He regarded everyone with skepticism until proven otherwise and even then he was always suspicious. At the slightest slip, Bernard would pronounce his victim untrustworthy and once again feel justified in treating others rudely and offensively. As the months wore on, Bernard's main purpose in attending his sessions was to defeat me. This goal took on more importance than obtaining insight into his worries and concerns. He seemed incapable of mentalization or of feeling empathy, and he seemed to have no interest in gaining understanding of his relationships. Because Bernard isolated himself and only exhibited hostility toward others, he had to convince himself that he had no need of others (ibid.). He was unable to receive anything I had to offer, such as concrete items (colored pencils) or more abstractly, inquiry into his mind.

In the clinical vignette, when hate in the countertransference got the better of me, and I almost literally called Bernard a terrorist, his "protective layer of invulnerability" was pierced and he could not allow himself to tolerate the pain, so he fled. "Self-hate is always cruel and merciless" (Horney, 1945, p. 207). Bernard hated in others exactly what he despised in himself.

Chloe's arrogance presented differently from Bernard's. Chloe had been emotionally neglected probably for her whole life. Before her mother moved across the ocean, she told me: "If my child and a stranger's child ran in front of a car, I would save one of the children, but it wouldn't matter if it was my child or the stranger's child." I understood Chloe's arrogant personality traits as a defense against profound emotional neglect. Arrogance combined with her superior intelligence protected her and saved her from more severe pathology such as psychoses, but had dire consequences.

When Chloe began treatment, she was performing poorly in her affluent, extremely academic private school, which enraged her father. It seemed like she had developed an inability to learn, and was no longer curious. "The disturbance of the impulse of curiosity on which all learning depends, and the denial of the mechanism by which it seeks expression, makes normal development impossible" (Bion, 1959, p. 299). Chloe's development was arrested as she isolated herself behind a cloak of arrogance where emotion was insufferable and "too powerful to be contained by [her] immature psyche" (ibid., p. 299). In Bernard's treatment and in the first three years of Chloe's treatment, when I demonstrated curiosity in them, it was met with incomprehension and arrogant contempt. I was then made to feel stupid and was blamed. I was aware that Bernard and I shared a subtle (or perhaps not too subtle) mutual contempt for one another (Britton, 2013; Zimmer, 2013). That did not occur with Chloe, which allowed the two of us to enter into a space of mutual understanding even in the face of her arrogant persona.

All three of the cases demonstrate that in the absence of an attuned mother and a modulating father, normal development gets stymied and often narcissistic defenses become distorted and magnified. According to Herzog (2004), in order for normal development to proceed, the child must develop a sense of self-with-mother, a sense of self-with-father, and most important, a sense of self-with-mother-and-father-together. Bernard's mother was anxious, depressed, and overbearing, while his father was absent. Chloe's mother was literally absent when she abandoned her children, but was not emotionally available to them before she fled. Chloe's father was overly harsh as well as emotionally unattuned. David's parents were so wrapped up in their own narcissistic vulnerabilities that neither parent was able to be attuned to his emotional needs or able to help modulate his overwhelming affects. In all three of these cases, the parents were emotionally estranged from one another. These children were left alone with their overwhelming aggression. Bernard, Chloe, and David were all "en route to the development of a perverse character structure in which the self is taken as object, and in which control of, rather than relating to, is the principal mode of interaction with others" (ibid., p. 894).

All three children had a seriously compromised ability to develop healthy self-esteem. They kept these vulnerabilities concealed beneath a false-self (Winnicott, 1965) of an arrogant self-assured attitude. They had all developed rigid coping mechanisms resulting in an arrogant, omnipotent sense of self. These children kept feelings of sadness at bay, making use of grandiosity to communicate to themselves and the world that they did not need anyone. Bernard, Chloe, and David all had grave difficulties in expressing love or gratitude, and displayed a disinterest in others. All three children devalued others in an effort to maintain a stable sense of self. In the therapeutic relationship, all three children played out with me their relentless attempts to remain disengaged, fearful that dependency and warm loving feelings might lead them to experience themselves as powerless and helpless. Over time, Chloe and David were able to allow their arrogant narcissistic defenses to begin to peel away, revealing new healthier coping mechanisms and defenses.

Undertaking and entering into treatment with children like Bernard, Chloe, and David is arduous, often stimulating intense countertransference feelings. The case of Bernard demonstrates where feelings in the analyst can be so intense that analytic thinking and behaving goes right out the window, derailing the treatment, and in Bernard's case, destroying the treatment. The analyst often feels boredom (as Chloe spent three years silently playing on her phone) and exploited (as I often questioned my allowing David to dump every toy in my playroom and to hide my precious belongings).

Last thoughts

When parents are emotionally unavailable, the child is unable to develop an efficient and adaptive method of communicating his or her needs. Very quickly, a system of gross misattunement is set up which sets the stage for dysregulation and distress (Slade, 1998; Stern, 1985). As the mother recognizes and finds meaning in her child's affects, the child is then able to see herself as a thinking, feeling, separate self. When the mother is unable to contain and reflect her infant's affects, the infant then becomes unable to self-regulate and normal development is at risk (Slade, 1998). Crucial to an infant's development is the parent's ability for attunement. In order to be properly attuned to their child, the parents must be able to differentiate their child's needs from their own. This, in turn, affects all future development.

Stern (1985) defines attunement as the "intersubjective sharing of affect" (p. 141). Several developmental and attachment theorists (such as Bowlby, Ainsworth, Winnicott, Stern, Karen, Fonagy, Beebe, and Steele, to name a few) all consider attunement to be critical to the psychological and physical development of the infant. As the infant cries and demands to have his needs met, the mother responds and thus gives meaning to the infant's signals.

Parents who do not have the capacity for self-reflection are unable to reflect on the inner states of their child. This child will, in turn, be unable to relate to his or her own inner world. The infant who does not experience attunement and mirroring may experience his emerging preverbal self as defective. This child is left to feel empty, helpless, and perhaps in severe circumstances, even without hope.

Winnicott (1960) conceptualizes the earliest parent-child relationship as a "holding environment" and emphasizes the importance of empathy, continuity, stability, and safety to the well-being of the child. "Being held in an embrace of safety is essential in nourishing the development of healthy intrapsychic structure and a sense of trust" (Paret & Shapiro, 1998, p. 302). These early social experiences usher the child into the richness of object relations and what it means to relate to another person. As the parents recognize and find meaning in their child's affects, the child is then able to see himself as a thinking, feeling, separate self. When the parents are unable to contain and reflect upon their infant's affects the infant then becomes unable to self-regulate and normal development is at risk (Slade, 1998).

The cases of Bernard, Chloe, and David demonstrate how pathological family configurations and dynamics can derail normal narcissistic development and result in children and adolescents who resort to arrogant omnipotence in order to cope with their world. These children are difficult to be engaged with and stimulate intense countertransference in the analyst, yet with patience and perseverance, and especially with parents who engage in the treatment, these children can get back on the path to normal development.

Chapter 4

Defensive arrogance in adult philanderers

Jerome S. Blackman

A long time ago, in a hospital far, far away, I was a psychiatric consultant to a cardiology unit. Joe, a cardiologist friend of mine, confided in me his disagreement with the generally accepted theory that people with Type A personalities developed more heart disease (Friedman & Rosenman, 1959; Rosenman, Brand, Sholtz, & Friedman, 1976). Being a skeptical sort myself, I thought we should investigate.

To that end, Joe consulted me on several of his inpatients who had just suffered myocardial infarctions. They all happened to be male. In a nutshell, I found that all the men were arrogant. They refused to stop smoking (one was secretly bumming cigarettes from visitors) and overeating (fatty foods). In addition, they drank alcohol to excess and did not sleep enough because of work. They did not exercise.

I concluded that Joe was right. These men had developed heart disease not because of their personalities, but because their personalities caused them to flaunt the usual medical advice to avoid risk factors. It seemed that the physiological factors were causing the heart disease, not the personality directly. Although Joe had told his patients to stop their self-destructive behaviors, they had not obeyed. As I visited and consulted with these men, I discovered that their arrogance had different causes. Some seemed to have remained omnipotent since early childhood, and would listen to no one; some had developed grandiosity as a defense against depressive affect, which, when confronted, led to sadness and recollections, with decreased negativism; a third group showed counterphobic defenses, which, when confronted, yielded to insight into lifelong patterns of toughness supporting skewed concepts of masculinity. In all those men, heart disease was connected to their ignoring of risk factors; the risk factors were aggravated because of their arrogance; and their arrogance had multiple etiologies, some of which were understandable dynamically. Joe agreed with me. He encouraged me to write a paper about it, and I eventually did (Blackman, 1987).

Over the intervening years, I have treated numerous people who showed arrogant character traits (Blackman, 2013, chapters 21 and 94), and have continued applying psychoanalytic ideas in attempting to understand how they got that way. More recently, many married men have consulted me for "internet porn addiction" or "sex addiction." The self-diagnosed sex addicts were invariably cheating on their wives, and the porn addicts were dreaming of doing so. Most of them showed arrogance.

Although both arrogance and philandering can have a multitude of causes (Marcus, 2004), in this chapter, I describe here a fairly common etiology that I thought was worth reporting because it is so treatable with analytic techniques. Specifically, the men I discuss used arrogance and philandering to defend themselves from re-experiencing pain and guilt from an emotional trauma that had occurred in their late adolescence or early adulthood – at the same time they were expressing hostility, getting themselves punished, and repairing their self-esteem.

The word "arrogant," adolescent etiology, and a bit of literature

Language usage varies with the era and the culture (Cao, Blackman, & Guan, 2016). Today, arrogance is a word used to denote a certain kind of criticism of self-centered individuals. I have also noticed that the word seems to be used more often by older people (like me, for example). Younger adults tend to use shorter, Old English-derived vulgar words, such as "asshole" or "dick." In addition, for native speakers of twenty-first-century American English, the term arrogance is almost always used to describe a certain type of man. Hence, it is not surprising that the patient examples I will describe in this chapter, as in my paper thirty years ago, are men.[1]

Finally, noting the masculine feature of the word arrogance seems necessary but not sufficient. In one of the few similarities English has to Mandarin Chinese, we often use several words together (as I just did) for emphasis, and refer to such a man as an "arrogant prick," or even more commonly, an "arrogant son of a bitch." The pairing of these words also seems necessary because etymologically, "arrogant" is multisyllabic and Latinate – a type of English that is, more often than not, also comparatively devoid of emotion – unless coupled with Old English words, which are usually more affect laden. The word "'arrogant" derives from the Latin *ad* (to) and *rogare* (to ask). To arrogate is to "assume, or claim (to oneself) unduly or without justification" (*Shorter Oxford English Dictionary*, 2017). Interestingly, this fits well the men I will discuss, although, on reflection, most readers will feel this definition is inadequate since there is something about arrogance that often involves showing off.

There does not seem to be much analytic literature on arrogance *per se*. Bion (1958) saw arrogance as an aspect of psychotic or criminal thinking. Kernberg (1994) described pathological narcissism in middle-aged men, warning that suicide attempts in such patients are more likely as narcissistic supplies become less available. Akhtar (2009a) further refined Bion's definition, viewing arrogance "... as resulting from narrow-mindedness in the realm of feeling and perception. This, in turn, is caused by the hostile obliteration of the concept of 'whole

---

1 That's not to say that there are no arrogant women. It's just that other terms are usually used to describe them, such as "stuck up," "self-centered," or "full of herself."

objects' . . . and their replacement by dehumanized figures" (p. 26). Zimmer (2013) added that attributes of internalized grandiose objects could affect the self-image of arrogant persons.

From a slightly different point of view, any character trait (including arrogance) might be described as preserving the concept of discrete, descriptively concrete traits, based on the concepts of multiple function and compromise formation (Boesky, 1983); that is, any character trait, including arrogance, is "supra-ordinate" – a sort of final common pathway that solves conflicts among wishes, reality, superego, affects, and defensive operations.

The finding of adolescent/early adult trauma as the major etiology of the conflicts in arrogant philanderers is in agreement with Blum's (2010) astute description of how adolescent trauma can be etiological of psychopathology in general. His arguments parallel Becker's (1974) interesting view of how emotional trauma (especially parental seduction) during latency can be etiological of adult borderline pathology (Kernberg, 1975) – sometimes not involving our current understanding of the importance of preoedipal object relations damage (Akhtar, 1998). Using case examples, Blum (2010) deftly demonstrates how adolescent trauma can become the main stimulus of adult psychopathology – regardless of prior oedipal and preoedipal resolutions:

> Adolescence has its own regressive and progressive forces, determinants of the restructuring of the personality. Trauma in adolescence may have permanent pathogenic effects, represented in masturbation fantasy, transference, nightmares, acting out. Adolescence is the gateway to adult life, and adolescents have maturing bodies, more mature ego resources, more developed sexual and aggressive capacities, and a modified set of values, injunctions, and ideals, as compared with children. Analytic reconstruction of childhood is essential, but the memories, reconstruction, and recapitulation of adolescence are all important in adult analysis. Later adolescent fantasies of future relationships and goals, with expectations concerning career, marriage, and parenthood may be stifled or extinguished.
>
> (p. 550)

Below are three case vignettes which I hope will illustrate how each man's arrogant philandering acted as a complex compromise formation that largely defended against painful emotional traumata from his late adolescence/early adulthood – and how I worked with each man analytically.

The case of Marc

Background information

Marc, age fifty-two, worked hard as a corporate defense attorney. He played fantasy football with the men in his large firm, was well-liked, competent, and financially successful. He came to see me because he wanted his fourth marriage to work out. The odds were against him because he was cheating on his wife, Nancy, as he had cheated on the other three. Nancy recently had gotten suspicious when she found condoms in Marc's attaché case, and was leery when Marc arrogantly accused her of being paranoid. He brazenly claimed that he sometimes masturbated at work, when tense, and used a condom to prevent making a mess. Marc told me he loved Nancy, but he "couldn't stop" sleeping with other women.

Marc did not form relationships, to speak of, with the women he bedded (unlike the men suffering from "the two-woman phenomenon" [Chessick, 1989; Weiss, 1987]). Because his legal practice involved national companies, he often traveled. Attractive, slender, and clean-shaven, Marc charmingly teased women, making fun of himself for being arrogant; no one could easily accuse him of coming on to women, since he was just being pleasant and social. From what I learned about him, lonely women between about thirty-five and fifty years old were drawn to him, especially when he had hidden away his wedding ring in his briefcase before traveling by plane or train. Marc had learned, over the years, how not to show his hand with women, but to "chat them up" and wait for them to seduce him. Even the women he used for sex did not retaliate or call him a "jerk." Many of them never found out he was married.

Marc was arrogant, and he knew it. For a time, I wondered if Marc were a psychopath. But he seemed to feel genuine guilt over hurting Nancy; he was critical of his two grown sons from his second marriage; and he seemed to have a rigid work ethic. I eventually came to the conclusion that although he had lied to his wives about his dalliances, his superego, although apparently unintegrated (Ticho, 1972), was mostly harsh. I interpreted to him, and he agreed, that he "broke" (i.e., used undoing as a defense against) any strict adherence to rules he believed in. When he did this, he became excited by letting himself off the hook (rationalizations) – which, to a degree, relieved his guilt.

The course of treatment

During the first year of treatment, Marc revealed that he had a rating system for women. He asked me if I was interested in hearing it. When I asked him if he were thinking of educating me, he laughed, and then realized he did not know my attitudes regarding cheating on women. He continued that, in his mind, he graded women as NFW, PFW, and AFW. That is, when he saw a new woman, he would consider her "not fuck-worthy," "possibly fuck-worthy," or "absolutely fuck-worthy."

Molly, he said, was AFW. She visited him from her job in the firm's copy room. He would give her a glass of thirty-year-old, single malt scotch, which she loved, and then have various types of sex with her. He laughingly explained that it was hard to talk himself out of "the fact" that when Molly left his office, "She's happy, I'm happy, and since I don't have to bother my wife for sex as often, everybody's happy." He paused to ask me, "Right?!" I considered, for a moment, Marc's hardened rationalizations, which we had already discussed, his ribald sense of humor, and his return to the structure of his cheating. I therefore decided to make a slightly funny, aggressive intervention to highlight all this, in the service of disrupting (Schlesinger, 1995) his concreteness, acting out, rationalizations, and anti-authoritarian attitude.

So I hesitated, while he waited for my reaction, and then quietly responded, "That's bullshit." Marc broke out laughing, hysterically, for a minute. He finally responded, sarcastically, "Bullshit! That's certainly empathic!" I decided to handle his manipulativeness with another bit of humorous repartee. I ironically claimed: "I failed empathy during my psychiatry training." He now doubled over with laughter, for what seemed like more than a minute without letup.

His rationalizations diminished after that exchange. For two years, I spent time looking at how Marc rebelled against authorities, including being rebellious with me (transferences from adolescence) and breaking rules at work. Invariably he got punished by his wives: He was now paying large sums in alimony.

As our work proceeded, Marc complained of increased sadness (Brenner, 1975) and pessimism. We eventually understood that this shift reflected some depressive affect at the same time as it protected him from feeling criticized by me. Our interpretive work had stirred up Marc's severe unconscious guilt, which he had easily externalized onto me once I had confronted his defenses of suppression, undoing, self-centeredness, rationalization, provocation of punishment, minimization, and humor (Blackman, 2003a). He reported even more painful, depressive feelings, but was unsure what those feelings were about.

From an interpersonal standpoint, he recalled not cheating on Nancy until she revealed, during pillow-talk some months after they were married, that she had once made love with a man whose penis, she laughed, was much longer than Marc's. When Marc was quiet, she tried to reassure Marc that Marc's penis was "better" and the other guy's had been "weird." Marc reassured himself that he had had plenty of sex with women who were satisfied. Nevertheless, as he reflected on that conversation, he realized that Nancy's humor, which he consciously enjoyed, also had caused some painful injury to his self-esteem ("castration depressive affect" [Brenner, 2006]).

During his second year of treatment, Marc recalled how upsetting it had been, when he was thirteen years old, to overhear his mother talking dirty with his pediatrician. He realized, at that early age, that his mother was having an affair with the pediatrician – and cheating on his father. This primal scene-like experience led Marc to dis-identify from his father's passivity: Marc would be the cheater, and find a new woman in order to repair his own self-esteem and castration depressive affect. Marc also eventually forced each wife to witness Marc's infidelity – taking revenge on his mother and identifying with her as the aggressor (Arlow, 1980).

This and other understandings only went so far. In year three of treatment, Marc had curtailed some of his philandering, but had not stopped it. I suggested he tell me more about his earlier marriages. He corrected me. There was a girl before the marriages: Joan, "The Saint" (his phrase). Marc met her during his second year of college. She was brilliant in economics, beautiful, and funny. However, she wanted to stay a virgin until married (hence his nickname for her, which she didn't mind). At that time, Marc was a virgin, too. After two years, and much sexual play, they declared their mutual love and decided to get married. They then had sexual intercourse. They planned to move together where Marc had been accepted to law school. Marc told his parents, who had an unexpected response. They told him that if he married Joan, they would not pay for him to go to law school.

Marc did not remember having an emotional response at the time. He simply told Joan that they could not get married for three more years, until he finished law school. Joan reacted with anger, stating that she had only made love with Marc with the understanding that they would get married. When Marc froze, and would not consider going against his parents' opinion, Joan got angry and broke up with him. He did not try to make amends. His friends reassured him that there was always another trolley car coming down the rails every ten minutes. Within a year, St. Joan had married someone else, and let Marc know about it. As Marc recounted this story, he was surprised to find himself crying.

I interpreted to Marc that instead of facing his painful feelings and anger (isolation of affect), he had passively caved in to his parents' blackmail and minimized and rationalized losing Joan. Marc became more upset and continued crying. It turned out that his callousness and philandering had begun after he had lost Joan. After meeting his first wife in law school, he immediately began cheating on her. And so on with his second, third, and fourth wives. Marc now revealed that he had contacted Joan every ten years or so, and once they had dinner. They never had sexual intercourse again. His reunions with her had the quality of established pathological mourning (Volkan, 1981).

Marc's loss of Joan had been traumatic – in that it had caused him overwhelming pain, but he had used a variety of defensive operations to quell his overwhelming loss. Until discussing his relationship with Joan in treatment, he had never realized he had been angry or suffered much pain due to his parents' destruction of his autonomy and his first love. He had used dedifferentiation as a defense at the time, as well as passivity, rationalization, and then arrogant philandering – a supra-ordinate character formation that incorporated solutions to many of his conflicts. There had been other factors that contributed to Marc's arrogant philandering. Partly, at thirteen, he seemed to have used splitting, and seen his mother as entirely degraded. St. Joan seemed to represent the other half of the split mother image (idealized), which partly explained why Marc did not expect her to be so upset about his parents' blackmail. The precipitating factor for his pathological solution of arrogant philandering, however, seemed to be the ungrieved loss of St. Joan, dedifferentiation from his parents, and rationalizations and isolation of affect defending against anger and guilt – about that forgotten emotional trauma from his early adulthood.

The case of Laurence

Background information

Laurence, age forty-one, was from a well-to-do family in Wisconsin that had made their money in the dairy business. After finishing prep school, he attended

University of Wisconsin-Madison, and graduated with a degree in chemistry. He first moved to work for a chemical company outside New Orleans, Louisiana. By the time he consulted me, he had already used family money and some of his savings from work to start his own oil service business in the New Orleans area. He was successful.

Laurence's wife, Jennifer, was a CPA but had only practiced for a few years before they had children. They had met at University of Wisconsin, and got married as soon as they both graduated. Laurence first mundanely mentioned that they had three children, a fifteen-year-old girl and two boys, ages ten and eight. His initial presentation was so filled with normalizations that they caused me to think of what, on the Rorschach test, are called "populars."

When I brought the normalizations to his attention, Laurence admitted he had consulted me because he was afraid Jennifer would soon find out that he frequented prostitutes. She had been asking him about fidelity lately. He thought she had a sixth sense about it, although he had been careful. He had had a hard time explaining the phone number Jennifer found of someone named Ursula. Jennifer had called the number, but when she asked the woman on the other end of the line how she knew Jennifer's husband, the woman hung up and would not pick up the phone after that. Jennifer was now angry and demanded an explanation. She would not have sex with Laurence until he "came clean." So far, he had tried to say Ursula must have been someone he had met somewhere who he did not remember, but Jennifer didn't buy it.

Regarding the mechanics of his liaisons, he explained that he usually took off for a long lunch hour. Since he was the CEO of his own business, no one asked him about his whereabouts, so he could just go to a hotel where a "high-class call girl" had been procured for him by a friend who "had connections. He felt "strange" about his "addiction" to going to prostitutes, but arrogantly asserted that it was "his life" with which he should be able to do whatever he wanted. When I asked if there were anything special he did with hookers, he admitted he liked to "go down on" (a colloquial phrase denoting cunnilingus) the hooker for quite a while before they had intercourse. He arrogantly argued that reading any meaning into that was useless. He felt what he did was "pretty usual."

The course of treatment

Over time, I pointed out the arrogant side of his argumentativeness to him. He at first was defensive, claiming he was a "model husband" who supported his family. His wife did not have to work. She was busy remodeling their kitchen at a steep price. He had just paid to install a fancy hot tub, and she had her own personal trainer. He rather arrogantly claimed that when Jennifer asked him to do anything, he always had to accede to her wishes.

As he described this aspect of their relationship, I brought his passivity (of which he was unaware) to his attention, and he begrudgingly admitted to this, though he rationalized that all husbands, sooner or later, learned to say, "Yes, Dear," when their wives wanted anything. He told me a joke: "A man in the locker room, after a shower, picks up the mobile phone and says, 'Sure, dear, if you want that $20,000 dining room set, go get it. The new Mercedes 500 series is on sale? Definitely. The beach house has been reduced to $2.5 million? Put in a bid pronto!' – then the guy hangs up and shouts into the lockers, 'Hey, whose phone is this?'"

I explained my opinion that Laurence used humor, made excuses for his own problem of passivity with Jennifer, and generalized and projected by assuming I would agree with him about "all husbands." He then agreed that acceding to one's wife might not be universal, and after some discussion, he finally saw that he was again making excuses for himself.

This led us to discuss the history of his marriage. He said he had enjoyed their first few years together, before the children. Also, his wife had been working back then, and he thought she changed after the first child. Maybe her self-esteem had dropped so she needed to focus on the house and the children, he thought.

They had both wanted the first child. He admitted their sex life withered after his daughter was born, as his wife wanted the child in their bedroom until the girl was about three years old. He had passively assented to that, although he would have liked the baby to sleep in her own room so he could have had more spontaneous and frequent sex with his wife. At that point, going to hookers didn't enter his thinking.

He was less motivated about having a second child. He tried to indicate this to his wife, but she was adamant. She wanted to "try for a boy." He assented. After his son was born, his wife became inundated with child-oriented activities, and seemed much less interested in sex. Laurence "sucked it up," but in retrospect, he saw he had been denying how deprived he felt (Levin, 1969).

He once tried to explain to his wife that sexual activity was necessary to him as a man. She responded by accusing him of being an "arrogant son of a bitch," cried, and insisted on her right to make her own decisions about sex. When he tried to defend himself, she said she didn't feel turned on if he was just "horny." He apologized, admitted he had perhaps been a bit unempathic, then went upstairs to his "man cave" and masturbated while watching pornography showing women with large breasts. Then he watched football and smoked a cigar.

This report gave me a chance to help Laurence see that his passivity with Jennifer caused him to feel like less than a man, and that he reassured himself of his manliness with the sports and porn. I linked the cigar with his interest in using his mouth on prostitutes. I suggested that this "oral" activity seemed symbolic of his wish to depend on a woman. But dependency made him ashamed – so he either sucked it up, or covered his shame by sexualizing his dependency wishes into performing oral sex or looking at breasts while masturbating. We discussed at length how going to a prostitute, while making him feel manly and sexual, also disguised his heretofore unconscious shame over oral dependency wishes (Volkan's [2010] "reaching up," related to, but sort of the opposite of Freud's [1926d] idea about how defensive libidinal regression includes drive symbolism).

As Laurence reviewed the situation in his marriage, he guiltily admitted that he had really not wanted a third child. He knew he would feel more deprivation from his wife, and told her this. She had threatened him: If he did not give her another child, she said she would never have sex with him again. He acceded to her wish. I was curious about his passivity in that situation, since he had so aggressively started his own business, and had to take on competitors, etc. Laurence thought about this, and replied, "I didn't want to lose her because of my arrogance." Again, dependency seemed an issue, but possessing her sexually (originating as wishes from the first genital and adolescent phases) and superego anxiety (fear of punishment) also seemed factors. Laurence was not sure if it was during the pregnancy or after the birth of the third child that he had started going to call girls. He still had sex with Jennifer once every month or two, when she was in the mood. He stopped pressuring her.

I shared my curiosity with Laurence about his fear of losing Jennifer, thinking, again, that he had more dependency wishes than he liked to admit. As he thought about it, he said he had "always" worried about losing her. He then related to me that he first met Jennifer during his sophomore year in college, when she came to a fraternity party. She was dating Jim, one of his frat brothers in college, who was a good friend. When Jim broke up with Jennifer, she was devastated, and Laurence offered to talk her through it.

She thanked Laurence for being a good friend, and told him she had been asked out by Skip, another frat brother, who was a senior. Laurence warned her not to date Skip. Skip was a womanizer, who charmed his way into a girl's pants, then dumped her. Jennifer, however, went ahead and dated Skip. Laurence saw them going into Skip's bedroom and sometimes heard them laughing. At the beginning of their junior year, Laurence found out that, as he had predicted, Skip had broken up with Jennifer. She was again devastated. She then apologized to Laurence for not taking his advice and agreed to date him. Two years later, they got married. Laurence had not thought about all this "for twenty years." At the time Skip had dumped Jennifer, Laurence was overjoyed that she was available. He felt he had won.

Only on reflection did Laurence realize how much pain he had felt by being excluded by Jennifer when she dated Skip. Bad enough that he knew she had had sex with Jim, but he hated Skip. In addition, he now recalled that after witnessing Skip and Jennifer going into Skip's bedroom, Laurence had had many sleepless nights obsessing about how he might barge in and confront (and fight) Skip.

Laurence had never realized that those early adult experiences had contributed to him feeling emasculated, fearful that Jennifer would reject him, and revengeful toward her. He had forgotten all about that when Jennifer agreed to date him, and never blamed her. He knew that, in a way, Jennifer was right: She had a right to date other guys, just as Laurence had had a right to date other girls. I suggested we explore why his previous experiences with his mother and father may have made him sensitive to Jennifer's "rejections" and his pain and anger about them, since those factors might contribute to our understanding of his chronic obsequiousness with Jennifer, contrasting with his secret arrogance in using hookers.

Laurence reported that his mother had brought him to a psychologist for evaluation when he was in sixth grade because Laurence was refusing to do homework, and she had caught him masturbating – which she thought was abnormal. Also, Laurence had received some poor grades, and his father spanking him had not helped. Laurence remembered little of the one psychologist visit except that he had felt humiliated. He promised his mother he would study harder. So, we had unearthed one aspect of his childhood history of passivity toward, and wish to please his mother.

During adolescence, Laurence's passivity diminished. He grew to be 6 ft. 5 in. tall, and told his father not to "mess" with him. His father backed off. Laurence associated his skill in business to the "training" his father had given him in handling male bullies. In high school, Laurence played basketball, and his condescending attitude seemed "cool" to some girls. He snorted cocaine and had sexual intercourse with one of the girls, whom he dated for several months. His mother did not like him dating.

But being cool was a "fake," and Laurence knew it. He actually was lonely and depressed. He was glad to finally go to college and get out of his home, hoping to make new friends. He had become close with Jim (the fellow who had first dated Jennifer), on whom he depended to share their thoughts and feelings on a wide range of subjects. Jim was not critical and stayed friends with Laurence throughout college, even after Laurence started dating Jennifer. When Laurence and Jennifer got married and moved away, Laurence had transferred his dependency needs almost entirely onto Jennifer.

We could see that Laurence had reacted to Jennifer's "rejection" of his wish for attunement and sexual pleasure. Because of shame over revealing his dependency wishes, even to himself, Laurence had not said much to Jennifer, remained passive and sometimes "cool" (which of course often irritated her), and later had turned to prostitutes. But he knew that when he eventually had to admit something to Jennifer about infidelity, he would inevitably be punished. Verbalizing the whole scenario led to our understanding Laurence's unconscious attempts to master being beaten by his father, while at the same time he was quite frustrated in his attempts to please his mother.

Laurence never admitted to Jennifer that he had gone to hookers. He concluded, himself, that "confessing" would expose her to the same kind of pain he had experienced when she had dated Skip. He did, however, eventually admit to her that he had been attracted to other women. He told her that his work in analytic treatment had brought to his attention that his passivity with her had caused him to be distant from her and to fantasize about other women instead.

He fibbed that "Ursula" was a woman he had met who probably was a hooker, but said he never went to her. He admitted that his conversations with Ursula and using porn were his way of taking care of his own "needs" for love and sex. Jennifer told Laurence she had intuited that he had been withdrawing from her, to which he admitted. When he brought up her blackmail about the third pregnancy, she was shocked: She had completely forgotten it. She then seemed less argumentative.

Jennifer was more understanding than Laurence had anticipated when he mentioned he had uncovered, during treatment, that he had had conflicts watching her go into Skip's bedroom in college. She told him she hated herself for being so stupid when they were young, and could see that her dating Skip must have bothered him – just like finding Ursula's name had had a jolting effect on Jennifer. They discussed how, as he became more passive, Laurence had lost some sense of himself. She encouraged him to be more direct with her. Their marriage improved. Laurence gave up the hookers.

Laurence initially presented as arrogant and philandering. As we analyzed these features of his behavior, we could see that Jennifer's sleeping with Skip in college had been an organizing trauma for Laurence. His emotional reactions had been repressed until Laurence's later uxoriousness with Jennifer could be understood as a compromise formation including passivity, reaction-formation, and stoicism as defenses. Laurence had guarded himself from the emotional pain and rage associated with his primal scene-type experiences watching Jennifer with Skip. Her confusion about dating, in college, had stimulated in Laurence a more primitive fear of losing her. Later, as his passivity became unbearable, and she became more demanding and demeaning of him, he defended against castration depressive affect, as well (Brenner, 1982).

Although childhood determinants of Laurence's arrogant philandering were also integrated during his analytic treatment, and the precipitating cause of his hooker use seemed to be a need to repair his self-esteem and reestablish autonomy, the emotional conflicts from his late adolescence were very important. At least, they made up a large contribution to his problems to which Jennifer could relate, and helped Laurence and Jennifer reestablish some emotional closeness. He eventually viewed his use of prostitutes as an acting out of masturbation fantasies (Marcus & Frances, 1975). Those fantasies, in turn, were highly overdetermined; and a significant part of the overdetermination involved the late adolescent trauma of rejection by, and primal scene-like exposure to, his wife to be.

The case of Rob

Background information

Rob was a married, fifty-seven-year-old, successful real estate broker. He had seen many mental health providers previously. He had been depressed for years, and spent a fair amount of time, initially, obsessing about antidepressant medications; none had helped. When I asked him about any sexual side effects from the antidepressants, he said he didn't know if it were from the medicine or just getting older – he wasn't as interested as he used to be. He blamed himself for the growing emotional distance he felt from his wife, Shony. They had been married for about fifteen years.

Rob's chief complaint did not involve philandering, but I found his tension and argumentativeness about medication annoying. In his second session, he brought me a copy of one of Otto Kernberg's books on borderline personality, and offered to lend it to me, since he thought he was a borderline. I diplomatically assured him that I was familiar with Kernberg's work. I realized later I had been annoyed with Rob's arrogance, and formulated that he was probably not aware of it (Blackman, 2003b).

When I pointed out to Rob that his preoccupation with medication might be keeping us from discussing any situation in his marriage that might cause him to be depressed, he surprised me by admitting that he kept thinking of Shony having sex with her first husband, Jeff. The thought was not constant, but would occur to him suddenly. He knew it was ridiculous because Jeff had been dead for many years. As I explored this obsessional symptom, Rob realized that the thought occurred to him mostly when Shony mentioned Jeff. Rob got mildly annoyed that when he talked about a particular city, Shony might say, "Oh, Jeff and I spent a week there," for example. If there was a bar mitzvah they were invited to, she might recall that she and Jeff had been to a different bar mitzvah at the same temple. Rob told me that he had been married previously, and had had many affairs with women after that, so he couldn't figure out why Shony's statements bothered him, and why he would suddenly think of her having sex with Jeff.

When I pointed out to Rob that rumination was usually a defense against guilt, he thought of how guilty he had felt about Jeff's death some years earlier. The details of that conflict took a while to figure out. We agreed that part of Rob's preoccupation had to do with Rob's intense love for Shony, where he wanted to exclude all others (an apparently oedipal theme).

I expressed curiosity about how he and Shony had met. Rob replied that they initially had met as children in Hebrew school, but he did not date her until they were in high school. They had dated for two years, had gone to prom together, and had "played around" sexually. They did not have sexual intercourse. Although he had suggested it, Shony had not assented; she was religious. Rob had given up religion after his bar mitzvah.

After graduating from high school, Rob and Shony had mutually agreed, before departing for different colleges, that they would stop dating each other so each would be free to date other people in college. They planned to remain friends. They both seemed to handle the separation with minimal disruption, and Rob recalled feeling relieved that Shony had not cried much.

In college, Rob became quite the ladies' man. He was on the baseball team, and reveled in the camaraderie with his teammates. They had many drunken parties. He began cataloguing the number of girls with whom he had sexual intercourse. Looking back, he said he was not proud of it: "I was an arrogant asshole."

It seemed at first that he had identified with his teammates, who believed that masculinity involved not making choices about sexual partners. The ego ideal of his team involved sleeping with as many girls as possible.[2] He joked, "The team was like *Animal House*, the well-known 1978 college frat movie."

The course of treatment

As we considered other factors causing guilt, I brought to Rob's attention his severe self-criticism for his sexual exploits in college (calling himself names, for example).

---

2 See Defense #48, Inhibition of an Instinctualized Ego Function (Blackman, 2003a).

He said he had three grown daughters from his first marriage, whom he loved, and he hated to think that they might have been used by a cad like he had been in college. His guilt about this seemed to contribute to his depression (Blatt, 1974).

Rob had had many losses which he shared with me. His mother had died when he was in high school from complications of Niemann-Pick disease. He felt consciously guilty that he had avoided her because he couldn't stand to see her frail and suffering. His father was a tough-love type of man, a manager of a retail store who constantly berated Rob, before and after Rob's mother's death.

His father, a baseball fan, had never played varsity baseball. It was therefore irritating to Rob that his dad took it upon himself to criticize Rob's athletic technique. They also fought over the length of Rob's hair (Rob wore it long). Rob finally stopped speaking to his father. He made his "Declaration of Independence" before he went to college, after his father mocked him for expressing interest in the US constitution and for ridiculing the Talmud.[3]

All of this history, of course, was important in understanding the losses and conflicts Rob had suffered. However, I had a strange feeling that he had told previous therapists about similar material, and when I brought this up, he admitted it. I kept thinking of Dorpat's (1999) paper[4] about "Type D" interactions:

> Although individuals with a false self organization who communicate inauthentically are attempting to relate affectively with others, they tend to do so in a compliant and ingratiating way. Their inauthentic communication tends to evoke a kind of relatedness in others in which the object is idealized and viewed as omnipotent.
>
> (p. 210)

After Rob and I discussed how he was simultaneously letting me in but keeping emotional distance from me, he finally told me a more emotionally genuine history of his relationships.

During Rob's senior year in college, Shony had contacted him over winter break. They had been incommunicado since high school. She said she needed to talk. He went to her house. Rob said Shony looked more beautiful than he remembered, but she was distraught. She confided in him that she had been date-raped at a party before she left for winter break. A boy she had been dating seriously for two years had just broken up with her, and she was depressed. She knew the boy who raped her, Jeff; he was in her history of art class. They had met at a party, both gotten drunk and smoked pot, and before she knew it, they were having sex in his apartment, which she did not recall allowing.

---

3 A long book of commentary about Jewish scripture.

4 In reviewing Langs's (1978) communication types, Dorpat (1999) stated the following: "The Type A mode is characterized by symbolic imagery and authentic affects, and it is the optimal mode for both therapist and patient. Projective identification is the defining feature of the Type B mode. The central and defining characteristic of the Type C mode is the absence of primary process derivatives, including affects, imagery, narratives, and metaphors" (pp. 209–210).

Jeff had dropped her back at her apartment but never called her. She had been avoiding their mutual class; she was afraid she couldn't go back and face him. She also felt guilty that she had been too rebellious against her parents' religious teachings. She had been a "goody-two-shoes" in high school, but when she tried to be freer in college, she had gotten dumped by one boy and then date-raped by another.

Rob comforted Shony at the time, and over several hours, they discussed how they missed their youthful dating, and agreed to get together again while they were home. They spent almost every day together during break. They wound up having sexual intercourse toward the end of the two weeks, pledging love to each other, but again did not put "strings" on each other when they returned to their different colleges.

Rob was happy, and continued corresponding with Shony. Toward the end of the year, however, she told Rob she had gotten engaged to Jeff, the same boy who she originally had complained had date-raped her. She told Rob that Jeff had eventually called her and apologized for not contacting her after their sexual interlude because he was too hung over and strung out. She had been dating him since she returned to school, but she had not wanted to hurt Rob's feelings, so she hadn't told him. Rob rationalized that he and Shony had not agreed to be exclusive.

Rob got depressed, however, and saw his first psychiatrist, who did not investigate the complications of Rob's experiences, emotions, or defenses. She simply gave him Prozac. He took it for about three months, then stopped it and joined his friends for more drinking and carousing. Rob went back to being an "arrogant asshole" with women. After college, he joined a real estate firm, where he met many women. As in college, he persisted in using women for sex.

Years went by. Rob was twenty-eight when he met Niki, a new female real estate attorney who worked with his agency. After a two-year courtship, he and Niki got married. But Rob cheated on her with other women he met working, sometimes in his private office. After about ten years of marriage, Niki asked him for a divorce. She had had a detective follow him, who had taken photos of Rob entering a motel with two different women.

The divorce was acrimonious. Rob lost primary custody of the children and had limited visitation with them. He also had to pay large amounts of alimony and child support. He got depressed. Again, he consulted a psychiatrist and was given antidepressant medicine, which again did not help. Sometime after the divorce proceedings ended, Rob received an email from Shony. In it, she reported that her husband, Jeff, had died in a car accident a few years earlier. She was fine now, but she had looked Rob up on the internet, found his email, and was curious about how he was doing. Rob, feeling lonely, responded to her inquiry. They started meeting, and enjoyed themselves much as they had in high school. They even went to temple. After dating for about a year, they got married. They were both forty-two.

During the period in treatment in which I was learning Rob's complicated history, and for months thereafter, we discussed the dynamics that underpinned his earlier philandering as well as his current obsession about Shony. Through the maze of Rob's sometimes confusing motives, conflicts, and defenses, we agreed that the first "organizing conflict" (Coltrera, 1979) had been the high school breakup with Shony. He had been in love with her, frustrated that they never had intercourse, and sad when they agreed to free each other after high school.

He had not grieved over her after that. He immediately added that he had never really grieved over his mother's death when he was in high school, either. Rob thought maybe Shony had been a substitute for his dying mother. I commented that his relationship with Shony may have partly kept him from grieving over his mother, but I thought that he had also avoided grieving over Shony herself. This discussion led to several sessions where Rob shared painful sadness with me.

Rob asked Shony to accompany him to one of his last sessions with me. She was concerned about Rob's moodiness and moping around whenever she mentioned Jeff. She volunteered, "It's the twenty-first century, and women have a right to have sex with whoever they want. And I married Jeff. And he died. Why should that bother Rob?"

I responded to Shony that she sounded like she felt a need to justify herself. She broke down crying, turned to Rob, and said, through her tears, "I feel stupid for having married Jeff! He was a bad husband, and I am sorry I didn't stay with you. I should have." I asked Shony if she meant she kept mentioning Jeff to relieve shame over having made a mistake marrying him. She responded, with more crying, "Yes. I wish I had never met Jeff. I hated myself for letting Jeff push himself on me that first time, but I tried to make it all right. I tried to make the right decision, but I was wrong!" We concluded that when she mentioned Jeff to Rob, she was relieving shame and guilt. She realized she had wanted it all to "be normal" and not so convoluted, but that the unintended consequence of her defensiveness in mentioning Jeff to Rob was that it stirred Rob up.

Rob was shocked. He told Shony he had always loved her, and that he had not grieved sufficiently over her at first. Maybe after they had had sex in their senior year, he should have made a commitment to her. She acknowledged she did feel a little rejected by his failure to do so, and that maybe that had something to do with her acceptance of Jeff – security, relief of shame, and maybe a way to hurt Rob for not making a commitment to her at that time.

During Rob's final sessions, he reported that his obsession of visualizing Shony with Jeff had disappeared. They had had very long discussions since their conjoint session, during which Shony had also faced the fact that she had not grieved over Jeff, another reason she kept mentioning his name. She also felt guilty; she had been secretly relieved when Jeff got killed because she had been planning on divorcing him.

Rob had not previously been aware of his late adolescent and early adulthood losses being painful; he had become a womanizer instead. When he rationalized in college that he was just one of the boys on the baseball team, he defended against his pain over losing Shony (and his mother). He was also unconsciously expressing some anger at women, symbolically.

What about his cheating on Niki, his first wife? Rob had returned to his callous philandering and arrogance after he experienced a roller coaster of emotions regarding Shony during their senior year of college. She first told him she had been date-raped, then slept with him, then later informed him that she was engaged to Jeff, the fellow Rob had hated for reportedly hurting her.

When Rob and Shony finally had had sexual intercourse during winter break in their senior year of college (after he had comforted her about the date-rape), he had strongly felt love toward her. He was therefore crushed by her call a few months afterward, when she told him she had gone back to Jeff. Rob then had given up on closeness with any woman, and slept around.

Years later, he "tried" to be married, but we could see, in retrospect, that his infidelity forced Niki to feel what Shony had made him feel. He had forced Niki, who loved him, to become aware of him having sexual activity with another woman. This unconsciously took revenge on Niki for the way Shony had forced him to become aware she was having sex with someone else (identification with the aggressor, projective identification of pain, repression, and displacement of rage).

At forty-one, after his divorce, when Shony emailed him, Rob had experienced a sort of oedipal victory on hearing that Jeff had died; in reclaiming Shony, he felt he had finally "won." But then Rob's obsession of picturing Shony having sex with Jeff started. Partly, ruminating was a means of punishing himself to relieve guilt over rageful thoughts toward Shony and Jeff. That rage, in part, caused him to form an unconscious wish to get rid of Shony whenever she mentioned Jeff – which he did mentally by giving her back to Jeff (in his head).

Rob had lost his mother to a terrible illness when he was in high school, but had never grieved over her. In a sort of "established pathological mourning" (Volkan, 1981), he had partly shifted his attachment to Shony in high school. He also experienced exaggerated oedipal competition with his critical father.

Some final thoughts

The particular configuration of dynamics I have described, that can cause certain men to develop an arrogant, philandering character, does not seem to be a new idea. Coen (1981), for example, suggests that "the term sexualization be used only to designate phenomenologically that aspect of sexual behavior and fantasy whose goals and functions are not sexual arousal and pleasure, but defense" (p. 907). He also provides an extensive literature review on the metapsychology of sex used as a defensive activity. Blos (1965) delineates how grieving over parents during late adolescence affects adulthood identity and superego formation.

My contribution to this issue has been to elucidate how arrogance and sexualization, even in later adulthood, may occur together, and how the purpose of these personality traits is to defensively abet "established pathological mourning" (Volkan, 1981) over a repressed traumatic loss from early adulthood or late adolescence.

To be sure, arrogance and philandering can have many etiologies. Marcus (2004), agreeing that extramarital sex often has little to do with sex, itself, describes ten common character types of philanderers, including the Adulteen, the Sampler, the

74 Jerome S. Blackman

Daredevil, and the Ponce de Leon. He gives examples from his clinical practice, and delineates the oedipal, preoedipal, and latency origins of his patients' problems. He sees the Adulteen as having a developmental delay, where adolescent narcissism, in particular, has persisted into adulthood. His Sampler type seems to be using sex as an antidepressant guarding against childhood loss. These types, in turn, are to be distinguished from psychopathic philanderers, who suffer no guilt (Cleckley, 1941). The man with superego lacunae (Johnson & Szurek, 1952) more frequently does not seek treatment, or if he does at the behest of wife or girlfriend, is untreatable because the philandering causes the man no internal conflict.

A defensive etiology of arrogance and philandering is found, as are many analytic observations, in language, arts, and music (Blackman, 2011). As early as 1922, the dynamics I have adumbrated appeared in the song, "Running Wild" (Gibbs, Grey, & Wood). There is both a male version, exquisitely sung by SPEB-SQSA's[5] Vocal Majority (1994), and a female version, first sung by "Miss Patricola" (1922); Marilyn Monroe also sang a variation in the Pullman-ukulele scene in *Some Like It Hot* (1959).

In the Vocal Majority's rendition, the man laments having been mistreated by a "hard-hearted gal." In response, he vows that his "poor, shattered, torn, tattered heart's got a brand-new start." From now on, no one "will make a fool" of him, and he will never be "blue"; he will be running wild, loving no one, and playing the "villain's part." He might have been romantic once, but because of the trauma from his "hard-hearted, two-timing, brow-beating, back-biting, man-hating gal," he has decided to stop loving any woman.

In other words, to relieve his pain and grief, he identifies with the aggressor (the woman who broke his heart), devalues women, generalizes, uses aggression as a defense, and sexualizes that aggression, all in the service of suppressing memories of humiliation and pain. He has developed narcissistic arrogance toward women. He now sees them as dehumanized objects to be used for displacement of his anger toward the woman who broke his heart in early adulthood.

In essence, the conflicts and compromise formations in the men I have discussed, and my formulations about them, seem to have been understood ninety-five years ago by three guys writing a song. It's a humbling thought.

---

5 Society for the Preservation and Encouragement of Barber Shop Quartet Singing in America.

Part II
Cultural realm

Chapter 5

Arrogance in text and in context

Apurva Shah

In the six months that it took me to research and write this chapter, I have had a persistent feeling that it is an arrogant act on my part to write about arrogance, and therefore to presume that I know more about the subject, and that you, the reader, would be interested in what I have to say. Where does this feeling come from? Am I insecure about my qualifications? Maybe, to a certain extent, but that insecurity has never surfaced to this degree before. And definitely not in this form. Perhaps it has to do with the subject itself. Has reading, writing, and thinking about arrogance made me more aware of my own? Possibly, even probably, so. Certainly, there could be a "priming" effect. But if so, it appears to be specific for this subject. I am not (consciously) ashamed about my chapter on "Shame" (2015), and do not regret writing about "Regret" (2017). What then is it about arrogance that lends itself so easily to reflection and apparent replication?

Do all academic endeavors have a certain degree of arrogance inherent to them? Perhaps, because there is an intrinsic imbalance, with the presumption of a superiority of knowledge on the side of the teacher. And yet few other writings have made me cringe quite the same way as some of the ones I read on arrogance. Blogs and articles on how to recognize or "cure" hubris and arrogance, one's own or others, or on how to recognize and "survive" a relationship with an arrogant person, seem to drip with the very toxin they promise to help eradicate. This is of course not true for most of the writings referenced here. Even so, one cannot help but wonder about the psychological disposition of the authors quoted.

Perhaps the key is in the recursive nature of any kind of reflection on narcissism, and all things related to it. It is nearly impossible to introspect on narcissism without making it a narcissistic exercise. For example, I feel that it is arrogant of me to have opened the chapter in such an informal tone and with my personal musings, even if I do rationalize that it led to a few insights. I will end this prologue here, with a modest invitation to read on, in the hope that you find something helpful.

Definitions and literature review

There are two features common to all literary definitions of arrogance: One is unwarranted or excessive pride, and the other is the feeling of superiority.

Etymologically, the Webster's Dictionary (1987) states that arrogance is related to the English verb *arrogate* – to claim or seize without justification – and both are derived from the Latin word *arrogare*, which means "to appropriate to oneself." It is related to pride, hubris, and conceit on one hand, and condescension, disdain, and contempt on the other. Correspondingly, depending on the predominant feature, many classify arrogance into two types, the conceitful and the contemptuous. There is a rich history of literature on arrogance and related concepts, including pride, hubris, humility, etc., in theology and philosophy, both Western and Eastern, much of which is beyond the scope of this chapter. What follows is a brief and highly selective review.

Perhaps the best description of arrogance is by Immanuel Kant (1797) who states, "Arrogance demands from others a respect it denies them" (p. 198). Working with Kant's ideas on arrogance, Dillon (2004) classifies arrogance into two types – interpersonal, which is "profoundly disrespectful" (p. 193) and always a vice; and primary, "an exercise of . . . power, in the service of desire, masquerading as a perfectly reasonable entitlement claim" (p. 198), which may, under certain circumstances, be a virtue.[1]

In psychiatric literature, arrogance is associated with pathological narcissism. In the *Diagnostic and Statistical Manual of Mental Disorders* (DSM), in the fourth edition (American Psychiatric Association [APA], 2006, p. 661), "arrogant behaviors" is one of the criteria for narcissistic personality disorder. However, it does not provide any further details or nuances.

Within psychoanalysis, arrogance is widely seen as a character trait of narcissism, specifically unhealthy narcissism. Nunberg (1979) lists it as one of the features of narcissism and convincingly points out its presence in the original myth of Narcissus. Hotchkiss (2002) considers it to be one of the seven deadly sins of narcissism. Vaknin (2014) believes it to be a core trait of narcissistic personality disorder.

Somewhat surprisingly then, arrogance does not find a mention in Sigmund Freud's (1914c) seminal paper, "On Narcissism." Reich is quite possibly the first psychoanalyst to talk about arrogance in a technical sense. In *Character Analysis* (1933), he talks about the phallic-narcissistic character as being "self-assured, sometimes arrogant, elastic, energetic, often impressive in his bearing" (p. 249). In a case example, he considers the arrogance to be defensive in nature and feels that the patient has "saved himself the repression of a certain amount of sadism through this form of defense, i.e., by absorbing the sadism into the arrogance of the character" (p. 228). Bursten (1986) also defines arrogance as a central feature of the phallic-narcissist, calling him a "man's man," the highest level of narcissistic personality organization, and suggests that this form of narcissism is more

---

1   According to the web page on Lehigh University website (2017), Dillon, in her new, not yet published, book on arrogance, appears to (re-)classify arrogance into two types – "status arrogance," which is the presumptuous sense of superiority with disdain and contempt for others, and "unwarrantable claims arrogance," which concerns unjustifiable claims of status, authority, etc. This would then roughly correspond to Zimmer's contemptuous and hubristic types of arrogance (see below).

common in men (pp. 385–386). He posits that the arrogance is often a defense against the shame of castration in men (p. 394).

Bion (1967b) appears to agree with Reich (although he does not refer to his work), and clearly and elegantly differentiates between self-respect, which is pride in a personality dominated by life instincts, and arrogance, which is pride in one dominated by death instincts. He goes on to reinterpret the Oedipus myth, keeping his arrogance – his insistence on knowing the truth at all costs – and not his sexuality, as the central crime in the story and the trait responsible for the tragedy. Bion connects the apparently disparate elements of arrogance, stupidity, and curiosity, both in this myth and in clinical situations, and suggests that they are signs of a "psychological disaster" (p. 86). In his later writings, according to Alhanati (2006), Bion elaborates on this disaster, now termed catastrophe, as resulting from the absence of a container, which causes splitting and fragmentation of the personality (p. 34).

Richard Zimmer (2013) elaborates on Bion's triad, adding a fourth element, that of surprise. He enumerates several possible sources of this surprise and posits that this triad (or tetrad) comes to the fore along with a retreat by both the analyst and the patient as a defense against the anxiety and frustration of being in contact with the other. Indeed, as Sartre (1946) writes, "Hell is – other people" (p. 45). Zimmer goes on to classify arrogance into two distinct types – hubristic and contemptuous – suggesting that the contemptuous type more accurately captures the full meaning of the word arrogance. In hubristic arrogance, the pain and frustration of not knowing is defended by omniscience or the quest for knowledge, and the aggression is turned inward, as in Bion's analysis of Oedipus. In contemptuous arrogance, there is a denial of the pain of knowledge and both an idealization and an intensified instinctualization of the quest for knowledge, and the aggression is directed at the other. Zimmer states that both types of arrogance are defensive in nature and can coexist in the same person simultaneously. They can exist in a milder form without a history of a psychological disaster.

Kohut (1971) regarded arrogance as a feature of narcissism that could be either a manifestation of the archaic grandiose self in the vertically split-off sector of the self or a defense against shame propensity, due to the archaic and unfulfilled needs in the horizontally split-off sector. Much along the same lines, Hotchkiss (2002) considers arrogance to be a defense against feelings of shame about personal shortcomings.

Vaknin (2015) takes a broad view on arrogance. Like Bion, he too refers to the triad of arrogance, (pseudo-)curiosity, and stupidity, calling these bouts "transformations of aggression taken to the extreme" (loc. 2325). But he also refers to arrogance as an armor that simultaneously protects him from the "everyday arrows of life" and makes him vulnerable and gullible due to a decreased contact with reality (loc. 3754). Finally, he suggests that arrogance can be a quality not just of the "noisy," entitled narcissist, but also of the aloof and withdrawn one, who is quietly grandiose and avoids the spotlight.

Collating, arrogance is in the realm of narcissism, but in the interpersonal space. It is almost always viewed as negative, a feature of unhealthy or pathological narcissism. As it is in the interpersonal space, arrogance may be more accurately considered as an attribute of an act or a relationship, rather than a character trait. This act either presumes or creates a hierarchy in the relationship. Arrogance, unlike pride or hubris, has a significant element of aggression, even sadism. This aggression is specifically directed toward the right of the other to equality within the relationship, at times going as far as to obliterate the subjectivity of the other. Following Zimmer (2013), arrogance can be classified as either hubristic and dominated by narcissistic elements, or contemptuous, with more prominent sadism. Integrating Kohut (1971) within this classification, hubristic arrogance can be nondefensive, a manifestation of the archaic grandiose self, in which the inequality may be presumed (and the arrogance more characterological?) or defensively grandiose. The contemptuous type of arrogance is always secondary, defending both against shame over the defects in oneself, and against acknowledging the limitations of one's grandiosity via the denigration of the other.

Humility

Before turning to some contextual issues relating to arrogance, a brief look at the concept of humility is warranted as it is so often juxtaposed with arrogance, especially in sociocultural studies. Both humility and modesty are considered to be the antitheses of arrogance. Of the two, humility fits better as the antonym of, and antidote to, the entire range of arrogance as described above. Like arrogance, humility has two facets: an interpersonal one involving deference (or in more extreme cases, submission and servility) and consequentially an acceptance of one's place in any given situation, and an intrapsychic one involving a modest self-appraisal (or low self-esteem and feelings of inferiority) and a decreased focus on oneself. Etymologically, Webster (1987) informs us that the words "humble," "humility," and "humiliation" share the same Latin root word, *humilis*, meaning "low" (see respective entries). The possible connection between humility and shame is discussed below.

Several authors have talked about different types of humility and whether it is a virtue or not. For this chapter, it will suffice to summarize a few of those opinions and consider three types of humility. The psychologically healthy humility is born out of a secure sense of self along with a lower investment in it. Van Tongeren and Myers (2017) give a succinct description of this type of humility, defining its three key components: an accurate view of oneself, a modest self-representation, and an orientation toward others (p. 150). The obverse to that is humility born out of an insecure self, in which the submission to the other may be defensive, in an attempt to fulfill and complete oneself. De Beauvoir (1949) elaborates on this in her chapter, "The Woman in Love." Finally, there is the humility imposed by those in power, where the person so humiliated does not have a viable alternative, as is evident in the two works cited. Ellison (1952) paints a compelling portrait of this in his novel, *Invisible Man.* Intrapsychically, these latter two kinds of humility do not really have a decreased focus on oneself, and need not extend to the entire character.

The social and cultural context for arrogance

If arrogance is a behavior within an interpersonal context, then it makes sense that social and cultural factors could exert a significant influence. Factors such as gender, ethnicity and culture, religion, and socioeconomic class have all been studied in relation to arrogance.

Arrogance is generally considered to be a masculine trait; humility, feminine. This is either explicitly stated or clearly implied by too many authors to enumerate. De Beauvoir (1949) writes about how women are the "Other" because they have submitted themselves to be that and have never tried to be the "One" (pp. 26–28) and hence, "the most mediocre of males believes himself a demigod next to women" (p. 33). Summarizing her writings from the same text about the woman in love, Tucker (2016) notes that "She [the woman in love] wants a god, he [the object of her affection] wants to be a god. . . . [They] work together to hide the flaws inherent in his pride and her humility" (p. 43). Dillon (2004) calls arrogance a "gendered concept" (p. 192), applied mostly to men and masculinized women. She associates arrogance with power and states that her research has showed that women are rarely called arrogant, even when they exhibit such characteristics. Reich (1933) talks of arrogance as a character trait of the phallic-narcissist, and goes on to describe his face as having "masculine lines" (p. 217) and how it is rare to see this disorder in women (p. 219). Bursten (1986) agrees with this and calls the phallic-narcissistic a "man's man" (p. 385). Vaknin (2015) declares at the very start of his book that "Most narcissists are men" (loc. 987).

There is a widespread belief that Asians, in particular, and people of non-European descent in general, are, as a rule, not arrogant, or at least, less arrogant and humbler than people of European descent. While commenting on the cultural variations in the need for positive self-regard, Heine, Lehman, Markus, and Kitayama (1999) refer to the Japanese custom of habitually emphasizing one's deferential position and taking on a self-denigrating and submissive stance (p. 773), customs which would lead to a greater degree of humility in most of their interactions. A prominent Indian psychoanalyst, Sudhir Kakar (2007), has hypothesized that Indian men have a significantly different Oedipus complex. He has coined the term "Ganesha complex" to denote this dynamic, wherein the renunciation of the boy's sexual desire for the mother and his withdrawal from the rivalry with the father is voluntary. He sees reflection of this attitude in the myth of Ganesha, whose surrender to his parents is held to be superior to his brother Skanda's wish for independence. This illustrates an ideal within the culture, as evidenced by how widely Ganesha is worshipped in India (pp. 115–117). Even though he does not explicitly say so, it is easy to derive from Kakar's theory that Indians show less arrogance and more humility in their interactions. Alan Roland (2011) has introduced the concept of the "we-self" or the familial self from his psychoanalytic work in India and Japan. He states that most of the world has some variation of this, and it is only the modern European/North American culture that has such a highly developed individual self. The Japanese and South Asian cultures are hierarchical, and the dual self-structure (with the individualized self being more private and secretive) allows for the observance of the etiquette of deference so integral to the hierarchy.

Conversely, many authors note the rise of personality disorders in the West, particularly the narcissistic personality disorder, from the second half of the twentieth century on (Lasch, 1979; Lunbeck, 2014; Roland, 2011). Referring to the controversy over the publication of a series of cartoons depicting Mohammad in a Danish newspaper in 2005, Rostbøll (2009) argues that the Western liberal values of autonomy and freedom of self-expression, derived from the Enlightenment, may lead to arrogance toward cultures or people who do not share the same values. Twenge and Campbell (2009) talk about the "relentless rise of narcissism in our [US] culture" (p. 1). Davies, Nandy, and Sardar (1993) have traced the origin of racism in the West, the tendency to see the "Other" as barbaric and subhuman, and hence, people whose subjectivity can be ignored, from the ancient Greek civilization through the history of European colonization and up to the late twentieth century. Furey (1986) bemoans the deliberate lack of humility in the American culture and feels that it hinders people from living with, and within, their limitations.

Religion too is very often cited as a generator of arrogance. Both Hitchens (2007) and Zingrone (2016) talk extensively about the arrogance of all religions, though the examples they use are mostly from the two major monotheistic religions, Christianity and Islam. In *Moses and Monotheism* (1939a), Sigmund Freud talked about religious intolerance, hitherto alien to the ancient world, being "inevitably born" with the first known monotheistic religion (p. 20). He also wonders how the Jews had the arrogance to label themselves as the "favorite child of the great Lord" (p. 65). This link between monotheism and arrogance is further amplified by Kirsch (2004), who states that monotheism inspires a ferocious fanaticism, which leads to religious intolerance and a "terrifying logic" (p. 2) that anyone who does not worship the one true God is an infidel who deserves to die. In other words, monotheism breeds an arrogance with an exaggerated importance of one's own value systems and a wish to obliterate the others' subjectivity, potentially even their very existence. Kirsch contrasts this with polytheism which he feels is an "open minded and easygoing approach to religious belief and practice" (p. 2).

Millon, Millon, Meagher, Grossman, and Ramnath (2000) bring an economic perspective to the creation of pathological forms of narcissism. They posit that a sense of entitlement increases as one moves up Maslow's[2] hierarchy of needs, and see pathological narcissism as one possible hazard to self-actualization. Individuals who "are too preoccupied with basic safety and survival needs" cannot afford to be arrogant (p. 333). In other words, beggars cannot be so arrogant as to be choosers. They go on to say that individuals in respected professions (law, medicine, science) or celebrities (in sports, entertainment, politics) are more likely to display pathological narcissism (pp. 333–334). Owen and Davidson (2009) studied the histories and biographies of all US presidents and UK prime ministers from 1901 through 2008 and concluded that seven heads of government of each

---

2   Referring to Abraham Maslow's theory, first postulated in *A Theory of Human Motivation* (1943).

country suffered from hubris, which they defined as "exaggerated pride, over-whelming self-confidence and contempt for others" (p. 1397). Even a cursory reading of the business news over the past decade or two would reveal several examples of arrogant CEOs and other kingpins of the finance world.

A few selected incidents from a popular Indian epic will be presented and dis-cussed in detail to understand some of the social and interpersonal dynamics of arrogance within a cultural context.

Arrogance of Lord Rama

Ramayana (c. 100 CE) is one of the best-known epic poems of ancient India. It is popular not only in India, but in several parts of South and Southeast Asia. It was passed on in the oral tradition for many centuries before it was scripted about 2000 years ago, and due to this, has over a dozen recensions and hundreds of versions. Ramayana is a much-loved tale, and most of the narrative details are known to almost every Indian. Importantly, the main protagonists of the story have become cultural ego ideals. Rama is regarded as the ideal son, man, husband, and king, Sita the ideal woman and wife, Lakshmana the ideal brother.

The story begins with King Dasharatha, Rama's father, who exiles Rama for fourteen years to the forest, in order to fulfill a promise to one of his wives. Despite Rama's protestations, Sita, his wife, and Lakshmana, his brother, join him. In the forest, Ravana, the powerful *rakshasha* (demon), kidnaps Sita. Rama and Lakshmana gather an army of allies and attack Lanka. After a fierce battle, Rama is victorious and rescues Sita.[3]

What should have been a joyous reunion of the royal couple becomes a near-tragedy. Rama, "apprehensive of public rumor" (p. 335), publicly states that he did not fight with Ravana for Sita's sake, but only to avenge his insult. He goes on to insinuate that she may have slept with Ravana while in captivity. Humiliated, Sita enters a fire to prove her innocence. Alarmed by this turn of events, gods descend from heaven, rescue Sita, and remind Rama that he is an incarnation of Lord Vishnu. They express surprise at his doubting Sita's purity of heart. Rama then accepts Sita and admits that "It was imperative that Sita pass through this trial by fire" to satisfy his subjects, lest they feel that he is "governed by lust" (p. 341). The story goes on to an apparent happy ending, as Rama returns to Ayodhya and assumes the throne that is rightfully his. He goes on to rule for ten thousand years, and no one is ever unhappy in his kingdom (p. 370).

However, there is an additional, seventh canto, called *Uttara-kanda*.[4] Most authorities (Banker, 2006; Griffiths, 1895; Menon, 2003; Sen, 1976; Shashtri, 1959) consider this to be a later addition, composed by another hand. However,

---

3 Everything so far, about Ramayana, is common knowledge for people raised in India. From here on, all quotes and references to Ramayana, unless otherwise noted, are from Shashtri (1959, vol. 3), part of a complete and unabridged English translation of Valmiki's Ramayana.

4 *Uttara* in Sanskrit, has several meanings – north, up, left, a sequel (or later addition), etc. Finally, and tantalizingly in this context, it can also mean response, answer, and revenge.

traditionally, it is included in the text and, indeed, is by all the authors mentioned above except Banker. The cause of Banker's discomfort in including the last canto (2006, pp. 819–820) is another twist in the relationship of Rama and Sita. Their idyllic relationship is described in some detail, and when Sita gets pregnant (p. 520), she states that she wishes to visit a sage and spend a night at his hermitage. Rama readily agrees, but before he can arrange for their visit, he hears that his subjects are questioning his decision to accept Sita back, given that she was "held in (Ravana's) lap." They bemoan the fact that they will have to do the same with their wives, as the subjects must follow the king's example (p. 522). Hearing this, Rama is "stricken with grief" (pp. 523–525). He describes to his brothers how anxious he had been about Sita's reputation before the trial by fire (p. 524). Then, he orders Lakshmana to take Sita to the hermitage and leave her there. She ends up living in Valmiki's ashram for several years, gives birth to twin sons, Luv and Kush, and raises them there.

As mentioned earlier, Rama is seen as the paragon of virtue. His humility is highlighted at various places – his repeated refusal to acknowledge himself as an incarnation of Lord Vishnu; his absolute obedience to his father's and other elders' wishes; his acceptance of his patently unjust punishment; and his sensitivity for his subjects. This is in sharp contrast to Ravana's character, which reeks of unbridled arrogance. Ravana defies and terrifies the gods; rapes several women; aspires to immortality and, of course, kidnaps Sita. And yet, it is Rama's arrogance, stemming from a supposedly higher morality, that shocks and puzzles us more.

Discussion

In psychoanalytic literature, arrogance is generally defined as a narcissistic trait within an interpersonal context. Several authors have described its quality, associated features, intrapsychic and genetic mechanisms, and clinical manifestations, including within the transference. What is missing is an adequate examination of the context. Arrogance, more so than any other characteristic of narcissism, is highly contextual, which is why it is better described as a behavior than a trait, a term that implies a certain consistency and independence from context. As demonstrated in the story of Lord Rama, even a paragon of humility may act arrogantly at times, depending on the context.

Before we explore the contextual element for arrogance any further, let us examine its relationship with humility. As mentioned earlier, humility is associated with women, colonized non-Western peoples, and the poor. One could add, as de Beauvoir (1949) does, the Jews (just post WWII), the proletariat, and the (pre-civil rights movement) blacks in North America. It is not a coincidence that humility is associated with precisely the groups that have been humiliated. In other words, humility may be merely a more or less forced acceptance of one's (inferior) station in life, and the ability to tolerate the concomitant shame, rather than defend against it with pride and rage. This then could provide a context for humility in what have been called "shame-based cultures," and for some cases of reactive arrogance to this. It is a common experience that it is difficult to resist the temptation to be arrogant with someone who is being overly servile and obsequious. Also the humiliated and vanquished can, and very often will, humiliate others, if and when the chance arises. As an example, Viorst (2016) argues that not just Israel, but revisionist Zionism rose from the ashes of the Holocaust.[5] Humility can both effect and be an effect of arrogance, hardly the antithesis and antidote, as is often assumed.

Indeed, the arrogance of true believers, with their abject humility and submissiveness to a god, has led to innumerable wars, genocides, and such, and continues to bedevil the world today. Worse, idealization of the divinity and an identification with co-worshippers is essential in overcoming the conscientious objections to the crimes committed.[6] In other words, humility becomes a precursor and a prerequisite for arrogance. The moral right to arrogate, to annihilate another's subjectivity, is derived from, and indeed can come only from, the god or other higher power to whom one submits, thus making humility and arrogance two facets of the same dynamic.

It is possible that I am referring to the "wrong" kind of humility. As indicated above, there do appear to be distinctly different types of humility. The humility of the subjugated could be posturing, forced. Ellison's (1952) narrator says as much when he talks about his much-acclaimed speech on humility as the very essence of progress: "Not that I believed this . . . I only believed it could work" (p. 14). Or it could be defensive, and arise out of the same insecurities that lead to arrogance, thus providing a "backdoor" connection between the two and explaining their coexistence in an individual.

Many authors talk about the "right" kind of humility, the one that comes from a secure sense of self, and is not defensive in nature. The concept of Van Tongeren and Myers (2017) has already been alluded to. Tucker (2016) defines it as "commitment, dedication and submission" (p. 10) and urges the reader to choose its object wisely (p. 14). Based on the worthiness of the object selected, the "self-dedicatory process" which is humility, may lead to "authentic pride" (p. 20), which he sees as a virtue. Furey (1986) gives two stages of development of humility: the psychological one of acceptance of our imperfection, followed by the spiritual one of accepting our place in the universe (p. 7).

Perhaps the best description of, and prescription for, the antidote to arrogance is to be found in Phillips's *Equals* (2002). He does not mention humility, but discusses the ideals of liberal democracy and egalitarianism, not as a reality, for gross inequality in almost all spheres is a manifest reality, but as an ideal, and a political hope (p. xiii). He believes that psychoanalysis as a listening cure can show the way, for it is important to listen to one another. More than that, it is crucial to allow the Other their own subjectivity, and an opinion of oneself which, even if contradicting one's own, is accepted as valid. In his formulation, arrogance is created due to the inability to tolerate differences and the resultant need to suppress conflict. Psychoanalysis, and its political counterpart, liberal democracy, aim to make these differences useful and bearable, even pleasurable (pp. 3–31).

---

5 For details, refer to the chapter on "Identification with the Aggressor" in Anna Freud's (1936) monograph, *The Ego and the Mechanisms of Defence*.

6 This is, of course, explained in some depth by Sigmund Freud (1921c) in his monograph, *Group Psychology and the Analysis of the Ego*.

It is a brilliant and provocative essay, with a lot to concur with; nevertheless, I have to insert my doubts here. Apart from the multiple difficulties Philips himself has listed, and he does call it an ideal hope, there are some historical and theoretical reasons to question it. Historically, the last few years have seen the liberal Western democracies struggling with the extent to which they can tolerate intolerance. Even prior to this dilemma, they have a very checkered record in regard to human rights, especially when it comes to its dealings with the Other – the non-Western peoples. It is almost as if the liberal, secular ideology becomes a religion in itself, and creates an egalitarian humility within the believers. However, it allows, even fosters, an arrogant dehumanization of the "infidels," leading to a disproportionate use of military might, xenophobia, inequitable distribution of wealth, and grossly imbalanced media coverage often in the name of fostering liberal democratic values, a proselytization almost as reductive as the one undertaken by the missionaries during colonization.

Hypothetically, if psychoanalysis has the capacity to mitigate the destructive power of the subjective difference, one should be able to discern that effect in people who have undergone psychoanalysis and gained this valuable understanding. However, the biographies of well-known psychoanalysts, presumably those most likely to have benefitted from these insights, as well as the widespread reputation of practicing psychoanalysts as being arrogant, appear to prove otherwise.

Even when and where egalitarianism is valued highly, as in the United States currently, where at least among the non-excluded groups some degree of equality is tangibly present, we find another form of arrogance, seen in the interactions of the "alt-left" and the "alt-right," who constitute what I call a "mutual arrogance society." This arrogance was underscored in the lead-up to the presidential elections in 2016, and remains easily evident in partisan debates on social media today, with its hateful language and total ignorance of, and disdain for, the Other's subjective experiences and reality.[7] The incredulity expressed by both the liberals and the conservatives at the others' beliefs in "fake news" is perfectly counterbalanced by their own gullibility. This fits well with Zimmer's (2013) hypothesis of the wider prevalence of the tetrad of arrogance, stupidity, pseudo-curiosity, and surprise.

In more hierarchical societies such as India and Japan, the social structure obviates the need for creating an interpersonal one. Both arrogance and humility are, so to speak, hardwired into the society. Their presence or absence appears to be determined less by the assumed differences in personality, and more by the assigned differences in social status. For example, it is very common to witness people in India being appropriately deferential to their elders and superiors, only to turn around and be astonishingly arrogant to those below them in the social order. Not only is this accepted, but in certain circumstances it is even expected. It is meaningless then to talk of arrogance and humility as being purely or even

---

7 The *New York Times* columnist, Thomas Friedman (2017), recently compared the mutual hatred of the Democrats and Republicans today to the sectarian strife between Sunnis and Shiites that is destroying the Middle East.

predominantly individual character traits. This is amply evident in the Indian tradition of the *chamcha*. A difficult word to translate precisely, it describes an ardent
sycophant, a lackey. The *chamchas* are extremely deferential, even servile, to
their object of worship, who is usually of a much higher status. At the same time,
they gain a huge boost in their own status from being associated with their idol,
but only as long as that association is publicly known and nonconflictual. They
make it a point to be arrogant toward those below their status, especially the ones
whom they leapfrogged because of their association. Sometimes, with people of
high enough status, even their *chamchas* have *chamchas*![8]

The difference in the very context of the arrogant behavior in hierarchical and
(relatively) egalitarian societies, in both the societal structures and the interpersonal interactions, precludes any glib generalizations. This confusion is con-
founded by the interdependent nature of humility and arrogance. Hence, most
comparisons of how arrogant or humble people from vastly different cultures are,
are deeply flawed. Having said that, overall humility is more valued, and less
prone to being seen as a weakness in hierarchical societies.

Another point to consider, which Phillips does allude to, is whether there can
ever be, even in a liberal democracy, a lack of hierarchy. In other words, perhaps
arrogance is a by-product of a basic psychic tendency. Certainly arrogance and the
arrogant(s) are very often rewarded. The sheer prevalence of arrogance in "news-
worthy" people, especially politicians, celebrities, and business tycoons, bears
witness to this. Some studies suggest that arrogance may be a very useful quality
in certain situations. Most studies (see, for example, Ou, Waldman, & Peterson,
2015) find that humility in CEOs leads to better outcomes; Zhang, Ou, Tsuic,
and Wang (2017) find that it is the combination of humility and narcissism in
CEOs, when they coexist harmoniously and are manifest in appropriate situations,
that leads to the best outcomes for the firms concerned. Some philosophers have
even glorified it – the writings of Marquis de Sade, especially *Philosophy in the
Bedroom* (1795), and those of Ayn Rand, notably *Atlas Shrugged* (1957), come
immediately to mind as rather extreme examples. Even Aristotle (c. 350 BC),
when he talks about the "great-souled men," appears to condone, even appreciate,
arrogance in them. Even though he specifies that they are not haughty or hubristic,
he lays out all the characteristics of arrogance while talking of these "great-souled
men" – they deem themselves to be worthy of great things and the greatest honors,
are contemptuous of honor from "random people" or of small honors, scarcely
need anything, will always maintain a superiority in relationships with others (by
always giving more than what they receive), and do not perceive anything else to
be great (pp. 75–79).[9]

---

8 I believe that the *chamcha* complex is an offshoot of the Ganesha complex, and explains the peculiar juxtaposition of arrogance and humility in Indians better than Roland's concept of the "we-
   self." I also believe shades of the complex are present in most individuals. But these are matters
   outside the scope of this essay.
9 Perhaps Aristotle had Lord Rama and his actions in mind when he wrote about the great-souled
   man? The description certainly fits well.

Phillips (2002) suggests that the fear of the ruling class for the masses is similar to the fear that the ego has for the id elements, that the primary characteristic of the id is not sexual or aggressive but destabilizing (of the established order) and that the psychoanalyst's task, as well as democracy's, is to open up new vistas for this new content to come out and to ascribe them equal value. And that is the crux of the matter. Whether you agree with Freud's (1923b) structural model, with its imagery of the humble ego trying to please the three tyrannical masters of id, superego, and reality, or whether you follow some other model of the mind, it is a truism, as Mitchell (1984) says, that the psyche is at war with itself. A very uncivil, civil war, between two, or more, factions that behave like ex-lovers – they can neither coexist peacefully nor can they become indifferent to each other, because each needs the other to define itself.

The experiences of arrogance and humility are similarly intertwined. The hierarchy created by an act of arrogance is only within the value system specified. As far as need is concerned, the arrogant person and the humbled person are on an equal footing. They both need the other equally. Indeed, Vaknin (2015) points out the vulnerability of the arrogant man, who can be manipulated precisely because of his arrogance (loc. 3755). That is what happens to Lord Rama, as, for all his divinity and virtues, he is manipulated by his subjects into abandoning the very person dearest to him. His arrogance lay not in his contempt for his subjects (the "others") but in his fear of losing their admiration by even the slightest degree. In other words, he saw them as being capable of only admiring him absolutely, and could not tolerate any other vision of them, could not tolerate them being full human beings with contradictions, doubts, and uncertainties. Very possibly, this is because he could not tolerate this ambivalence within himself, having been set up with an ideal too high to meet – that of an incarnation of a god.

To return to the possibility of an "ideal" form of humility, consider the statement, "I am humble," or "I know myself, and I am a humble person." It comes across as braggadocio, (called a "humblebrag" in slang), even if one assumes that the speaker has been well analyzed. In other words, the very act of self-observation destroys whatever humility there may be, as the subject's focus will necessarily be on the self, and not directed outward to others. The introspection leads the subject to assess his abilities in relation to either some ideal or to others. This comparison, whether it leads to an under- or an overvaluation, becomes a narcissistic exercise. Consequently, such an idealized concept of humility can be just that – a hypothesis based on observations and theory, but not verifiable by analysis or introspection. Therefore, it is unable to be differentiated from the defensive variety of humility. This is why all self-professed acts of modesty or humility smack of an attempt to seek admiration and attention (narcissistic supply) – including my reflections at the beginning of this chapter.

Chapter 6

Literary portrayals of arrogance

Nilofer Kaul

Arrogance is frequently accompanied by a fear of it. Most literary and personal narratives deal with arrogance either by acknowledging it or rejecting it. While the register of tragedy accepts it, the register of Christianity forbids it. As a result, narratives are born out of the tension between the flight to grandiosity and its inevitable crashing. Invisible shields of omnipotence promise an escape from unbearable helplessness. An arrogant posture helps preserve the brittle armor against omnipotence.

Omnipotence is discussed as a recurrent, almost quintessential trope in myths and while narratives seek to abjure it, recurrence points to its inevitability. The skirmish between its stubborn return and the subsequent fallout seems to engender narrative itself. The next section looks at heroic discourse and ponders on its register which seems to be culled out of an insouciance for life, and deeper yet, an evacuation of emotion. Gandhi's (1957) self-fashioning autobiography is read as embodying paradoxically both a need to carve a new kind of boldness and to negate the arrogance implicit in such a project. This anxiety is sought to be contained by a vocabulary of humility, passivity, and God's will. Is it possible to create a narrative without traces of arrogance/omnipotence? If so, where can we locate the Other to arrogance? Finally, we look briefly at Samuel Beckett's (1946) *The End*, which presents yet another landscape of death-in-life. The abjectness of the protagonist and his complete indifference to life create an idiom as remote as possible from arrogance. This effacing of meaning and the negating of the self engender an anti-narrative. And except for stray moments, we can see nothing but the debris of a self.

Preamble

Greek gods, like those of many mythologies, may be read as omnipotent versions of their human counterparts – bestowing benedictions or destroying at will. Most stories emerge from the confrontation between wishes for magic and the dread of such an arbitrary world. What divides men from gods in these mythologies is power, and mortals aspire to be gods. One such myth is that of Aphrodite: A beautiful goddess falls in love with the all-too-mortal shepherd, Anchises. Dazzled and awed, he is deceived by her momentarily into believing she is mortal too. Aeneas – the invincible one – is born from this union of man and god, which embodies the tragic quest for perfect coupling. Before bidding Anchises an inexorable farewell, Aphrodite says:

> If you could only stay the way you are, in looks and constitution,
> staying alive as my lawfully-wedded husband,
> then *akhos* would not have to envelop me and my sturdy *phrenes*.
> But now wretched old age will envelop you,
> pitilessly, just as it catches up with every man.
> It is baneful, it wears you down, and even the gods shrink back from it.
>
> (Homer, c. 500 BC)

In Aphrodite's haunting words, we can read the disappointment at being merely human. In an interesting intertextual moment, Aphrodite cites the story of Tithonus (in which the goddess Aurora or Dawn fell in love with Tithonus, the beautiful shepherd). Aurora had pleaded with other gods to have him immortalized but failed; Aphrodite knows better than to ask! In Tennyson's (1859) languidly melancholy rendition, Tithonus now haunted by immortality looks at his once beloved Aurora and the pain underlying his envy of her eternal youth allows the sadness to wash over envious longing:

> How can my nature longer mix with thine?
> Coldly thy rosy shadows bathe me, cold
> Are all thy lights, and cold my wrinkled feet
> Upon thy glimmering thresholds, when the steam
> Floats up from those dim fields about the homes
> Of happy men that have the power to die,
> . . . Thou seëst all things, thou wilt see my grave:
> Thou wilt renew thy beauty morn by morn;
> I earth in earth forget these empty courts,
> And thee returning on thy silver wheels.
>
> (pp. 65–76)

Myths are often haunted by this shadow-line that is crossed and then either betrayed by tragedy or proved illusory. And yet one could well say that without what Aristotle calls "hubris," there is not just no tragedy; there may well be no narrative. Hubris seems the closest Greek equivalent to arrogance. It is often glimpsed in a gesture of defiance of gods, followed by nemesis. The core of hubris, or arrogance, seems to point to the inability to accept the constraints of being human.

Etymologically "arrogance" (Latin, late Middle English, via Old French from the Latin verb, *arrogare* – claiming for oneself) suggests an undue sense of one's entitlement; implicit in this is a rejection of the other's claim. Like narcissism, arrogance only sees a mirror, while otherness remains a foreign language. It must deny mortality, finitude, incertitude, and so sweep away the truth of human existence, making an exaggerated claim for itself. What the Greeks called "hubris" appears to be an equivalent term. Here I will look at the intertwined nature of omnipotence and arrogance; in order to sustain itself, the ego calls upon arrogance to aid and uphold its omnipotence.

Aristotle (c. 335 BC) in *Poetics* observes that the tragic hero must have a flaw (*hamartia*) that undoes his fate. It is remarkable that hubris was recognized as central to tragedy and a sense of waste, despite the immediate sense of distaste that the word itself evokes. "Aristotle argued that hubris is what destroys a city. One can not destroy the other without destroying the self" (Willett, 2001, p. 184). In his more political writing, Aristotle will proclaim it a crime to be banished, but "privately" – in his poetic theory – he laments how it destroys the best of men. This bifurcation is very much the heart of the matter here. I will refer to these two responses as tragic and moral, perhaps suggesting that narratives are born out of a skirmish with arrogance. But in itself this will not suffice. Are there narratives that elude arrogance – its grammar and its idiom?

The tragic response: arrogance as fatal flaw

Writing about the tragic, Arvanitakis (1998) observes, "Aristotle's belief . . . was that tragedy was born when a member (*exarchon*) of the choral fusional mass broke off and started acting independently and speaking in his own voice, thereby becoming the first actor" (pp. 957–958). There appears to be a paradoxical link that connects the act of individuating with arrogance, ergo tragedy. The roll-call is pretty formidable: Odysseus, Oedipus, Antigone, Prometheus, Sisyphus, Adam and Eve. Aristotle's masterly stroke really is to see that hubris is innately tragic. There is an unspoken imaginative sympathy implicit in this. He imagines the audience moved by the spectacle of the hero's fall on account of his hubris. The hero has to be good enough and the structure must be one of a fall of fortune. And somehow this fall must be caused by his moral flaw and this "hamartia" or flaw is usually "hubris" or pride – or some version of it, at any rate. This brings us to the proximity between arrogance and omnipotence which I will discuss in the third section of this chapter. It is tragic because the choice Oedipus actually has is between submitting to his destiny or trying to fight it. Hubris is in fact everywhere: What was Laertes thinking when he got rid of his child? Or Jocasta when she remarried? How did they dare to think they could defy fate?

Aristotle's master, Plato, saw it too, but his response was more terrified: Poets ought to be banished from the ideal state, because they did not organize narrative to ensure that good would be rewarded and evil punished (Plato, c. 380 BC). Plato intuitively felt that poetry ran counter to the ordered structure he sought. It is only one short step away from what the argument here is assuming, that narrative itself is born out of the knowledge of this inevitability of this fatal flaw. What is profoundly interesting is how pervasively it is dreaded. So much narrative seems to be infected with a fear of arrogance. And even as different voices endeavor to disengage themselves from it, "mnemic traces" of it may be found everywhere. So what would be its other? And where would it be? Can it sustain narrative?

Every generation, as we know – not from Oedipus alone but from Antigone locked in war with Creon, from Prometheus who tried to steal fire, and Satan who tried to defy God, from the challenge by Oedipus to Laertes, by Krishna to Kansa, and by Christ to Herod – represents a threat to the previous generation. So is *Oedipus* about this threat or is it about trying to undo fate? Is *Oedipus* actually about the arrogance of youth or is it about arrogance itself? And who is being arrogant? The one who thinks he can question established wisdom (Antigone, Oedipus, Prometheus, Faustus) or the one who feels nobody can question his omnipotent hold (Herod, Cronos, Laertes)? Lear's blindness to his daughter's love has a counterpart in Cordelia's cussed refusal to humor an old man in his dotage. The brittleness of his arrogant shell collapses and roles are tragically reversed.

An interesting variant on the oedipal theme is Yayati's story in *The Mahabharata* – an ancient tale with dubious ethical codes. It is discussed at length by both Ramanujan (1999) and Goldman (1978). Ramanujan referred to it as the reversal of the Oedipus myth (pp. 385–387). It tells the story of yet another ambiguous hero, King Yayati who consorts with a beautiful princess, Devayani. Some years later, he has a chance encounter with her "waiting woman". That woman, of noble birth, is 'in her season' and in urgent need of a man who could impregnate her. She argues and equivocates with him till he succumbs to her persuasive beauty. When Devayani discovers this, she is livid and complains to celestial powers who curse Yayati to premature decrepitude. He asks for it to be reversed, which is not possible, but if he can get one of his five sons to agree to swap his decrepitude for their youth – that can mitigate the curse. The four refuse, but the youngest, Puru, agrees. And for a thousand years, Yayati is able to feast on a prolonged and borrowed youth. Puru is then rewarded with the gigantic kingdom. The cultural twist it brings to the oedipal tale quite apart, what we can also take away is that Yayati is unable to accept the consequences of his choice. He tries to hold onto his omnipotence (embodied here in a powerful kingdom, abundant beauty, plenitude) and by a thread – by "reversing the charges" onto his son – he is able to do so. Interpreted in this way, the myth can be read as dealing with a denial of reality, or a fantasized postponing of death, a promise of plenitude in one form or another. So how do we read this: Does the inevitable clash between generations give birth to tragedy or is it more profoundly a trigger for the intrapsychic wrestling between the quest for omnipotence and a dread of just such a fate? Is the intergenerational rivalry contained by its oedipal dynamic or is it a part of an overall hatred of temporality?

Bion (1958) seems to suggest the latter when he writes about Oedipus who, as we know, has the temerity to think he can reverse his destiny:

> I shall rehearse the Oedipus myth from a point of view which makes the sexual crime a peripheral element of a story in which the central crime is the arrogance of Oedipus in vowing to lay bare the truth at no matter what cost. This shift of emphasis brings the following elements into the centre of the story: the Sphinx, who asks a riddle and destroys herself when it is answered, the blind Teiresias, who possesses knowledge and deplores the resolve of the king to

search for it, the oracle that provokes the search which the prophet deplores, and again the king who, his search concluded, suffers blindness and exile.

(pp. 144–145)

Bion suggests a link between knowledge, truth, and arrogance. Here and else-where, he writes of the drive to know the truth and while this is Oedipus's claim for himself (*arrogare*), he demands to know the truth, but fails to see it all the time. This is the quintessential tragic paradox – that some powerful force within us seeks to know the truth, but when it confronts us, we are terrified – unable to bear it. And perhaps that is the tragic moment.

The moral response: dread of arrogance

Christ

While narrative as we discussed in the section above arises from ambiguity, Chris-tianity warns consistently against the deadly sin of pride and through this it wishes to dispense with ambiguity. The quotations above are instances of how it warns of pride in no uncertain terms, as something that will be punished. The Bible and its commentators repeatedly warn against pride and vanity, but one finds these dire warnings belied by actions. Like a hydra-headed monster, arrogance returns in changed forms. So while The New Testament entreats us to submit pride, it upholds itself as the "true faith," condemning all others to being heathens who chase "after strange gods."

We can perhaps safely assume that no story endorses arrogance. So even though "pride goeth before a fall" in every narrative, the location of the narra-tive can fall broadly into either the phobic (paranoid-schizoid) or into the tragic (depressive) pattern. Paganism allows tragedy, while Christianity inhibits it. This can be traced from the myths to Christianity and even to psychoanalytic narra-tives. Christ – as the son of man – gives a strange new twist to the idea of divinity by embodying his mortality. Compassion replaces omnipotence and cuts away radically at earlier more anthropomorphic, willful notions of gods. Christ dis-arms with humility. But when we look closer, he triumphs, and not just morally, he also performs miracles. He makes water into wine, he cures the lepers. This contravenes the spirit of the lamb, the son of man, the redoubtable ally of beg-gars and thieves. The incredulity of this is immortalized by Blake (1794), when he addresses "the fearful symmetry" of the "Tyger burning bright" . . . "Did he who made the Lamb make thee?" (p. 23). If God creates both lamb and tiger, he must be a very split figure.

But finally, it is story of resurrection that actually put paid to this endeavor of an all-too human Christ. That this mere mortal can return to earth after he is crucified is a telling drama in itself: While the story of Christ can be seen to represent the wish to renounce omnipotent strivings through immortal legions of gods, it seems as if the psyche finds it too hard to sustain such renunciation. Philip Pullman's *The*

Good Man Jesus and the Scoundrel Christ (2010) actually is a story born from the incompatibility inherent in the story of the messiah: that in fact, the humility and passivity seem to run counter to the miracles and mysteries.

The gravitas of its theme notwithstanding, it cheekily unpicks the two impulses embedded in Christ's story by splitting. This fork is represented by making it about a pair of "un-identical" twins. The passionate, charismatic, and radical Jesus, and his rather diminutive twin, Christ – the shadow of the big man. Weak in flesh and spirit, he follows the rather potent Jesus around surreptitiously, scribbling down his words. Finally, he is commissioned to write the story of Jesus's life. And here is the really clever twist: In order to ensure posthumous influence, the crafty plan is to incorporate the register of miracles. When Christ demurs, the stranger who is allegorically the Church or institutionalized religion, says:

> The Spirit is inward and invisible. Men and women need a sign that is outward and visible, and then they will believe. You have been scornful lately when I have spoken of truth, dear Christ; you should not be. It will be truth that strikes into their minds and hearts in the ages to come, the truth of God, that comes from beyond time. But it needs a window to be opened so it can shine through into the world of time, and you are that window.
>
> (Pullman, 2010, p. 227)

And a little later we watch:

> Christ sat . . . he couldn't help thinking of the story of Jesus and how he could improve it. For example, there could be some miraculous sign to welcome the birth: a star, an angel. And the childhood of Jesus might be studded with charming little wonder-tales of boyish mischief leavened by magic, which could nevertheless be interpreted as signs of greater miracles to come . . . if the child born in the stable had been not just a human child, but the very incarnation of God himself, how much more memorable and moving the story would be! And how much more profound the death that crowned it!
>
> (p. 243)

Its irreverent tone notwithstanding, the book captures the impossibility of renouncing omnipotence in any absolute way. So even as Christianity attempts to reinvent the spirit by anthropomorphizing God, this impulse is overridden with the desire to be in the presence of something awesome, reverential, infinite. The paradox between man's desire to know the truth and his terror of finding it unbearable is embodied in the way the Christian hero is man and yet, son of God.

In the next section, I look briefly at a particular refrain in Gandhi – another prototype of Christ – who eschews omnipotence, who represents humility and attempts to redefine heroism and courage by stripping down, rather than arming;

defying through surrender rather than fight, by emasculating rather than muscularity. But it is only a particular moment I wish to examine.

Gandhi

In *My Experiments with Truth*, Gandhi (1925) "retells" a particular "story" three times. Each of these episodes that "retell" can be clustered together in Gandhi's term as "faith on its trial" (p. 26) where there is a life-threatening illness, and he is faced with the predicament of dying or allowing a contamination of purity, which he rather simplistically equates with vegetarianism. The first time it is the son, Manilal, whose life is endangered, the next time it is his wife, Kasturba, and finally it is himself. I would like to speculate on the repetitious nature of these trials of faith and what is being established:

> Though I had hired chambers in the Fort and a house in Girgaum, God would not let me settle down. Scarcely had I moved into my new house when my second son, Manilal, who had already been through an acute attack of small-pox some years back, had a severe attack of typhoid, combined with pneumonia and signs of delirium at night . . . The doctor was called in. He said medicine would have little effect, but eggs and chicken broth might be given with profit . . . Manilal was only ten years old. To consult his wishes was out of the question. Being his guardian, I had to decide. The doctor was a very good Parsi. I told him that we were all vegetarians, and that I could not possibly give either of the two things to my son. Would he therefore recommend something else?
>
> (pp. 298–300)

He goes on to narrate his obdurate refusal of the doctor's advice and persistence with hydropathy. The fever remains unabated. We see here the "if this, but then . . ." obsessive syntax of defiance followed by guilt and finally a recourse to God's will. Gandhi's voice skims past the logical lacunae: What would people say of me? Do parents (father) determine right of life? God is invoked here as the arbiter, but this apparent "surrender" is in fact a very active choice:

> I knew Kuhne's treatment, and had tried it too. I knew as well that fasting also could be tried with profit. So I began to give Manilal hip baths according to Kuhne, never keeping him in the tub for more than three minutes, and kept him on orange juice mixed with water for three days . . . But the temperature persisted, going up to 104 degrees. At night he would be delirious. I began to get anxious. *What would people say of me?* What would my elder brother think of me? Could we not call in another doctor? Why not have an Ayurvedic physician? What right had the parents to inflict their fads on their children? *I was haunted by thoughts like these. Then a contrary current would start. God would surely be pleased to see that I was giving the same treatment to my son as I would give myself. I had faith in hydropathy, and little faith in allopathy. The doctors could not guarantee recovery. At best they could experiment.*

The thread of life was in the hands of God. Why not trust it to Him, and in His name go on with what I thought was the right treatment?

(p. 300)

The justificatory tone, the sliding quickly past his own preferences, the foreclosure of "God's will" point towards an attempt to render invisible his active and even obstinate choices. The certitude of his beliefs seems to be at complete variance with the professed passivity (and humility) of submitting to God's will. He writes that God will be pleased with what he decides, but the assumption itself, that it is possible to know God's mind does not trouble him. Needless to say, he elides over what he raises earlier: "My mind was torn between these conflicting thoughts" (p. 300). Fortunately for him there is a happy ending and the ruminations end with a recovery. Renunciation and hard decisions are rewarded. This is again the language of miracles. We see this particular anxiety in his language – the fear of his belief in omnipotence:

Today Manilal is the healthiest of my boys. Who can say whether his recovery was due to God's grace, or to hydropathy, or to careful dietary and nursing? Let everyone decide according to his own faith. For my part I was sure that God had saved my honour, and that belief remains unaltered to this day.

(p. 301)

This is an especially interesting construction. Manilal's recovery may be attributed to "hydropathy" or careful dietary and nursing or "God's will"; the offhand tone underplays the dilemma for a professed believer. If God's will is supreme, why is this in question? More to the point, we see it was "God who saved his honour" (p. 301). Subtly the concern slides from gratitude about Manilal's recovery, to relief over his defiant choices not being punished.

A similar episode appears towards the end of Gandhi's book. A chapter called "At Death's Door" describes him following a diet of groundnut butter and lemons. He contracts violent dysentery and lies dying. But he writes, "All interest in living had ceased, as I have never liked to live for the sake of living" (p. 549). This appears to be the kernel of Gandhian courage. It is what makes him voraciously seek causes. His life can well be read as a fervent pursuit of causes followed with scrupulous zeal, the tenacity of which becomes the source of gratification. Here as he lies nearly dying, refusing all sources of nourishment for the sake of his dearly beloved (vegetarianism is the overvalued ideal object that is picked over real human relationships), the ". . . doctor too took up the strain: 'If you will take goat's milk, it will be enough for me,' he said" (p. 552).

We see how lightly Gandhi holds an attachment to life and how hungry he is for a cause that can tempt him to live. The entire narrative can be organized as his fight against temptations – whether it is sex, alcohol, or meat – in fact all symptoms of life itself. Being overattached to life seems to make for a lack of courage:

I succumbed. My intense eagerness to take up the Satyagraha fight had created in me a strong desire to live, and so I contented myself with adhering to the letter of my vow only, and sacrificed its spirit. For although I had only the milk of the cow and the she-buffalo in mind when I took the vow, by natural implication it covered the milk of all animals. Nor could it be right for me to use milk at all, so long as I held that milk is not the natural diet of man. Yet knowing all this I agreed to take goat's milk. The will to live proved stronger than the devotion to truth, and for once the votary of truth compromised his sacred ideal by his eagerness to take up the Satyagraha fight. The memory of this action even now rankles in my breast and fills me with remorse.

(p. 552)

Truth – the idealized object of Gandhi's life – is a rigid, morbidly absolute, almost persecutory object, which is pitted against life. Heroism is about renouncing everything to its absolute command and all desires for life are seen as temptations that steer away from the path of righteousness. Conquering desires (linked with pleasures of living) forms an omnipotent armor against the uncertain rhythms of life.

Omnipotence: flight to arrogance

The pervasive fear of arrogance is an acknowledgement not just on account of its ubiquity, but also, because it is linked with the fear of madness within us, it feels unmanageable and as a patient put it, as a blowfish can not help inflating when it senses danger, the flight to grandiosity on the wings of arrogance hurtles into omnipotence, then crash-lands! Altogether a flight into madness and a return to sanity that feels cataclysmic.

Freud hears echoes of childish omnipotence almost everywhere. *Totem and Taboo* (1912–13), written in the form of speculative history or anthropology – may also be read as an allegory of the psyche, if we replace "primitive man" with "primitive parts of our mind." Freud imagines the primal experience of helplessness, that needs must be countered first by a flight into omnipotence. When this seems to flounder, animism is born: *If I can not do this, someone else can* – the renouncing of the wish is harder than the transferring of power. So when I am disappointed in myself, I look towards my objects, and when they disappoint, a god is summoned and religions created. Spirits and objects are reposed with omnipotence. Sorcery, Freud implies, is the handmaiden of animism – it creates rituals by which to appease, mitigate, or vanquish these omnipotent spirits created by the disappointed ego. By contrast, magic ignores these animated presences and looks to create its own treasury of rituals by which it can maneuver its fate. Writing here of the difference between animism and magic, Freud says, animism imputes attributes of life to inanimate objects (projection) to then seek some degree of control, while magic is more directly assuming an omnipotence of thoughts (if I think this, it is bound to be – or not). The contrast as Freud builds it here between magic and animism is analogous to that between narcissism and love: It is either an overvaluation of the self (narcissism) or the other (anaclitic). Fundamentally both postures deny the surrender to what the ego experiences as the essentially unbearable experience of helplessness.

Let us briefly consider how closely the syntax of arrogance resembles that of omnipotence. The mythical figures we know embody attributes that bypass human frailty in one way or another. It seems that the narrative impulse arises from a search to bypass the constraints of being human and it is countered by a recognition of not just the futility but also the inevitable danger of such flights. So even as Achilles represents invincibility he is belied by his heel, Tithonus's desire for immortality is foiled by omitting to ask for youth.

Orpheus is unable to exercise restraint on his longing to see and so he loses Eurydice forever, Tiresias's omniscience is rendered useless by his equivocating, Narcissus is destroyed by the loneliness of a stance of being involuted. The Three Fates (allegorical in themselves but figuratively speaking here) loom large over the whole canvas of drama – destiny can be translated as unwanted reality that the characters fight – an act at once futile (Sisyphus), foolhardy (Icarus), and tragic (Oedipus).

In and through our patients, we often catch glimpses of our own "bastions" – our little fortresses that hide pouches of primitive omnipotence. I am thinking of a patient who was always late, who would be shocked that the clock had moved. Time ought to have stood still for her; it always shook her that it hadn't. My grey hair was something that shamed her – she colored her own assiduously. Time should have stood still for me too. Time is the great antagonist, the most powerful warrior in the enemy camp. The underlying refrains in her talk vary between: "I can fix everything, I am not going to die, life and time stand still for me, I can wrestle like a man and give birth like a woman, I am both man and woman. I can heal everyone. I can renounce anything. Death will not come to me. I am immune." She taught me a great deal – chiefly that I could not help her. But she appeared to learn nothing from me.

In these strains of arrogance, there is embedded the poignant plea to be spared harsh reality. Narcissus, haunted by absence and mocked by echoes of himself? Lear uses this syntax of narcissism. His affections are trampled by his injuries which he cannot distinguish from insults. And such insults destroy all relationships. In the lonely rantings of patients, there's longing to be autonomous, to be freed of the inevitably disappointing vagaries of relationships; to rise from their own debris, if not ashes. And that echoes the Phoenix myth. The myth of giving birth to oneself, the variations on the myth of self-sufficiency. Grotstein (1997) refers to something similar as "autochthony." Thoreau's (1854) *Walden* is a more secular, contemporary version of the same. And we see these not just in psychotic states but in the psychotic syntax, the primitive part of every psyche. "I don't need anybody's help. I do not depend on anyone." Touchingly, it is an ode to survival.

Effacing the self, the anti-heroic: The other to arrogance?

From here we just need to retrace our footsteps, and look again at all the heroes mentioned in the first section; what emerges as one common attribute is being intrepid, courageous, and willing to die. So is this the other side of the hubristic coin? In the final leg of this chapter, I would like to examine the syntax of Samuel Beckett with whom perhaps high modernism reaches a kind of apotheosis. Beckettian protagonists are indistinguishable from each other, which is already symptomatic of the effacement that may be read as the other to arrogance. The tone is an unvarying insouciance about life, and an affectless waiting in a landscape of death, and is perhaps most remarkable in creating an idiom that evacuates life and meaning from existence.

Cheated into impoverishment and rendered homeless, the narrator of *The End* wanders around aimlessly:

> I unbuttoned my trousers discreetly to scratch myself . . . It passed the time, time flew when I scratched myself . . . It was in the arse I had the most pleasure, I stuck in my forefinger up to the knuckle. Later, if I had to shit, the pain was atrocious. But I hardly shat any more . . . Normally I didn't see a great deal. I didn't hear a great deal. Strictly speaking I believe I've never been anywhere . . . You become unsociable, it's inevitable. It's enough to make you wonder sometimes if you are on the right planet. Even the words desert you, it's as bad as that.
>
> (1946, pp. 25, 29)

Relentlessly, there emerges a bleak, objectless landscape – unforgiving, ruthlessly empty. These anti-narratives usually end without conclusion, for to give closure suggests sequence and implies meaning. This is a syntax I have heard in a patient with autistic defenses too. She lost her parents in quick succession between the ages of eight and ten. Understandably, mourning was not possible then. I begin to feel it is not possible now or ever. Session after session, I hear her steady stream of words, like a leaking tap. Unable to feel anything, she mimes other people and denies all connections. There is neither anger nor bitterness directed at anyone. But in the rhythm of a language drained of affect, sometimes, a line may jump out which gives a clue, a flicker of life. It dare not last. So I will conclude with a passage from Beckett's *The End* in which the harsh and arid landscape may momentarily flicker with life, an object might appear. It is hard to tell whether it is an oasis or a mirage:

> I knew them well, even as a child . . . It was evening, I was with my father . . . I would have liked him to draw me close with a gesture of protective love, but his mind was on other things . . . the fires turned from gold to red . . . I knew what it was, . . . How often had I set a match to it myself, as a child . . . The sea, the sky, the mountains and the islands closed in . . . The memory came faint and cold of the story I might have told, a story in the likeness of my life, I mean without the courage to end or the strength to go on.
>
> (p. 31)

This line about "father" quietly slips in in the midst of such consistent disaffection for life, almost as if it needs to go unnoticed, as if such sentiments were beside the point, and the only real point was of being indifferent to life, and yet it is a revelatory slip in a text that obstinately refutes the possibility of meaning. To repose meaning in any object is to relinquish control over it. Beckett's oeuvre seems to be forged from an indifference to life and it can be seen as the other end of the spectrum of narratives from the myths of omnipotence. The debris-self of his characters is as far as possible from the godlike figures discussed. As if in fact the arrogance of the divine pose concealed the terror of this debris-self within. Is this "the other" to arrogance? Or is the refusal to attribute meaning the last bid to preserve some control? While this is the furthest we can travel away from arrogance, it yet is an attempt to survive the onslaught of an inherently changeable and hence perilous world.

Conclusion

In this contribution, I begin by looking at how arrogance or "hubris" is integral to myths and narratives. Aristotle recognizes hubris as a fatal flaw that precipitates tragedy. This "tragic" response is indicative of its inevitability. By contrast, Plato's response to tragedy is a "moral" one, which is echoed in Christianity. Freud (1912–13) in *Totem and Taboo* writes about how the primitive mind is linked to magical thinking and omnipotence. From here, it is argued that our failed omnipotence underlies arrogance. It is the inability to bear our disappointments and failures that underpins a flight to mania, grandiosity, and arrogance. The morality against arrogance in Christianity runs counter to its own claim as a supreme faith. Pullman's (2010) contemporary take on the story of Christ seems to undo the tragic-moral binary by revealing the need for the register of omnipotence. Gandhi's (1957) autobiographical account, *My Experiments with Truth*, offers another kind of self, like Christ's, that fashions itself as embodying the antithesis to the scintillating heroes – he is humble, flawed, passive. But on a closer look, this too reveals its fissures. So the distinction I make at the beginning between two responses to arrogance as tragic and moral seems to sag in the middle, if not snap completely. Finally, we look at Beckett's (1946) antihero in an antinarrative, *The End*. Surely this abject figure, standing at the last outpost of civilization, must mark the furthest distance from the language of arrogance. And Beckett does indeed create an idiom where the self is effaced. In doing so, he turns the tables on life. The evacuation of all meaning from life forges an insouciance to life and apparently disavows all possibility of attaching value. This resembles the patient who is in the grip of a death wish, who elects objectlessness over mourning and in doing so, replaces life with death. Unlike "heroism" where courage demands that death is not feared, here in Beckett, death is awaited as the only certitude, while the uncertain pleasures of life are seen as pointless. This indifference to life forges its own form of vocabulary of antiheroic and yet hubristic rejection of life. Yet, every now and then, something slips in almost against the grain of this fabric which reveals the unbearableness of disappointment and it is in such breaches that we may hear faintly the terrors against which we arm ourselves with arrogance.

Part III

Clinical realm

Part II

Chapter 7

Arrogance and aloneness

Kathleen Ross

In a recent comprehensive paper, Leon Wurmser (2015) describes the beginning years of what became a half-century of thinking and writing about shame and shame conflicts. "I was startled to find," he says, "with a few exceptions . . . very little about this affect of shame and these shame conflicts in the psychoanalytic literature of the time . . . Yet, wherever we look there it was, like a will-o'-the-wisp, here and there and everywhere" (p. 1615). During the time – fortunately months, not decades – that I have considered the concept of arrogance while researching this topic, I have often felt a similar dilemma. There are more than a thousand mentions of arrogance in the literature, but most include the word only briefly and in passing, without according it any special importance or differentiation from other descriptors used to characterize a patient. Most frequently, arrogance figures as part of a list meant to illustrate a patient's narcissistic tendencies, one feature of the defenses such a person deploys against underlying feelings of shame and inferiority.

I will give a few examples, taken from a variety of theoretical orientations. From ego psychology, Broucek (1982), lists "arrogance, competitiveness and phallic grandiosity" (p. 375) as a way to counter the shame of feeling weak and castrated. From an object relations perspective, Ogden (1995), examining the experience of aliveness and deadness in the analytic process, presents a clinical discussion of his patient, Mr. D: "The patient carried himself and spoke in a way that conveyed a sense of arrogance, aloofness and self-importance; at the same time, this deportment had a brittleness to it that made it readily apparent that the patient's superior tone of voice and demeanor thinly disguised feelings of fear, worthlessness and desperation" (p. 699). A last example from an interpersonal and relational orientation is Bromberg (1983), in his well-known study of narcissism, "The Mirror and the Mask," where he asserts that "the defining qualities [of narcissism] are most often described in the psychoanalytic literature as a triad of vanity, exhibitionism, and arrogant ingratitude, which . . . is what the word 'narcissism' has come to mean in popular usage" (p. 360).

Narcissism has reentered our politico-cultural scene and popular usage of late with a vengeance, as has arrogance. The resurgence of many, if not all, of the above-listed qualities in public discourse, arguably with arrogance most prominent, assaults us on a daily basis. Now more than ever it seems pertinent, and even crucial, to understand arrogance as it manifests in the clinical setting, both as a feature of the inner world of patients, and as their response to the larger cultural surround. Moreover, I am interested in exploring how patient and analyst, separately and together, confront arrogance when it enters the consulting room. I see arrogance as connected with agency, or the lack of agency, fantasized or real, in a person's sense of self. I will be discussing patients whose arrogance stems more from powerlessness than power, and the analyst's stance with such patients. First, however, I wish to return to a review of the psychoanalytic literature, in order to arrive at a more precise definition of arrogance as I will use the term in this chapter.

A brief review of literature

As a starting point, let us briefly consider narcissism, the larger psychoanalytic concept within which arrogance resides. Sydney Pulver (1970) states in his elegant study, "Narcissism – the Term and the Concept": "In the voluminous literature on narcissism, there are probably only two facts upon which everyone agrees: first, that the concept of narcissism is one of the most important contributions of psychoanalysis; second, that it is one of the most confusing" (p. 320). Unraveling that confusion – which continues and has only multiplied as I write this nearly fifty years after Pulver – goes far beyond the scope of this chapter.

Nonetheless, for the sake of clarity and completeness, before entering into a discussion of the literature on arrogance, I will touch on the main contributions regarding narcissism. Akhtar (2009a), and Auchincloss and Samberg (2012), in their respective compendiums of psychoanalytic terminology, both provide extensive and illuminating entries on narcissism that put a great deal of order into this thorny area of theory and psychopathology. I refer the reader to them for a more comprehensive discussion of the literature, as well as explications of the many related terms (e.g., narcissistic injury, narcissistic rage) that make narcissism such a multifaceted and extremely complex concept.

Freud's (1914c) "On Narcissism," while not his first mention of the term, is his most complete elaboration of it. Notable in this essay is the expansion of narcissism, which previously had been a term used to define a kind of sexual perversion, to explain a much wider range of phenomena. Three in particular stand out: a kind of object choice (narcissistic object choice) based on identification with some aspect of the self; a mode of object relations, which Freud used to account for states of withdrawal from objects, such as schizophrenia and psychosis; and self-regard. The last, as considered in Freud's description of the new concept of the ego ideal, perhaps most interests us in the present context. "On Narcissism" lays a foundation for the theories of self-esteem and its vicissitudes which have followed.

The concept of pathological narcissism, associated with British Kleinian theory, will also be important to my essay. As Auchincloss and Samberg (2012) put it,

"Klein argued that even earliest infancy is not objectless, as Freud had proposed, but rather is characterized by primitive object relations" (p. 164). The theory of pathological narcissism that begins in infancy forms the basis for Bion's "On Arrogance" (1958), to be closely read below.

In the decade of the 1970s, the brilliant and very different pioneer thinkers Heinz Kohut and Otto Kernberg built on these earlier theories of narcissism to develop their own distinct ideas with crucial technical implications for psychoanalytic treatment. Kernberg, in works such as his 1975 *Borderline Conditions and Pathological Narcissism*, elaborated on Kleinian concepts to study how early defensive operations, such as splitting, lead to a distortion in the basic structure of the self and a resulting pathological psychic structure. Kohut (1971), moving in another direction, produced a theory of both normal and pathological narcissism that would eventually become known as self-psychology. His book, *The Analysis of the Self: A Systematic Approach to the Psychoanalytic Treatment of Narcissistic Personality Disorders*, along with other important contributions, posits narcissism as an essential part of psychological life, with its own narcissistic line of development. For Kohut, narcissistic pathology reflects an environmental deficit, caused when a child's developmental self-object needs are not adequately met.

Lastly, Bromberg (1983) in his aforementioned "The Mirror and the Mask," makes a major contribution towards the synthesis of theories of narcissism with the interpersonal school of psychoanalytic thought, taking social factors into greater account than other orientations. This essay argues that the insistence by ego psychology on interpretation as the *sine qua non* of analytic technique must be revised and rethought to make room for the very different work an analyst needs to do to reach a narcissistic patient, who is developmentally stuck between ". . . the mirror and the mask – a reflected appraisal of himself, or a disguised search for one, through which the self finds or seeks affirmation of its own significance. Living becomes a process of controlling the environment and other people from behind a mask" (p. 361). Bromberg's work is now a cornerstone for what has come to be known as the relational school of psychoanalysis.

I will now return to the specific topic at hand. Arrogance, as we saw earlier, merits mention by many psychoanalytic writers, but specific definition by almost none, save Bion (1958) in his famous formulation of "curiosity, arrogance, and stupidity" (p. 144) in "On Arrogance." For Bion, arrogance is a phenomenon reflecting disastrous early object relations that deny the normal use of projective identification to the developing infant. As I understand Bion's highly condensed and almost poetic prose, the pursuit of truth at any cost in the analytic enterprise, achieved through verbal communication, lies at the core of the triad of references to arrogance, curiosity, and stupidity in the material. What is felt by the patient to be the analyst's "claim to a capacity for containing the discarded, split-off aspects of other personalities while retaining a balanced outlook" (p. 145) evokes envy and hatred, and a regression to psychotic mechanisms that interrupt verbal communication. A primitive superego emerges that prevents the patient from depositing bad feelings into the analyst and establishing the dyadic contact that in turn provides a foundation for verbal communication. The process is short-circuited until these mechanisms can be uncovered and understood in the analytic pair.

In "Attacks on Linking," Bion (1959) further explicated his thoughts on curiosity, arrogance, and stupidity. The image of the patient's psyche as a "primitive disaster" (p. 311) here receives some refinement, taking into account the dynamic aspects of the analytic situation. It is not a static situation within which the analyst works, but rather "a catastrophe that remains at one and the same moment actively vital and yet incapable of resolution into quiescence. This lack of progress in any direction must be attributed in part to the destruction of a capacity for curiosity and the consequent inability to learn" (p. 311). Only concrete questions of "what," rather than "how" or "why" are tolerated by the patient at this stage of the work. The link between objects created by mutual problem-solving falls under attack, as ambivalent feelings of gratitude and hostility coexist towards "the analyst as the person who will not understand and refuses the patient the use of the only method of communication by which he feels he can make himself understood" (p. 313), namely, projective identification. As a consequence, "[T]he links surviving are perverse, cruel, and sterile" (p. 315).

Viewed through a psychoanalytic lens, then, arrogance as part of a patient's presentation in the consulting room may be but one of several aspects of an overarching constellation of narcissistic defenses. It may also signal a more profound poverty of capacity for connection and the ability to join in a mutual inquiry. Death rather than life instincts predominate in such a person (Bion, 1958, p. 144) and pride felt as self-respect cannot develop.

Both of these formulations focus on the patient's psychology as the locus of arrogance; the analyst's role is that of interpreter and/or container of the wound or early trauma. But what might the analyst's own arrogance contribute to the process? Zimmer's (2013) "Arrogance and Surprise in Psychoanalytic Process," a recent addition to the literature, reads Bion's work in the light of our present understanding of two-person psychology and enactment. I will comment on several innovative ideas of Zimmer's that have helped me think through my own clinical experience with arrogance, before moving into a presentation of material from my practice.

Zimmer (2013) adds to Bion's triad the fourth element of surprise, in the form of something new and not yet understood by either member of the pair in an analytic treatment. At moments when surprise and the unknown emerge,

> Each member of the analytic pair retreats into a state of arrogant self-satisfaction, ensconcing him- or herself in an internal relation with what is known, excluding and condescending to the other member of the pair, as a way of retreating from the anxiety and frustration of being in contact with the other, and from the unknown contents that threaten to erupt within that contact; and the familiar Bionian triad of *arrogance, stupidity* and *curiosity* (Bion, 1958) comes to the fore.
>
> (p. 393, italics in the original)

Thus for Zimmer, both patient and analyst engaged in a psychoanalytic process are subject to states of arrogance, which Zimmer defines somewhat differently from Bion. In Zimmer's view, what Bion focuses on is better termed hubris, over-confidence leading a person past the boundaries of human limitation into potentially fatal error. Contemptuous arrogance, encountered clinically, is a broader concept having to do with aggression and contempt turned against the other, as "[A] presumption of authority or superior knowledge on the part of one member of the dyad is accompanied by a projection of ignorance and lack of understanding onto the other, often with aggressive attacks on the other's actual capacities for thought" (p. 407). Since the analytic situation requires the pair both to think together and to think independently, "The contemptuous attribution to the other of ignorance, stupidity, or lack of understanding readily engenders a relation of mutual contempt, though this may be unconscious in one partner or both" (p. 407).

When the members of the pair retreat from the new and unknown, signaled by surprise at the material coming to the surface, they do so in asymmetrical ways. The analyst may retreat to familiar analytic theory or technique, or the model she currently holds of the patient. The patient retreats to "a sense of him- or herself as the ultimate expert on his or her (henceforward his) own experience of his inner world, his own theoretical model of that inner world, and to unspoken experiences of the analyst's shortcomings as analyst" (p. 394). The capacity to embrace surprise in a spirit of shared curiosity may thus be lacking at any moment in the patient, the analyst, or both, but tolerating material not yet understood is fundamental to the forward movement of the process.

Zimmer further suggests that surprise may come from many sources: "The impact of insights gained from the analysis, together with pressures from the external world or shifts in the transference" (p. 394) may bring surprises for the analyst, while the patient in turn may be surprised by shifts in the analyst's reactions or behavior as the analyst's own thinking about the patient evolves. Moreover, each patient actively struggles

> . . . to meet the day-to-day challenges of his life and as he does this, he is simultaneously constrained and guided by the remnants of his past and actively experimenting with jettisoning some of those remnants in the service of survival or expansion in the present and the future.
>
> (pp. 409–410)

This constant adaptation to changing external circumstances and demands, as I understand it, implies not only the usual practical challenges with which every analytic pair must deal, but also a challenge to the process itself: Will the unexpected be met with shared curiosity, or arrogant contempt?

My perspective and clinical experience

My own definition for arrogance will follow Zimmer's lead as I discuss vignettes from two analytic patients. Each is a composite of more than one case and many details have been altered to protect confidentiality. I am thinking of "surprise" in the broadest sense of something as yet unknown, and of arrogance as a hesitation or failure of one or both parties to welcome that newness when it emerges in the work. Moreover, in these discussions I also add another dimension to arrogance as I have encountered it in my patients: that of aloneness.

In my work with deeply traumatized, although still fairly well-functioning adults, I have found that contemptuous arrogance, both conscious and unconscious, extends out from a core of profound aloneness. Perhaps this is another way to conceptualize Bion's (1958) theory of arrogance resulting from the disastrous denial of projective identification to the infant. A child left alone with disturbing affect, given no help to process it, develops a core experience of aloneness. One adaptation to this frightening situation can be precocious self-sufficiency, a conviction that "I don't need you anyway" when dealing with emotionally distant, highly critical, or unattuned caregivers, and the combination of self-reproach and unconscious grandiosity (Cooper, 2010) seen in adult patients. In the countertransference, the analyst too can feel alone, impotent, and at times arrogantly certain that she has answers without first asking needed questions.

Clinical vignette I

Linda, a woman in her mid-forties from an immigrant family background, came to treatment with a significant trauma history. Growing up with a short-tempered father and a chronically depressed mother had left Linda with a constricted range of emotions, notably bottled-up anger she could not express for fear of exploding into murderous rage. There was domestic violence in her home, and she remembers covering her head with a pillow as a child so as not to hear the fights going on between her parents. Prior psychotherapy had allowed her to move forward somewhat in love and work but there were still many things she wanted to achieve, including a better job and a stable romantic relationship. Linda suffered from chronic depression and anxiety, as well as low self-esteem. She entered analysis with me feeling hope, gratitude, and a positive maternal transference.

As our work went forward, I wondered when she might start feeling more of the negative emotions she denied herself – envy, anger, jealousy – but my attempts at any interpretation in that direction were met with what Zimmer (2013) refers to as "pseudocuriosity" (p. 401). Linda would acknowledge the possibility of such feelings then quickly change the subject to something else. Sensing too much fragility and Linda's profound need for a consistently good new object, I backed off and decided to wait. Eventually, I became aware that I, too, felt safer this way. I found myself sometimes ruminating on what felt to me like underlying arrogance on Linda's part when she made late payments or otherwise stretched the analytic frame, always with an excuse and an apology.

I also sometimes became sleepy in Linda's sessions and wondered why. I realized that I was holding all the anger for both of us, in effect sitting alone with negative affect, and feeling sleepy was a way to avoid confrontation. I started wondering privately, when I became sleepy, where the missing anger was, and sometimes was able to identify and name it in the session. This way, I did wake up, but we didn't get much further, for Linda's fear of rupture prevented her from joining me in a truly curious inquiry. She had been through a lot in her life, and wanted peace with her analyst. Threats to that peace and stable holding felt like potential world war, not just a friction that could be repaired and even leave the relationship stronger after being worked through. Such a positive resolution lay entirely outside what Linda and her family had ever experienced, and curiosity felt like a foolish luxury that just might set off a lethal land mine.

Linda and I sometimes touched on her immigrant family background and her feelings towards me as a native-born citizen. I wondered to myself about her lack of curiosity towards other aspects of my personal history that are public knowledge and of which I knew she was aware – for instance the fact that I am a bilingual Spanish speaker – but any inquiry by me in that direction was again deflected. Linda was afraid to overstep and offend, and terrified of her powerful underlying feelings of envy and painful loss. She frequently arrived late to session, and acknowledged that by coming late, she avoided getting too close or going too deep. It was just safer that way.

Leary (2007), in a discussion of two papers on difference and sameness in psychoanalysis, remarks that both arrogance and humility are required in the art of clinical psychoanalysis. Referencing comments made by Ambassador Lakhdar Brahimi, UN special envoy to Iraq and Afghanistan in the early 2000s, Leary applies his view of the relational nature of his work as a mediator to the analyst's efforts to create a process with her patient: "Mediation, he suggested, is to be understood as the willingness to accompany people who are in conflict" (cited in Leary, 2007, p. 470). One needs arrogance in order to intervene in problems seen as insoluble, and humility in order to be willing to risk failure, and the analyst, to be effective, must "stake a claim at the border" (p. 473) of the two.

The analyst, confronted with a patient different from her, where issues of race, class, and culture may come into play, struggles to find a place on that border from which such differences may be engaged in the service of the patient's development and growth. She may offer an opening for engagement on the field of difference between the pair, but must also consider the patient's individual need for sameness, in the form of positive transference, love, and containment. On that border between arrogance and humility, akin to Bion's (1958) description of the analyst's "capacity for containing the discarded, split-off aspects of other personalities while retaining a balanced outlook" (p. 145) in addition to envy and hatred, the analyst may find aloneness in the transference and countertransference.

Back to clinical vignette I

Over time Linda did get better in many respects. I continued to contain her more primitive, preverbal affects and felt alone with them, even when I articulated them in session, for Linda never fully joined me in exploring their roots. I understood my aloneness in the countertransference, and my reluctance to push Linda further, as an indication of how potentially dangerous her anger was to both of us. Looking back on this through the prism of arrogance, I also believe that Linda unconsciously imparted to me the stupidity and presumption of a person who, never having experienced the trauma she and her family had endured, would never really understand her, and would be as incapable as her parents were to help her manage the damaging effects of violence. She retreated back into the known (Zimmer, 2013), for to venture out into the unknown with me, a flawed and inexperienced guide, would make her too vulnerable. I retreated back into my own working theory of her need for peace with me, and did not challenge her assumption.

Linda began to talk about making some changes in her life, including buying a new car. The one she used to get around the city was rather old and not reliable, especially in bad weather. It was also at times the reason she was late to session. She debated spending the money a new or relatively new car would cost, and taking on the loan she would need to finance it. Linda recognized that she would feel a lot more confident with a recent model that had more safety features. Her thinking about this went back and forth. I listened and we discussed the underlying question of whether or not she deserved such security in her life, a familiar theme for us. Linda's car, meanwhile, developed more problems, and I sometimes worried about her driving home at night from her job. I wondered to myself how much danger and risk both she and I could tolerate, and how and when I might intervene.

One day, Linda began her session by talking about all the repairs she was planning to have done on the old car. They were going to add up to quite a bit of money, but she had figured out how to pay for it. There was a mechanic in her neighborhood that could do the work. She had an appointment to take the car in the following week. I was surprised, taken aback, and somewhat alarmed by this turn of events. "You've been talking about replacing the car," I said, "not fixing it. I wonder why you're talking about repairing it now all of a sudden." "I guess I was saying that," Linda replied, and then she explained to me that in her family's culture, you used things until they fell apart; not to do so was wastefully arrogant and selfish. She wanted to avoid being accused of such things by actual family members, and by their internalized harsh voices populating her inner world. Her idea of buying a new car had just raised too many conflicts. Part of her wanted to go with the idea, but another part of her had shut it down.

I thought to myself about metaphors of breakdown, of the fixable and the hopelessly damaged, and realized how much more there was to this material than the rather consumeristic question of whether or not Linda deserved good things in life. Was I the mechanic who could tinker and get the old car going again, saving it from abandonment? Was I a car dealer who might sell her an expensive new car she wanted but couldn't really afford, getting her into even more trouble? Was I both at different moments? Many new questions arose, opening what ultimately grew into a new and deeper phase in the work.

Clinical vignette 2

Alan, a white man in his mid-thirties, entered analysis at a crossroads in his life. He had grown up with a learning disability in a small town where competent help for his needs was lacking. His fundamentalist Christian parents looked to God and prayer as the answer to problems; his father was harshly critical, and clearly favored Alan's very bright older sister. Despite so many challenges, Alan had managed with great effort to do well enough in school to leave home, support himself with blue-collar work, and graduate from college in his late twenties. Since then, he had been underemployed in a series of dead-end office jobs. He wanted to advance but felt paralyzed and unable to take steps towards enrolling in a graduate program or looking for a better position. Alan engaged in merciless self-criticism whenever he did experience success; nothing he did ever seemed good enough to matter much.

Alan's fragile narcissism made it difficult for me to interpret without being attacked with arrogant contempt as clueless. "You don't get it," he would say angrily when I invited him to explore the reasons why he was so stuck. "Just imagine what it's like to have people think you're stupid. Can you imagine that? And you're saying it's my fault." Alan's profound social isolation and mistrust of well-meaning but incompetent professionals often left me feeling like just one more useless helper. I felt as stupid as he had been made to feel as a child.

Our work was slow and progress was incremental. Alan railed against slights both real and imagined. I struggled to find a way to join him; for each step forward towards a true therapeutic alliance, it felt to me like there were several going back. While I was never consciously afraid for my own safety, and he always respected physical boundaries, Alan's abusive language towards others, towards himself, and occasionally towards me was deeply unsettling. I sought out consultation on several occasions when Alan's pain was too much for me to bear alone.

Alan always felt like he was about to fall off a cliff, and I was right there with him on the edge. He wanted me to help him, and was clearly committed to our work, but if my efforts triggered bad memories of ridicule and bullying, he quickly pushed me away. A lack of understanding and empathy for his disability from any responsible adult in his young life had left him feeling profound shame and self-loathing. His identification with the aggressor kept him locked up in an internal prison, as well as the external jail of work that was stultifying and beneath his capacity. He longed for escape but feared that worse would befall him in freedom.

Over time we were able to name the cumulative trauma (Khan, 1963) of his childhood experience both in school and at home. Understanding himself as a traumatized child resonated to Alan and lessened some of his burden, but he still could not trust anyone, including me. He often reminded me of this. The fact that he said it with anger, not coldness, kept me from feeling entirely disconnected from him. I admired Alan greatly for all he had done in life despite heavy odds, but he could not take in my admiration and found it suspicious, remarking that I was paid to say such things. At times I wondered how to reach him, and whether his inability to join me in mutual, open-ended inquiry meant that our work would be necessarily limited. Alan had me locked up in a professional prison that mirrored his own.

Since his elementary school years, Alan had developed a hard shell of anger and aloofness, and had consciously made up his mind not to trust anyone or let them get too close. He was convinced that no one who really knew him could accept and love him as he was, rather than as he appeared to be. He looked "normal" but felt like a "freak." Along the way as an adult, Alan had gotten more competent professional help, and a diagnosis that aided him with the demands of college. He accepted these accommodations with ambivalence; they made his life easier, but his crushingly harsh superego sat in judgement and saw them as a crutch and a weakness. His disability had lessened but would never entirely disappear. This was the sad reality he had as yet been unable to grieve and mourn, for to Alan it meant that he was defective, and too broken to be lovable to anyone.

Alan's profound shame had roots in the repeated experience of incompetency and inefficacy. A vicious circle is created by such experience, for "the shame reaction itself heightens inefficacy and augments the original shame response because of the cognitive impairment, uncoordinated motor activity, and autonomic disruption which are characteristic of the shame experience" (Broucek, 1982, p. 370).

Alan experienced this cycle over and over again as he tried to master learning tasks beyond his capacity. A harsh father and passive mother meant that there was no respite or comfort at home. Their scorn became Alan's own internal voice, mocking and cruel, always comparing himself to someone else like his favored older sister. The absence of a loving father or other paternal figure was particularly devastating to Alan. Herzog (2004) observes that the deformed narcissism of children exhibiting contemptuous arrogance "reveals the absence of an effective paternal authority sanctioned by the mother" (p. 893). Such a child is left alone to deal with their aggression, and if there is no other appropriate intervention, the result is "the development of a perverse character structure in which the self is taken as object, and in which control of, rather than relating to, is the principal mode of interaction with others" (pp. 893–894). Alan's fear of ridicule and rejection led him to seek out others he could control. However, once they were within his control, he held them in the same contempt he felt towards himself, never allowing intimacy or tender feelings to emerge.

As Wurmser (2015) explains regarding his patient, Sonya,

> Others are being treated with the same scorn and are punished with the same pitiless harshness, as the "inner judge" deals with everything she does and feels . . . Simultaneously with this turning of the archaic superego's aggression against the outside world, we encounter the narcissistic attitude of arrogance and entitlement.
>
> (p. 1626)

Alan was terribly lonely, but felt safer within his protective shell. Our work proceeded steadily as I respected his need for a safe distance from me, along with providing a consistent frame that could contain his aggression. Again I cite Wurmser (2015): "In many cases, much of psychoanalytic work may consist in listening to the sense of slights that seem to confirm the feeling of one's own unworth" (p. 1627). In the process of this repetition of wrongs, Alan began to allow himself a glimmer of trust. Nonetheless, he held tight to his view of his own experience as beyond anything I could ever understand. At times I agreed with him, yet I persisted in chipping away at his shell. Working on the border of arrogance and humility with Alan sometimes left me frustrated and often feeling alone, when the quantity of humility needed seemed like more than my own narcissism could handle.

Back to clinical vignette 2

At one point several years into treatment, as Alan repeated the familiar "You don't have any idea what it's like to have a disability no one can see," I found myself saying, "Well, actually I have experienced something like that." I told Alan about a congenital bone defect in my left arm, discovered in childhood, which had kept me from participating in sports and physical education at school. More than once, my peers had accused me of making it up to get out of gym class or a softball game, not believing that anything but visible bodily limitations actually existed. Until I mentioned this to Alan, I had never thought of my experience as akin to his and I was surprised at my own spontaneous self-disclosure. Alan, too, reacted with surprise, keeping himself at a safe distance, but listening without contempt and with some measure of understanding. Although this moment did not magically change the course of our work, I do believe it created a reference for the greater trust and curiosity that later developed in the treatment.

Discussion

When analysts think about arrogance in their patients, people like Linda and Alan might not be what first come to mind. Someone more like the public figures of our current political landscape to which I referred earlier, someone with power and the will to stay powerful, might fit a more typical image of an arrogant patient. Linda and Alan suffer from arrogance of another kind, stemming from trauma, shame, and loss. I have shown in these vignettes two moments when the transference-countertransference enactment caused me to engage that arrogance in a way that surprised both me and my patients, breaking through a precocious self-sufficiency covering over profound aloneness.

Linda could not manage her own anger, to which she did not feel entitled. The overwhelming experience of violence in her home left her feeling that closeness equated danger. While she readily joined me in pseudo-curious inquiry, her positive transference to me as a good mother was too valuable to risk losing. Only when I actually acted like a good mother, protecting her child from doing something potentially risky, did I realize how Linda's conflict over how well she could be fixed, and whether or not her new self would still be loved, was playing out in the process. She imagined I would rather have her keep her old car as her family did, unconsciously expecting me to judge her as arrogant for wanting something shiny, safe, and new. My response challenged that expectation and revealed the underlying terror of being rejected and left alone if she strayed too far from the fold.

Alan's anger had saved him from despair and depression, and enabled him to move forward on a somewhat normal developmental track through his youth. Now at the cusp of middle age, he became stuck in his arrogant, protective shell. He desperately wanted to connect and end his isolation, but could not really mentalize others, only use them. I see my unplanned self-disclosure as breaking out of the prison where Alan's contempt had placed me, and as an invitation to him to break out with me. My efforts at empathy having only gone so far before they were shot down as false and untrustworthy, I revealed something about myself that Alan could not dismiss as untrue. If in the transference I had been the father and mother who denied his pain and could never understand, my countertransference response was to feel as misunderstood as Alan, and to protest against my own persecution. Perhaps I was modeling for Alan another way to present the experience of childhood difference and isolation.

Conclusion

I would like to end by returning to Leary's (2007) description of analysts staking a claim on the border of arrogance and humility in their work. She follows that powerful image with the statement that "The psychoanalytic profession is only just beginning to come to terms with its organizational history and organizational present" (p. 473). In his account of the psychologists' lawsuit against the American Psychoanalytic Association that was settled during his presidency of that group, Richard Simons (2003) is unsparing in his appraisal of the conflict: "The American was guilty of . . . something that is very difficult to prove in a court of law. It is called arrogance, or swollen pride, if one wants to recall one of the Seven Deadly Sins. We were so proud in thinking that we were the best, and in the process we forgot Voltaire's warning: 'The perfect is the enemy of the good'. . . I think many of us . . . had simply lost touch with our organizational humility, just as in some ways we may also have lost touch with our clinical humility and our personal humility. I think at least some of us may have forgotten what we analysts have in common with other human beings" (p. 269).

When confronted with a patient we perceive as arrogant, as analysts I believe we would do well to remember where we came from. Our legacy of cultural and professional arrogance, of foreclosing curious inquiry and discussion in the name of smug certainty, is our recent history. When considering our patient's arrogance we might first look in the mirror, and wonder about our own.

Chapter 8

Arrogance in countertransference

Dhwani Shah

The arrogant psychoanalyst is a pervasive stereotype in our culture. "Why are psychoanalysts so damn arrogant?" This question has haunted me in countless ways – at conferences, dinner parties, and in casual conversations – even by strangers upon discovering what I do for a living. In an absurd, memorable, moment ten years ago, a woman dressed in a banana costume, dancing and singing on Park Avenue in New York, began chanting: "Freud is an arrogant fraud" when she discovered I was in psychoanalytic training. It feels as though the general census within and outside of the psychoanalytic community is that we are an arrogant bunch. While it can be reassuring to brush these comments off as envious and aggressive projections, there is of course a long tradition of arrogance in psychoanalysis that is a painful reality. The "origin story" of psychoanalytic societies began with arrogance – Freud's ruthless methods of alienating colleagues who had contrasting perspectives; most notably his notorious "secret committee," which demanded absolute professional and personal submission with secret rituals and loyalty rings, is the most striking example (Grosskurth, 1991). The tradition of arrogance continued in America with the ascent of psychoanalysis as the dominant model of understanding human psychology beginning in the 1930s, reaching its zenith in the 1950s-1960s. In the highly influential and widely published *Elementary Textbook of Psychoanalysis*, Brenner (1955) confidently wrote: "At present, interest in psychoanalysis is expanding. . . . it seems likely that the current interest in psychoanalysis on the part of psychiatrists and associated workers in the field of mental health will continue to grow" (p. 243). This obviously did not come to pass.

The barring of nonmedical specialties from psychoanalytic institutes and training (which Freud was against) and the infiltration of psychoanalysts to prestigious posts in medical education cemented psychoanalysis as an elitist occupation. This culminated in an overt use of psychoanalytic theorizing to validate heteronormative cultural values including homophobia and sexism (Dean & Lane, 2001; Wright, 1992). It also led to psychological reductionism and ignoring complex genetic and organic factors most notably in autistic and psychotic disorders (Shorter, 1997). The ascent of psychoanalysis in America also led to widespread arrogance within training institutes, promoting submission to orthodoxy and a squelching of curiosity and creativity (Kernberg & Michels, 2016). Other notorious examples of arrogance include numerous boundary violations of patients (Celenza & Gabbard, 2003) and a greedy pandering to the rich and elite (Shorter, 1997). The unfortunate outcome of this widespread institutional arrogance is an enduring stain on the image of the psychoanalyst, who is usually depicted in the stereotype of a snobbish, fussy, and privileged white male who makes his living barely engaging with his equally wealthy clients who could care less. This is in striking contrast to the psychoanalysis that is radical in its understanding of human relationships and the unconscious as well as traditions within psychoanalysis that promoted social activism and freedom of thought and expression. As Aron and Starr (2013) state bluntly in their book, *A Psychotherapy for the People: Toward a Progressive Psychoanalysis*:

> In the 1950s, at the height of its success in America, psychoanalysis made a choice. The choice was to define itself narrowly in order to maximize its status and prestige. A sharp divide was erected between analysis and psychotherapy, thinking it would keep the treatment pure . . . and that it would justify high fees and the high cost of training. It seemed like a good thing to make psychoanalysis an elite medical sub specialty. It became a high cost, high class, elitist, exclusive practice for an exclusive clientele.
>
> (p. 28)

It must be said, however, that everything written above has been documented and discussed at length by scholars within and outside of the psychoanalytic tradition. But to focus on this obvious overt arrogance in our profession feels too convenient and smug – the joy of sneering at others for their arrogance at a distance is seductively pleasurable. What about our own arrogance and how it affects our practice on a daily basis? I have a colleague who every year after our annual psychoanalytic meeting turns to me and remarks, "What a bunch of arrogant narcissists!" I always laugh and unwittingly encourage his comments but secretly feel anxiety about my own cringe-worthy moments of arrogance with my patients and wonder how much we gleefully project our own arrogant fantasies into "these narcissists." The realization of my own arrogance was a painful experience, which was not easy to tolerate. Mostly it was pointed out to me by my patients who, within their rights to speak freely, did so in a manner that exposed me to my blind spots of arrogance that were disconcerting and always unknown to me in the moment. As psychoanalysts, we cannot ignore our context or our history of internalized elitism and arrogance within ourselves. By doing so, we risk losing our ability to access vulnerability in our patients and become overly identified with mastery and success. In its identification with the wealthy and elite, psychoanalysis dissociated its vulnerability by projecting it into other "lesser forms" of psychotherapy and onto "difficult" patients, leaving psychoanalysts in the role of identifying with the heroic and masterful (Aron & Starr, 2013).

In this chapter, I would like to focus on our arrogance in the clinical setting and its effects on our clinical work with patients. Considering Bion's theory of psychotic and nonpsychotic parts of a personality in all human beings, extended by Akhtar in his discussion of prejudiced and unprejudiced parts of the personality, I believe that, like psychosis and prejudice, we all have arrogant parts of our personality that we are vulnerable to that can emerge in various ways often implicitly (Akhtar, 2007). This is a way of avoiding the temptation of declaring some individuals arrogant (usually referred to as "the narcissists") and others – conveniently including oneself – as free of arrogance. This allows a more nuanced and personal vantage point in which to explore the ways in which arrogance plays a role in the clinical encounter.

For heuristic purposes, the analyst could separate out transient arrogance that emerges in the analytic space at various times, and a more fixated chronic arrogance that can be pervasive, which informs his approach to his work, often in a manner unknown to the analyst. Faced with the terror of the unknown, the analyst and patient can each retreat into a state of arrogance, the analyst enclosing himself in an internal cocoon with what is known, excluding and condescending of the patient (Zimmer, 2013). The analyst is "reduced" to arrogant ways of being to ward off the bewildering and frightening state of affairs that is erupting in the room between himself and his patient.

Defining arrogance

Arrogance results from a narrow-mindedness in feeling and perception (Akhtar, 2009a). Two aspects of arrogance that are present are a combination of superiority and a feeling of certainty, which leads one to feel a heightened sense of narcissistic satisfaction and omnipotence. There is an exciting, seductive, at times sexual experience of knowing and being self-satisfied: "It all makes perfect sense after all." There is a curious lack of anxiety or shame and a feeling of clarity, of being comfortable in being the knower. One's tone of speech transforms to a more declarative and omniscient quality.

Self-righteousness is often present. Others observing the arrogant behavior often perceive smugness, stubbornness, and rigidity. Arrogance is a nonreflective self-state of mind. It is only after it is pointed out or reflected upon later that one realizes one has in fact been arrogant. It is perceived first by the person who is the recipient of the arrogance. The other is perceived and feels he is inferior and is demeaned. This leads to the other feeling oppressed and forced to either agree with the arrogant person or rebel against him. In the "arrogant moment" the arrogant person is not aware of this, specifically the aggressive and demeaning aspects if his behavior, which reflects a kind of stupidity. "I'm not being arrogant, I'm just stating the truth – why are you getting angry?" Another quality of stupidity in the experience of arrogance is how complexity and depth of human experience are reduced to linear "facts" and rigid concepts, which will be discussed further below.

Bion's celebrated and enigmatic paper, "On Arrogance" (1958), describes a constellation of widely dispersed, seemingly unrelated references to arrogance, stupidity, and curiosity, in a seemingly neurotic patient who has psychotic mechanisms of thought. There is transference to the analyst as arrogant, stupid, curious, or suicidal, and the patient also identifies with these qualities, so at any moment either the patient or the analyst can inhabit these attributes via projective identification. Bion attributes this syndrome to a "psychic disaster" involving the patient's relation with an early object who is not capable of the infant's need for emotional containment and communication via projective identification. This results in a disruption in the patient's ability to develop a creative and meaningful link in relationships through emotional communications. In the analytic situation, this creates a retreat on the part of the analyst and patient – for the analyst, the retreat is often to his relationship with analytic theory and his current way of thinking about the patient. This is truly a "disaster" because it disrupts the analyst's ability to have access to and be with the patient's most primitive and vital forms of communication (Zimmer, 2013).

The analyst's arrogance

The analyst's ability to live with and contain the patient's unbearable psychic suffering via projective identification in the countertransference is vital to create a safe "home for the mind," for the patient can then contain and transform his unspeakable pain (Ogden, 2008). Arrogance cocreated in the analytic field blocks this vital process of unconscious communication. Below I will describe the four ways in which the analyst's arrogance can have this effect, including (i) the analyst's disruption in his ability to experience failure and the depressive position, (ii) a collapse of depth, surprise, and a sense of awe, (iii) a disruption in curiosity, and (iv) the hidden pleasure of seduction.

Arrogance, failure, and the depressive position

Failure haunts the practice of psychoanalysis. The well-worn analytic clichés of our profession, being "impossible," speak to how difficult it is to constantly be in a position of not knowing and grasping at the unconscious which of course is never fully knowable. The terrifying uncertainty and intimacy of the clinical encounter can easily lead to arrogance as a way of warding off the possibility of failure and not knowing. The analyst's capacity to contain doubt and the unknown, our "negative capability" (Keats, 1899) to tolerate the pain and confusion of not knowing is severely tested by our failures. Negative capability can be defined as the ability to tolerate the pain and confusion of the unknown rather than imposing certainties upon an ambiguous or emotionally unbearable situation. Our patients invest an incalculable amount of time, effort, and expense in us and feeling the effects of our failures is truly unbearable. It must be someone else's fault! As Goldberg (2012) notes about his failure to help a patient:

> Somebody else was to blame for this sad state of affairs, and that somebody was probably the patient. Or anyone but me. I later learned that almost everyone who

fails as a therapist has a storehouse of excuses that can be called up, examined for usefulness, freely discarded, and just as freely embraced. Failure has no friends.

(p. 29)

The temptation to resort to some form of arrogance in these situations is incredibly high. Importantly, it is not just the failure of our individual cases that we feel the need to protect ourselves from, but often in the ebb and flow of a daily session where our patients are letting us know how we are failing them in direct and indirect ways all the time. Probably the most common way of warding off these unbearable communications from the patient is to lapse into blaming the patient in subtle (and sometimes not so subtle) ways. Casement's (2002) wonderfully honest book, *Learning from Our Mistakes*, highlights this:

> Psychoanalytic practitioners sometimes slip into a position of arrogance, that of thinking they know best. Thus, when something goes wrong in an analysis, it is often the patient who is held accountable for this, the analyst assuming it to be an expression of the patient's pathology rather than perhaps (or at least partly) due to some fault of the analysis. It is unfortunate that analysts can always defend themselves by claiming special knowledge of the ways of the unconscious. But analysts can become blind to their own mistakes. And even more importantly they can fail to recognize that it is sometimes the style of their clinical work itself that may have become a problem for the patient.
>
> (p. xv)

Because of our training and our supposed "understanding of the unconscious," we can easily lapse into the arrogant trap of using our explanations as a cover for our anger and confusion in not knowing. In fact, our training in making connections often can be used in the service of expressing our arrogance:

> Let's face it: analysts and therapists become experts in making connections. We can connect almost anything with anything! And we can always use theory in support of this, however wild these connections might be. Then, when things don't fit exactly, we can assume the patients are employing whatever forms of defensive thinking best lend themselves to our own way of seeing things . . . in fact, we can use theory in almost any way we wish. And yet there are times we are bound to be wrong. But if our style of working is to be too sure, it can become a real problem for the patient when the analyst is getting it wrong.
>
> (ibid., p. 4)

This can lead to various forms of arrogance that we are all familiar with, including lecturing the patient, offering unempathic reassurances, interpreting the patient's actions we do not like as resistance or aggression, or offering practical suggestions and strategies that are of limited use. Experientially, we often feel this in ourselves in moments when we are being clever and overeager to provide explanations or help. Britton and Steiner (1994) refer to this phenomenon as an overvalued idea on the part of the analyst:

> It is recognized that an observation which may at the time be convincing to the analyst, and even perhaps to the patient, is often inaccurate and sometimes mistaken. Among such errors some are determined by the defensive needs of the analyst, and we refer to this type of false insight as an overvalued idea. An awareness of the possibility that an insight may be an overvalued idea helps to alert the analyst to the need to sustain doubt and to examine subsequent clinical material to evaluate his understanding. At the same time it is clearly important that the analyst interprets with conviction, so that his capacity to entertain doubt must exist alongside a willingness to commit himself to a point of view which seems right at the time, and yet be willing to relinquish this view if subsequent evidence demands it. The experience of a moment of insight or discovery may give a sense of excitement and achievement to the analyst, but it is our experience that once uttered the interpretation often loses some of its conviction and that the importance of doubt, guilt and other feelings associated with the depressive position are an inevitable part of the experience.
>
> (p. 1070)

Steiner (2011), describes this phenomenon as "narcissistic helpfulness". (p. 119) Rapid interpretations given with a certainty and a quickening pace can be a clue that this type of "helpfulness" is operating in the analytic space. The aim of the intervention by the analyst unconsciously is not to deepen the analytic process, but to give the analyst and patient relief from the unbearable experience that is occurring between them, often involving a state of complete helplessness and vulnerability. As Steiner notes:

> My over-activity concealed an inner feeling of helplessness. I could see that I was colluding with the patient's phantasm of omnipotent repair and that I too had been trying to prevent a disaster and restore the patient to reason. It then became possible for me to admit to myself that I could not protect the patient from his acting out, and my feeling of helplessness gave way to sadness . . . once I accepted my helplessness, I seemed to be able to be more thoughtful.
>
> (p. 126)

Steiner goes on to say that narcissistic helpfulness is rarely successful because it ignores the actual needs of the object. It also involves a concrete type of thinking in which the object has to be materially restored, and as a result it betrays omnipotent fantasy rather than genuine reparation. Casement (2002) offers a useful and pragmatic method of combating this tendency by cultivating our ability to perform "trial identifications" with our patients, considering from the patient's point of view either what we have said or what we are thinking of saying. The analyst's comfort in working also means that he thinks about the unintended effects that his participation is having on the patient. This combats the tendency towards facile cleverness and unempathic interpretations based more on our inability to tolerate our patient's unconscious communications.

However, overly identifying with the patient can lead to arrogance as well. If the analyst feels too identified with or guilty towards the patient's lived experience, others can become the target of blame and arrogance as well. I am always struck in clinical case discussions and also in my own countertransference with patients by how tempting it is to blame the patients' pathology on their parents or significant others and transform these living human beings into caricatures of bad objects. In one case conference I attended, the discussant – a psychoanalyst – spoke about how a patient described her parents leaving the bedroom door unlocked when she was a child and how she had felt she had hidden access to their lovemaking because of this. A member in the audience gasped loudly and shouted, "What the hell were they thinking! They are not truly parents!" Where did this outrage come from? This is not to underestimate the trauma and unspeakable pain that is disclosed to us by our patients about their past. I am speaking more to the manner in which we can arrogantly transform people into almost cartoon-like caricatures for our own arrogant purposes – which is to maintain a feeling of moral superiority, leading us to "stupidity."

The truth of the matter is that our work as psychoanalysts is by default incomplete, unsettling, and uncertain. Living in this "depressive position" and reflecting on ways in which we move towards omnipotence is essential to help our patients attain this as well. Even after a productive and meaningful analysis, we will contend with easier and more difficult parts of ourselves, but our lives will continue to be out of joint in certain ways. The analyst holds this unsettling narrative in the service of helping the patient to better contain this incompleteness (Cooper, 2016). This capacity to accept incompleteness allows us to be more available to our patients' interiority and their struggles with living in "ordinary misery." Arrogance can block our patient's ability to access this within us. This also applies to our internalized representations of our teachers and theories – arrogant clinging to a particular model or theory without an understanding of its incompleteness maintains an omnipotent and walled-off analytic stance.

This ability to accept the depressive position and live in incompleteness and to tolerate failure and uncertainty should not be confused with self-deprecation or self-loathing. When we choose not to blame the patient or the people in the patient's life, the "bad" one often turns out to be us. The temptation to give in to self-loathing and vicious self-attacks seems to be a professional hazard for almost all of us at some point. As we see in our patients, attacks on oneself often involve an unconscious grandiosity that is arrogant as well. As Cooper notes, self-criticism "rests between the silent acceptance of disappointment or shame on the one hand and on the other a clearly disproportionate level of grandiosity about our ability" (2011, p. 21).

Arrogant compliance and the collapse of depth and surprise

A deepening analysis is a jarring and confusing experience for both the analyst and patient. What we were told as "facts" about a person initially become infused with conflicting meanings and emotional truths. Michael Parsons (2000), reflecting on this process, writes:

> To genuinely enter into a patient's viewpoint can involve an unexpectedly profound shift of position. We know something matters. Then something happens which jolts us into seeing it afresh and throws into relief just how much it really does matter. We did realize it was important and we knew why, but from where we stand now, seeing how acute its significance truly is, our previous attitude cannot help seeming a bit bland and superficial.
>
> (p. 36)

This experience gives rise to the possibility of surprise and depth. Psychic depth can be viewed as the experience of what is known in the foreground (subject) surrounded by a less articulated and perceived background which is "there" but its meaning is unrealized at the moment, an affective resonance and fullness that would otherwise be flattened (Stern, 2015). Depth allows for emergent possibilities and the possibility of surprise, a crucial element in the psychoanalytic process. A cocreated analytic space of depth and emerging possibilities allows for experiences of awe, surrender, and vulnerability, crucial in the analytic process for the patient to be able to reclaim a sense of self and psychic experience (Ghent, 1990).

Because of its emphasis in domination and solipsism of knowledge, arrogance collapses depth into a flattened experiential world. In contrast to the patient feeling instinctively safe to surrender and have faith in his relational freedom with the analyst, he feels he must submit to whatever worldview the analyst considers is correct. Boredom, cocreated stupidity, and dry intellectualized interpretations can follow from this. The arrogant analyst has "figured it out" and has already understood what has unfolded – he just has to convince the patient what he is saying is correct. Bromberg (2011) notes the differences in the impact this has on the patient's mind:

> Each patient analyst couple must strike its own balance of safety and risk, but for any patient, confrontation with the analyst as a separate center of subjectivity will be most enlivening and safe if the analyst is not trying to figure things out on his own and then using his own truth about his patient as a means to a good therapeutic outcome. The more an analyst's communication is based on sharing his subjective experience because he wants it to be known, as opposed to wanting it to have a preconceived impact on his patient's mind, the more it will be felt by the patient to be "affectively honest."
>
> (p. 103)

As stated above, when an analyst takes on the position of the knower "figuring out things on his own," the other is reduced to either submitting or rebelling. For a vulnerable patient desperate for help, this is an impossible choice. Casement (2002) notes, "Patients get put in a situation where they do not have sufficient say concerning what is being assumed about them, and they may be at times exposed to interpretations that cannot effectively be challenged. They then have little choice but to leave that analyst or capitulate" (p. 13). An attitude of arrogance where the analyst's reality is correct can go unrecognized by the analyst but have profound effects on the patient. Interpretation outside the alive quality of the cocreated experience between patient and analyst often feels like indoctrination and produces compliance. In order to survive and protect their inner world from being invaded and colonized, patients develop a false compliant self that can go unrecognized. This leads to a deadening of the lived experience between the analyst and patient and a lack of depth in the material.

> What is happening between us what I think it is, nothing more, nothing less . . . depth, ambiguity, and mystery collapse – the analytic space becomes flat . . . there is a certainty about things that are perhaps left uncertain, because uncertainty allows possibility. The possibility of new meanings is shut down. Things are what they are, nothing more.
>
> (Stern, 2015, p. 8)

This type of false compliance in a two-dimensional space destroys the opportunity for playfulness. Giving out interpretations as unquestionable "facts" to the patient does not give him the opportunity for joining and play, "kicking it around whilst offering other angles that could also be considered" (Casement, 2002, p. 105). In order for an interpretation not to be indoctrination, the patient has to creatively make use of it, changing and transforming it in the process if needed.

Clinical vignette I

Molly, a fifty-seven-year-old magazine editor and a mother of boys aged eighteen and sixteen, began treatment with me after her analyst of two decades passed away. Despite a twenty-year treatment, Molly was significantly impaired in her ability to function due to severe anxiety and somatic symptoms including intermittent pains in her throat and neck with no clear medical cause. She spoke in a rapid and loud fashion, staring straight ahead with only intermittent eye contact, with a flurry of complex ideas and verbiage that often caused me to feel confused and worried that I could not understand her. I began to also feel ashamed that I could not keep up with her complex ideas and thoughts that seemed to relentlessly take up the entire session. Most of her associations involved angry struggles with her ex-husband and her two sons, both of whom had developmental delays and behavioral issues. Molly felt overwhelmed by facing her sons' needs without any help, which reflected her past as well. Molly was the fourth in a family of eight, born prematurely with a neurological disorder that affected her ability to walk. Growing up, Molly watched her brothers and sisters play together without her. Her mother, diagnosed with lupus, was often bedridden. When she was awake, she preferred the company of her eldest son, leaving Molly alone with her books.

I felt flooded in our sessions together without the ability to self-reflect and contain much of what she was saying. I found myself resorting to often repeating what she was saying back to her in an effort to enter her experience or make empathic comments, neither of which seemed to resonate with her. I also tried to help her make connections between her past experiences, struggling with her own disability and maternal neglect, with her current overwhelmed helplessness in assisting her sons with their needs and how possibly she was searching for help here with me in a similar way. None of my comments seemed to reach Molly. She would usually not pause after I spoke and made a few intellectualized remarks about possible connections between her past and the present, and then continue to talk about the details of her daily struggles with her two sons and ex-husband's unavailability. She also explicitly ignored any comments about our relationship and its emotional meaning for her. This went on for several months and I began to feel trapped in a flatness of relating to her – it seemed there were no moments of emergence, surprise, or depth in our relating with one another; it felt as though she was "just reporting" the events as she saw them. I found myself starting to become more and more "stupid" in my comments and not able to think or reflect clearly.

In one session, Molly began the discussion by talking about how a friend was supposed to take care of her two sons for her to have a night out. Right before her leaving, the friend called and cancelled. Molly was enraged and spent the session ranting about how she had no one in her life that could help her with anything, and that she felt others around her were either incompetent at helping or did not care. Unable to contain myself, I blurted out, "Which one am I to you? Incompetent or uncaring?" Molly looked visibly shaken by this comment. She paused for a moment and then replied, "It's always about you, isn't it – god damn you." I was taken aback by this comment – she had never spoken about her feelings towards me prior to this and certainly had not expressed anger towards me. Uncertain how to respond, I mumbled, "Thank you for the honesty. Please do whatever you feel you need to do with what I said to you." Over time, Molly began to open up more about her feeling that I was not connected to her inner world and felt I was arrogant in my tone of speech and method: "I feel like you are just saying things out of a book sometimes and want me to agree with you. I don't feel you're a real person in here, but you're all I have right now." Later in the analysis she was able to express her grief and anger over the sudden death of her analyst who she loved deeply and how seeing me brought up intense longings for him, and how it was painful to allow herself the vulnerability of receiving help.

Without realizing it, my comments and analytic stance towards Molly were arrogant. Flooded by my own reactions to Molly, I retreated emotionally from her into a defensive intellectualized "textbook" way of relating to her. This enactment reflected her early childhood experiences and narrowed our ability to emotionally relate to one another. Another consequence of this was a disruption in my curiosity and genuine interest in Molly.

Curiosity and arrogance

Bion (1958) describes a constellation of arrogance, stupidity, and curiosity as a "psychic disaster" that is linked to psychotic parts of the personality. At first glance, this is puzzling because curiosity – the drive towards obtaining knowledge and understanding – is essential to the psychoanalytic process for both the analyst and patient. Curiosity promotes and allows for the patient to internalize self-reflection, mentalization, and wonderment for his inner affective life. Why would Bion add this to a "disastrous" constellation including stupidity and arrogance? Curiosity considered carefully is a complex and multidetermined process that can have varying configurations and motivations. For heuristic purposes, one can separate two distinct types of curiosity that can be forms of arrogant curiosity: pseudo-curiosity and instinctual curiosity.

Pseudo-curiosity is rooted in the sense of a person not genuinely interested in understanding others – he is more interested in his own ideas being of value. Akhtar (2009a) notes,

> A peculiarly naive curiosity about others accompanies this dehumanization . . . however this curiosity does not express a genuine wish to understand others. Rather it reflects puzzlement about their motivations on the part of an individual who has little knowledge of his own intrapsychic life.
>
> (p. 26)

The pseudo-curious analyst wants to understand what he (or she) already believes to be true and needs validation of his own internal truth – curiosity is a method proving his own ideas as correct. Listening is perversely transformed to finding out his own thoughts inside another person's subjectivity. The other experiences this as oppressive and dehumanizing and the subjective alterity of the other is abolished. As one of my patients said to me, "You may think you are asking me a question, but what you are really doing is trying to prove to yourself that you have the right answer to the question you just asked."

Instinctual curiosity: In his discussion of the triad of arrogance, stupidity, and curiosity, Bion (1958) reinterprets the Oedipus myth as a quest to "lay bare the truth at any cost" rather than a focus on incestuous and patricidal wishes. This aggrandized search for the truth regardless of the consequences lays bare the instinctual aspects of curiosity that can predominate in an arrogant state of mind which is oblivious to the consequences of this overzealous curiosity (Zimmer, 2013). This type of instinctual curiosity can take the form of the analyst relentlessly searching without regards to a patient's boundaries or a private space in the mind away from the analyst's intrusion. As Poland (2013) writes in his wise and measured essay, "The Analyst's Approach and the Patient's Psychic Growth":

> There is an inevitable tension built in between those two forces: curiosity to satisfy oneself and respectful regard for the needs of the other. [He goes on to write] What is specifically psychoanalytic in clinical work arises from the force of the analyst's curiosity tamed in the desire to utilize that curiosity primarily in the service of the patient . . . the tension between the analyst's curiosity and wish to advance inquiry, on the one hand, and the analyst's staying sensitive to the patient, on the other hand, demands creativity on the analyst's part. This is a large part of what makes clinical work an art . . . it was from the marriage of curiosity with respect for the other that clinical psychoanalysis was born.
>
> (p. 834)

This taming of instinctual curiosity in the service of the patient with respect is lost in an arrogant state of mind that disregards the need for privacy from the analyst's penetrative searching.

Clinical vignette 2

I met Sarah, a twenty-four-year-old chemical engineer, for an initial psycho-therapy and medication consultation. She reported a history of panic symp-toms and longstanding inhibitions surrounding social relationships. She had several close friends but had difficulty initiating or sustaining relationships with romantic partners. Being an only child, Sarah felt she was very close to both her mother and father but felt her mother could be at times anxious and controlling. As a varsity lacrosse player in high school and later in college, Sarah felt a great deal of pride in her physical athleticism but also strug-gled with her body image as "muscular and too big" for a woman and often felt shame around viewing her body in pictures or being in locker rooms where others could see her not fully clothed. In our initial consultation, Sarah brought in a novel with her that piqued my interest, *The Brief Wondrous Life of Oscar Wao*, by Junot Diaz. I had recently read the book and found myself wondering if the book had meaning for her in regards to her intimate relation-ships with others. I felt a strange pressing need to ask her about it, for unclear reasons at the time. Towards the end of the session, I finally said, "I noticed what you are reading – does it bring up any feelings or thoughts?" She looked slightly uncomfortable and said "Why, is it important?" I replied that if the book brought up any feelings or thoughts, it could be a way of us understand-ing her inner world better. She half-heartedly seemed to agree with this and afterwards I felt the session went well. Later that night, Sarah called asking to speak with me. She wanted a referral for another therapist and for me to only prescribe her medications. "I think a woman therapist would be a better match for me – I don't feel comfortable speaking with a guy about these things."

It seemed clear that my unchecked curious inquiry frightened Sarah. Without being consciously aware of it in the moment, my interest in her was laden with instinctual wishes to know about private areas of her life without the restraint of respecting her privacy. My wishes to know about her private life also may have enacted a seducing other that was overstimulating and frightening to her.

The seductive power of arrogance

In contrast to the deadness that arrogance often imposes on others, there are clinical moments when arrogance can induce thrilling and seductive fantasies enacted by the analyst and patient. Arrogance can be an intoxicating and exciting experience – full of omnipotence and certainty, the analyst conveys a special kind of magical power that can evoke powerful fantasies. These can include sado-masochistic fantasies of erotic submission and rescue fantasies of being saved by a powerful other. The analyst's certainty and conviction combined with an often unconscious wish to assume a sexually exciting authority position can provoke these scenarios. The enactment between arrogant male analysts and female patients with hysteric character styles has been extensively written about elsewhere (McWilliams, 2011). That subtle forms of these types of seductive arrogance occur, however, on a more frequent basis in a variety of clinical situations is often overlooked. Enjoying the potency and thrill of being in a position of power is not just something that narcissistic men experience – we are all prone to these seductions.

Clinical vignette 3

Jenny, a forty-nine-year-old physical therapist of Haitian descent with a history of alcoholism and depression, began treatment after her youngest child graduated from high school. After her son's graduation, she began drinking heavily at night to cope with the emptiness of the house and her emotionally unavailable husband who was absorbed in his successful roofing business and hobbies. Jenny felt comfortable in the treatment right away and began to make improvements over the first several sessions. She had never been in psychotherapy before and felt "liberated" being able to speak freely to me. Growing up, she felt her mother was superficial and fragile and often felt the need to play the role of a caretaker for her. Jenny felt more of a connection with her domineering and powerful father who was often absent because of his own struggles with alcohol. I found myself feeling affectionate towards her and pleased with myself that she took to the process of therapy so quickly. After several months of psychotherapy, her drinking had significantly reduced and she was able to begin to make changes in her life that she felt proud of. A few weeks after Jenny began working again, she left a desperate message on my voicemail asking me to call her back. I happened to be free when she called and was able to call her back right away. She disclosed that she had a relapse of drinking alcohol and was frightened about falling into old patterns again "before I saw you." The conversation was brief but had a lasting impact on her. At our next session, Jenny felt "incredible" and said the fact that I was so responsive to her needs made her feel better than she had for years – "It was as if a veil was lifted off of me." As she was saying this to me, even though intellectually I knew that this moment had to do with her experience of me that was informed by her transference and early longings as a child, it felt incredibly validating and exciting to have had the power to have helped her this way. I found myself congratulating myself on how my relationship with her had such an impact on her. After this session her depression improved but she began to drink heavily at night again, leading to hangovers during the day. What I was not able to see at the time which later became clear was that her relapse occurred after she began working as a physical therapist again and she was deeply conflicted about her autonomy and power. Her fantasies of me being an omnipotent rescuer were enacted in ways I was not fully con- scious of until later in the treatment, when I began to realize the manner and way in which I spoke to her conveyed a firm but loving parent who wanted to take care of her and protect her; this way of relating to me helped her feel more safe and secure but also protected her from her wishes to be assertive and powerful which frightened her. Although my unspoken arrogant way of communicating with Jenny was helpful for our therapeutic alliance, it led her to be cautious about challenging what I said and speaking freely about anger and disappointment with me as well.

With this being said, we should be careful to not be "arrogant about arrogance" and dismiss it as something that needs to be completely avoided. In the ebb and flow of our clinical work, we are all vulnerable to an onslaught of frightening affects, fantasies, and defensive reactions to them. It can be frightening, uncer- tain, and confusing. We all succumb to psychic retreats (Steiner, 2011) to protect ourselves from this emotional storm of intimacy and I would include a position of arrogance as a method of coping in this way.

Concluding remarks

This chapter is an attempt to better understand the experience of arrogance by the analyst in our clinical work. We all have to contend with our internalized institu- tional arrogance and elitism based in our culture and history as psychoanalysts. The experience of arrogance was described as having aspects of both certainty and superiority, both of which are unseen by us but experienced by others. Arro- gance was discussed as a retreat from the terror of the unknown and unbearable. Four aspects of the effects of an analyst's arrogance were described including the disruption in our ability to experience incompleteness, failure, and the depressive position; a collapse of depth, surprise, and a sense of awe; a distortion of curiosity and the role of arrogance in seduction.

Before ending, we might consider some possibly healthy and developmental aspects of arrogance. These are described in the literature on the narcissism of adolescence which highlights its defensive and adaptive purposes for the development of self-esteem (Blos, 1965). Perhaps there is a similar developmental arc for psychoanalysts in training – allowing oneself to experience and be a person of authority is an important aspect of our work that requires time to be comfortable with. Often, arrogance persists unconsciously in the form of chronic self-doubt and secret envious attacks on others when we are uncomfortable with our own desire for power and clinical conviction. These moments can easily descend into anxiety-ridden arrogant stances with patients and colleagues. When arrogant experiences are not allowed to be put into words and enacted in moments with our supervisors and early cases, we risk banishing them to the unconscious where they cannot be reflected on and worked through.

Chapter 9

Managing arrogance in child analysis

Susan Sherkow

Arrogance, like entitlement, appears to me to be a by-product of multiple determinants in a child's development, a character trait arising from intermingling threads of nature and nurture woven together over time. Unlike character traits that are thought to have a strong genetic contribution – shyness and boldness, musicality and tone-deafness, athleticism and weak or diminished gross motor co-ordination – arrogance seems more likely to be a product of instinct and defense, compromise formations colored by identifications.

I have rarely encountered an arrogant child who does not have at least one arrogant parent, although the topic upon which parent and child hold forth as experts is rarely shared, and the parent is often entirely at odds with her child as a direct result of the arrogant stands the child takes. This is not hard to parse: After all, the arrogant child believes himself to be an expert, a supreme judge, head and shoulders above everyone else in his domain, sometimes extending his assertion of expertise from his own field to all others, and this perforce includes lording his superiority over his parents, teachers, and psychoanalyst. As a case in point, I can think of no better way to demonstrate such a child than to present the development and course of treatment of a boy whose family and educators suffered from his extraordinary degree of arrogance.

Introducing Ethan

I saw Ethan through three periods of psychoanalytic treatment, four-times-weekly starting at age two and a half for about two years, then twice weekly at age six for about a year, and again at age eight and a half for another year. During each treatment period, I saw his mother or his parents together weekly. The best way to introduce Ethan is to let him introduce himself, as he did through his "Autobiography?" This essay was written at age nine and a half years in response to a class assignment given over the Christmas vacation to "Write your autobiography." Not only does the content fully demonstrate the extent of Ethan's characterological arrogance, but the writing process does as well.

But first, to contextualize the writing sample, one needs to know that Ethan was a brilliant child, which was not only obvious in conversation with him, but was confirmed by neuropsychological testing. Second, Ethan loved to write, and one by-product of his arrogance was that he ignored his teacher's instructions about the pragmatics of any writing assignment. Invariably, he wrote about ten times more words or pages than asked for, and regardless of the form or person making the request, Ethan characteristically refused to follow suggestions for edits or a requirement to pare down. For example, asked to write a short sentence using a vocabulary word, Ethan wrote a minimum of three to four very long sentences, free-associating to each adjective he employed. Thus, the resulting plethora of words collectively embodied his conflicts and anxieties while also asserting his self-importance.

Although Ethan excelled at spelling, and boasted of his Scrabble scores, it was beneath him to check spelling or grammar when writing a class assignment. He would literally look down his nose, peering at the teacher or me out of the corner of his eye, and declare that he did not need to follow tedious rules. Even the title (all caps, in italics) of his autobiography bespeaks arrogance: N.B. I have cut and pasted his essay verbatim below, leaving the grammar and spelling as is.

Who is Ethan Oliver Johnson and his auobiography?

I, Ethan Oliver Johnson, was born on May 10, XXXX. At the time, I had an older sister, Melody, and my Mom and Dad. They were all watching me when I came out of my Mom's stomach yet I was feeling uncomfortable because I was in a hospital and it was the first room I had ever seen in my life. My sister said, "I always hoped for a sibling" and it so happened that it was me. My mom said that I was the easiest child to go through just being born. On My Dad's side of the family, there was his parents who were called Nana and Papa, there was Papa's sister, Aunt Jane, and her husband, Uncle Max. Unfortunately, Uncle Max passed away early when I was 4 years old. I also had my cousins, my cousin Nancy was born just 8 days after I was. Ben, the other cousin, was born when my Uncle Tony opened the world famous Las Vegas Mammoth Hotel. On my mom's side of the family, there is her sister, Aunt Beth, Uncle Joseph, and my cousins Michael and Mary.

When I was 1, my family went to Italy. My parents said "I was their best sleeper". I went to a wedding but I don't know who it was for. At age 5, I started kindergarten. I did not start at Melody's school. My mom wanted me to go to a school that was smaller and less crowded. I liked that school but after 2nd grade it got boring because I did not get enough of a challenge. At that time, I would sleep with my little sister Tess. One night and all night she was saying the same word over and over again. It was Weewee. I realized after that night that the word really meant Ethan. My sister had already said words before. Her first word was Dada, her second word was hi, and she also learned how to clap. I started baseball session and the very first time I was up to bat, I was out. I was crying and screaming and yelling. I also started to play tennis. I am athletic because I played tennis but so did my whole family. Tennis was at a country club that I went to all the time in the summer especially because it is closed in the winter. We would also go there for special occasions and events. Plus we would invite many people that were not members of the club so it made it more fun for us and for them. Every friday we have a jewish occasion called Chabat. It is when you sit down for a family dinner with absolutely no phones or screens.

My mom could prepare thanksgiving dinner for over 20 people. At seven years old, I was in second grade. I started to watch cooking shows and fell in love with them. When I memorized on how to make cake, I gave it a shot and actually did it. Everyone thought I was the smartest kid in the grade although I knew I wasn't. I loved to go out of the box but my writing was very messy. I was a class clown and came up with a name called the murky turkey. When I said the name out loud at first everyone laughed even though I didn't say anything funny. Maybe that is the reason Thanksgiving was one of my favorite holidays. My mom could prepare thanksgiving dinner for more than 20 people.

At age six, I started first grade. My grandmother, Nana taught me how to play scrabble. 2 years later, I was an expert scrabble player. 3 months in with scrabble, I could already beat my mom as if I used the best word all the time. My name Ethan means "a great protector". To me it means a brave person and a friend. In baseball I felt like a more important person on the team. One of our first games I had a stuffed neck, yet I still forced myself to try on the field and at bat. I got 4 hits and I crossed home plate every time and I was ninth at bat. My Mom loves to host parties and hosted a cocktail party for my school. She did that 2 or 3 years ago. I thought I would be annoyed but in fact I wasn't. for halloween I was in the hamptons picking pumpkins, Going out for lunch, but then a bee stung me (again) in the head. We discovered that there was an area with tons of bees. For halloween I knew just what I wanted to be and that was an angry bird. The big black bird. My Mom found the costume that I wanted in a store. For winter break, I went to ski in Colorado for spring break. Even on the coldest days, I forced myself to ski every day but It was still a blast. I had more friends than in kindergarten, but I had more internal rivals too. My internal rivals were actually my best friends when it was the end of the year. On roof we usually were with another 1st grade class. We played soccer or kickball and usually they would win or they would cheat but one time my class crushed them and made fun of the other class and we had to send in a big postcard as big as a poster and do nothing in school except for sit there. I loved to hula hoop and try to teach my cousin Maya how to get better. I showed her jumping, 360's, kneeling, standing up, walking and spinning but still didn't get as good as I wanted. The next time I saw her, she was great! For summer, I went to Nantucket, Italy, Paris, and London. In Nantucket, I enjoyed the fourth of July, and also sailing around In a boat coming to a beach and picking up shells. My sister was at sleepaway camp so she missed the fun and the warmth. In italy, we went in a boat as well, just Melody was there too. I devoured the seafood and pasta on my plates for lunch and dinner and for dessert The chocolate would melt in my mouth. Every night I had trouble sleeping because of the light but in the morning I would get to play outside with scooters and bikes. to see the. even my mom(who was in the shower). After school every day I would go to get a big, rich, creamy black and white cookie. I also had a swim teacher. It was painful swimming. and every time I jumped in the water, I felt if I was going to throw up. My music teacher was funny and never strict. I was very into music and had so many CDs you won't even believe it. I had a psychologist to help with my behavior and feelings, but I never knew who a psychologist was at that point. It was so devastating to lose one of my grandparents and now I had lost one of my uncles too. My grandfather Papa who lost my other grandparent Granny, wanted to remarry at a old age and found a girlfriend. Her name was Marg. My sister Tess never even Got to meet Granny. I went to see the movie Charlie And The Chocolate Factory for the first time. In Paris, I got to see the Eiffel tower. There was a chocolate factory that produced over 2,000 chocolates(yum) so I didn't know which to choose. Italy was hot and we went on a lot of boats and went to seafood restaurants. the beach was always open and it never rained.

The reason why everyone laughed was because it was the name of a spanish restaurant. I played scrabble at an expert level and what better to be a scrabble board for halloween. My Mom found a giant size for me but I still was very pleased. During December, my writing got better and I was able to help people on work. Lots of the people in my school were Jewish and Chanukah was a big hit to talk about. I went to Colorado again. I again skied every day. Luckily, the days were warmer. After that, my parents told me that I was going to go to Melody's school, I was crushed. Until I went there for 3rd grade, it was on my mind all the time.

When I was eight, One million things were happening. 3rd grade seemed fine and not as challenging as I thought it would be. I knew what my dream would be. A chef. I made breakfast every day. I went on a 16 mile bike ride to the little red lighthouse next to the George Washington Bridge. I went to Mexico to zipline and have fun with my cousins. I stayed at the hotel, I went to a waterpark where I ziplined and had fun on water slides and in the water. It was hot there and I swam every day but the beach wasn't open because there was a idiotic boat that leaked and they had to make the beach 4 feet higher. I liked everyone in 3rd grade but there was never anyone that I could play with. Sometimes I felt lonely. Sometimes people laughed at me or bragged but I ignore that and never tell teachers anything because it will turn into an argument and I will lose the argument. So this is the reason why I have never told on a kid in my class ever.

At age 2, I was in this group that was kind of like preschool. There were 4 teachers to help us. I also went to Elmo's World. Unfortunately, I did not remember or go on any of the rides until I came back when I was 7.

At age 3, I would not eat anything but pasta. So my Mom had to stuff veggies, meats and protein inside the pasta. I started real preschool at the XXXX. Although I was the oldest in my class, I still made lots of new friends. I went to Florida also. there I touched a dead bee and I was stung!

At age 4, I started to take gymnastics with one of my friends. My baby sister Tess was now a new addition to our family. I went to mexico with everyone in my family. I also was on a trip with my grandparents, my cousin and my older sister.

When I was in Florida, I made my sister giggle first out of everyone by doing the chicken dance with small maracas. I showed it to everyone. That summer I went to my aunt and uncles house at the beach When 2 weird things happened. first I got a splinter, and then my babysitter opened one of the doors and a random, stray dog came running all over the place. Luckily I got 3 new babysitters who wouldn't cause cause that much commotion.

Treatment phase I

The outline of Ethan's essay reveals the basic facts of his life, despite patchwork order. The references to family members and historical sequences were recognizable to me, revealing his conflicts and wishful thinking – *"my sister wanted me"* – *"everyone stood around watching me be born."* I also recognized the fantasy elaborations and associations to various experiences that lent color to the events as he remembered them, such as being bitten or hurt. They were consistent with similar other fantasy constructions of notable events, such as a description he wrote elsewhere of Tess's birth: "Tess was born on an airplane on the way to Colorado! My mother was very unhappy! We all watched her be born."

Ethan's description of his extended family was accurate: he had a four years older sister, Melody, and a four years younger sister, Tess; a maternal aunt, uncle, and cousins to whom he was very attached; and he spent much comfortable time with both his maternal and his paternal grandparents. At the point in time that Ethan wrote this document, he had been seeing me, whom he called his "psychologist," for all his "remembered" life. Importantly, I was a very real presence even when not seeing him in my office, through his mother's mental representation of me as a very essential helper in her quest to raise her children in general, especially this difficult boy, at the level of *excellence*, and to bring her husband and extended family on board. Thus, my persona as a super-doctor; mother's reliance on me to be a super-achiever on her and her son's behalf; some degree of arrogance on my part, including arrogance about my ability to help this child with neurobiological differences achieve a mainstream existence; all likely contributed to his arrogant character development.

Ethan had been brought to see me for evaluation at age two years four months for failure to make eye contact or to respond to his parents' verbal requests, as though he were deaf. He was showing little capacity to mirror actions, and his communications leaned toward repeating sentences in a sing-song voice; neither did he indicate his wishes or needs. Ethan fell in the category of "uneven development," a diagnosis that falls short of ASD. While he was precocious in vocabulary, puzzles, math, and verbal games, he was delayed in other areas, for instance, in separation-individuation and in anal body awareness/toilet training/genital awareness. Gender identity was frozen, as is often the case with children on the spectrum or with "uneven development." His play had not moved beyond concrete use of objects.

At first blush, one would take Ethan for being an utterly cheerful and charismatic little boy, who did make eye contact with me. However, from the first evaluation session I noticed his shallow, restricted affect when with his mother, indeed appearing very two-dimensional, with little evidence of modulation of between "pleasure" or "distress." Ethan's play demonstrated he had internalized that he was "broken." His behavior with his mother also demonstrated (and this was clearly observable to me) that her frightened and frightening eyes appeared to penetrate him as though she could eradicate his symptoms through her willpower – literally "will" them away.

His parents' description of how Ethan seemed to "manage" his mother by either demanding CDs or her credit cards, else he became hysterical, was also apparent in our first meetings. She bowed to his wishes rather than "fight" what seemed to her like a losing battle, reinforcing his use of CDs and credit cards in other domains and to manage an increasing range of negative emotions. He seemed to have found a way to self-regulate by displacing his aggression onto concrete objects.

Following the consultation, Ethan and his mother met with me in dyadic therapy four-times-per-week with additional weekly sessions with his parents. In my office, I would track when Ethan would reach into his stroller for his own CDs, a loose stack of four to eight discs, observing how his need for them was associated to the emotions that began to emerge during our work: issues mostly reflecting his anxiety about separations, changes, transitions, and to a lesser extent, sibling rivalry. I also observed that once Ethan discovered that I had my own packet of CDs in the office, and a CD player, he began to use the CDs and player to identify shades of musical "emotions," differentiating instruments, sounds, textures, and degrees of "scratched" or "broken" CD tracks. This play enabled us to help him differentiate between his own emotions, developing a repertoire of "sad," "missing," "worried," "angry," "frustrated," and "other" (those CDs or DVDs that belonged to his sister, his father, and his grandparents).

Ethan was particularly focused on the CDs that were scratched before he touched them, and ones that were scratched from his handling of them. The theme of feeling "broken" and defective was amply demonstrated in his obsessional collection and cleaning of CDs, and using them as more than transitional objects, as deeply rooted substitutes for mothering. His concern with being broken seemed to stem from his sense of being viewed by his parents, but most especially his mother, as defective from the moment she noticed that he was different, and different from his older sister Melody, who, as an "object," served as a mental representation of mother-projected-onto-Melody, a phenomenon enabled by Melody's ability to live up to mother's idealization of the perfect little girl.

One particularly interesting variation of the "broken" play was an instance in which he labeled a disc that was damaged so that the music, when played, sounded "wobbly" on the turntable: "It's wobbly!" he exclaimed. Of course, I heard this as an emerging metaphor: If we were going to acknowledge feelings, we all three were on "wobbly" ground! This became a regular feature of ensuing sessions, especially about a Paganini disc that was "born," as far as Ethan was concerned, with a scratched and unplayable track. Identifying himself with the "born defective" and literally, "unplayable" CD, his first application of a more nuanced use of expressive language came about in the context of his struggling to play this "unplayable" track of the CD. "It's broken," he said, rather quietly, but without intonation, still distanced from the experience of identifying something about him we could interpret. Indeed, to have interjected at that moment, "Ethan, I think *you* feel broken," would have registered intellectually, but not at the level of his gut feelings. I felt like I needed to wait until there was some bit of emotional connection to the idea. With much repetition, he then extended his observation a few days later to include himself for the first time, although at first what he said was still lacking a subject – he said, "It's bothering" several times, a *totally new referencing of an internal experience.* Then, again after repeating himself several times, as though practicing how to synthesize his inner experience with his evolving language capacity, he said, referring to himself in the first person, "It's *bothering* me."

This moment in the treatment seemed to be an example of the transforming work of therapy in the development of cognitive and emotional connections, a moment of being in a transitional space between experiencing something outside and experiencing something inside. My hunch was borne out when, several minutes later, he attacked the Paganini CD that was "bothering" him by biting on it as one might bite on one's "blankie" in a moment of anger at one's mother. It seemed that he identified in every respect with the broken CD that he worried his mother had destroyed, and conversely, he was enraged at his mother that he was "wobbly"!

Through this work, Ethan started to project his feelings onto toys in symbolic play. He called a teddy bear "broken," and repaired him by covering him with scotch tape. At the same time, he then also became fixated on playing only scratched tracks, until I asked him, "Are you practicing something that *doesn't* work?" Experimenting with the experience of "non-working" and broken, Ethan wanted to know whether the broken tracks and broken teddy would *stay* broken, or could be made to magically work. Insofar as the broken tracks represented his mother and himself as a working pair that had been damaged, his play showed concern about how well he and his mother "worked" as a couple struggling to be connected and stay connected with each other, through moments of negative feelings and separations. He kept trying to play the broken track to see if it could magically repair itself, and it then became clear that this particular play represented also my work with him – would we overcome his difficulties?

A successful part of Ethan's process of individuation from his mother and from me was visible in his development of a strong and playful capacity to tease me by seriously searching my office for a disc he knew he had stolen. And then there was the added torture of his knowing that he had scratched a particularly favorite track of mine on a vocal CD, and would pretend that we were about to hear it, playing dumb. At first, I fell for this, but after a while realized he was working successfully to get my goat. He similarly tortured us by putting on CDs that were educational material, or DVDs that, of course, could not be played at all. I then began to see that Ethan purposefully meant to cheat me while also damaging the CDs by abruptly removing them. I realized that in these instances, Ethan controlled me. I was his pawn, his victim, and he increasingly withheld the music, exquisitely able to start and stop the player before it emitted a sound from the disc, snapping the discs in and out, and tossing them to the ground. Sometimes, he varied his control of me by putting the music on "pause"!

Another aspect of his increasing individuation was Ethan's developing an interest in his genitals and urinary prowess: A very gratifying moment for him occurred when he pulled a cart of building blocks off of a shelf and, straddling the pile of blocks, pretended to "pee" on them, shouting "Pisshhh!" For a time, he regularly put his hands in his pants when worrying about the damaged tracks. His body habitus evolved from seemingly gender-neutral to boy-like.

Through variations on his newfound, multilayered establishment of control, Ethan was in effect projecting back onto the toys the introjected fear of being his mother's broken object. In doing so, he was increasingly able to tolerate the use of language and softer forms of transitional objects than the CDs and credit cards. He maintained the defense mechanism of withholding from his mother and me, but in the form of part-objects, rather than whole object representations. And, over time he began to allow us to play the actual tracks on the CDs, playing not only track 1, but multiple tracks, and allowing some of them to play to their conclusion. One sign of his increasing differentiation and internalization of a separate, good-enough object was in the following inquiry to his mother – he asked, "Which one do *you* want, Mommy?" (referring to the CDs and their tracks).

How does this all relate to the development of Ethan's arrogance? His essay conveys his early awareness – to him, from birth – of his mother's hyper-vigilance. "Everybody is watching!" combined with how different he must have seemed from his sister Melody in every respect, how "broken" he was. Ethan compensated for the ensuing rupture in the internalization and thus the separation/individuation processes by compulsive "quirks," his attachment to CDs as replacement objects, and to his avoidance of his mother. These consequences then exacerbated his mother's hyper-vigilance that in turn triggered performance anxiety and further exacerbated his symptoms, creating a vicious cycle of display and angry retreat. His sense of "specialness" (i.e., "different-ness"), for better and for worse, must have been the earliest seeds planted in his characterological "superiority" and arrogance.

School

During the initial phase of my treatment with Ethan, I observed him in his toddler program, where he engaged in parallel play at times, although he did not "fit in" to the activities that required more regulation, rules, or structure. His preferred activity was watching the other children from a distance. His teachers saw nothing peculiar in his behavior in the two-hour classroom, so they had little comprehension of why he was in intensive treatment! The advantage of their lack of sensitivity about his emotional state was that he did not perceive himself as "different" or defective in that setting.

However, Ethan's mother was determined that he attend the nursery school Melody had attended, one of the most sought-after and structured in the community. At age thirty-nine months, twelve months after we had begun analysis, Ethan began that nursery school. Here he was clearly "different" than the other toddlers, but he withstood the demands of the two-year program through a moderate amount of intervention and through self-isolation and imperviousness to the opinions of his teachers. He had, indeed, developed the capacity to relate to his peers to some extent, as well as follow instructions and maintain some of the regulatory demands expected of him in the school setting.

But surely his defensive posture toward succeeding when one not only does not fit in, and is "not really interested or needing buddies," probably vulnerable at all times to peers who are conflicted about one's success, and also vulnerable to not being included by other children who were "less intellectual," were contributing factors to (or set the stage for) his characterological sense of superiority and arrogant dismissal of those who did not understand or even care to understand how he felt or processed his environment.

Ethan's ability to appear to succeed gave his parents hope that he would be able to enroll in the grammar school of choice – that to which Melody attended, and their alma mater. Again, Ethan rose to the occasion and was accepted at that school, on the condition that he delay entry for a year. His parents chose to enroll him in a school that was less demanding academically but would keep him on track with his intellectual ability, and where socializing would be less important than learning academics. They also felt he needed a "break from treatment" and arranged for us to terminate during the summer before kindergarten began. By now, Ethan had demonstrated more communicative and social skills that bespoke his having "evened-up" his development, was superior in so many respects, and certainly, literally for all intents and purposes, had lost whatever diagnosis he had had. No one took him for a child "on the spectrum." In short, we took an eighteen-month "pause."

Treatment phase II

Ethan's mother, who had been in fairly regular contact with me, contacted me when Ethan was halfway through first grade, asking me to see Ethan for a consultation, to determine if he needed further treatment. This time, her major concerns were about his difficulty managing his relationships with boys, both academically and athletically. Ethan was struggling to relate to his father, avoided physical or competitive activities with his father or other boys outside of school, and was contemptuous of the boys who were athletically superior in gym class and after-school sports.

At nearly seven years old, Ethan was slightly built, wiry and strong but not capable of playing team sports alongside the more robust classmates. He had compensated by being the academic star of his class, and often tutored other boys in math off the cuff. He learned to play Scrabble in three languages, even playing and winning against the computer. He had begun to imitate the hooligans in his class to become as popular as his sister. When he was called to the principal's office, he was as thrilled as he had been in "urinating" on my blocks: a show of masculinity!

At the same time, Ethan had begun to show an interest in cooking, was an avid reader, liked chess, but more to the point of his character development, had developed a variety of reaction formations to his performance anxiety of toddlerhood. Among them were: practicing at being a stand-up comic; enjoying being "class clown"; also a "cousin's club clown," which included stripping naked for the girl cousins with no sense of shame or embarrassment ("above reproach," was his attitude) and performed as emcee at family events, again with no self-consciousness whatsoever, but often to the embarrassment and anxiety of his parents and grandparents. He also had begun sexual games with his younger sister.

In the ensuing phase of a one-and-a-half-year period of treatment, Ethan described and demonstrated all of the above performances in our sessions as I observed his multiple gifts in language, processing of emotional information, especially in understanding the dynamics between not only his parents but all of his family members, and the extent to which he had also identified with me in areas in which I took personal pride – reading, writing, wordplay, word games, puns, jokes, sarcasm, forcing me to examine my own leanings toward a sense of superiority, but on my side balanced by an ability I also have to poke fun at those very attributes, to joke about them upfront so as to be the first to pseudo-brag about how I could be arrogant or the smartest one in the room!

Ethan worked in our therapy to develop some self-observing ego, but was too cognitively immature to be able to fully develop the necessary awareness of the impact he had on other children, to learn to pull back; neither was he consciously willing to give up his "trump cards." We worked steadily on his anger and resentment toward the demands placed upon him by his parents to perform, to fit in (when he observed that they, in many ways, were as iconoclastic as he was) and their intense competitiveness in so many domains where he was the "tool" toward their sense of security and accomplishment as parents of a boy, a boy who in addition had overcome the potential label of ASD and could eventually go to Melody's school, the sign and symbol of our – Ethan's and my – success.

Ethan's struggle with his emerging competitiveness was painfully obvious to everyone – having not yet processed how to "work toward" success by practicing and indeed, skipping this step somehow between treatment gains and treatment flaws, and inadequate parental education, and inexact or inadequate parental identification. Ethan had no tolerance for practicing: only an arrogance, a supercilious denigration of "practicing" anything. He thus had no empathy for practice on the part of another child: one time, furious, Ethan physically assaulted a teammate in baseball practice who struck out. He verbally assaulted a good friend whose piano playing seemed inferior to Ethan: He walked up to him on stage and gave the child a dressing down, and tried to sit down and play the piece correctly himself.

Moreover, Ethan's projection onto his male classmates of his struggle with prowess – substituting physical prowess for social-emotional prowess, and muscularity for emotional muscularity, resulted in his formation of a compromise formation in which he embraced being the class "asshole," the negative-attention getting clown, the cut-up who gets sent to detention, and the child whose mother is called midday to the rescue. The turnaround was so astonishing to his school faculty that they could not take his acting up as authentic, which led to despair on Ethan's part, and a renewed desire on mother's part to transfer Ethan to Melody's school.

And that she accomplished. Ironically, the transfer was accompanied by another demand for termination of treatment, so Ethan could be given a chance to see what he could do "on his own." The gender issues had been barely addressed; like many children with uneven development, Ethan had not accomplished consolidation of gender identification during his pre-oedipal years; the phases of pre-oedipal and oedipal were blurred, and superego development was distorted by the lack of differentiation or clarity about both subtle and not so subtle positive and negative identifications with either parent. I was not a "gendered" person in Ethan's eyes.

In retrospect, the seeds of Ethan's arrogant posture of superiority toward peers and to almost all adults were visible in his intensifying his special interests during this period, due to his ability to take pleasure from words, language, writing, and verbal games. This posture served, at the same time, as defensive distancing from his siblings and his classmates, admiring and "hanging out" with only the gods of his universe – a few teachers, the chefs on TV, his mother, and me. Only baseball drew him in; he developed a pitching arm while in this second phase of therapy, further nurtured in his third phase, that served as a compromise formation between his need to be me, to show off for me, and to be masculine.

Treatment phase III

Thus, at the beginning of third grade, at age eight and a half, Ethan was on his own in a far more demanding academic and social environment, a day with many transitions between subjects, teachers, and classrooms. By late winter, Ethan's parents again contacted me, as did his school psychologist.

Ethan now presented with a massive case of performance anxiety, to which he brought meager defenses: denial, avoidance, physical retreat, and a case of arrogance/superiority/moral superiority equal to the degree of failure and approbation on the part of the faculty. The gender issues were being expressed in Ethan's singling out susceptible girls for verbal attacks on their femininity, using language to accost them that he barely understood, but associated with feminist causes, for example, girls who chose to wear pink, and look girlish, should be mocked for their "backwardness." He worked harder than ever to be class cut-up and class clown, without getting a laugh – these classmates were themselves too arrogant or simply sophisticated to pay attention to his infantile behavior. He also mocked his teachers when they failed to live up to his standards, corrected them, and ignored their attempts to correct his work. At a school where the expectation was to hand in multiple consecutive drafts of an assignment, incorporating the teacher's and sometimes other students' remarks and corrections along the way to the production of the final paper, Ethan almost never corrected his work. Without knowing his psychiatric history, his teachers and school psychologists could not make sense of Ethan's behavior other than to label him as having ADHD, learning disorders, and oppositional defiant behavior, and asked to have him tested and evaluated. More than anything, they were struck by his arrogance.

While Ethan was in the process of undergoing a neuropsychological evaluation, we continued treatment twice weekly. The sessions in content were bipartite, addressing his competitiveness from two angles – baseball and cooking. From the start, these sessions took place in the context of baseball practice, largely pitching a rubber ball or tennis ball at my playroom wall, while I sat to the side of the trajectory and hoped not to be bonked by a ricocheting ball. Occasionally, we played a version of handball, either standing side by side, trying to catch a ball that ricocheted off the wall, throwing it back to the wall, keeping it in play, or, facing each other, a simple game of throw and catch. When my shoulder took a beating after the first few months, Ethan kindly allowed me to sit out while he did all the throwing, racket ball, or pitching, asking me politely whether I was up to playing with him. He was an amazing athlete, as his parents attested, not only in these skills but in tennis, but had no faith in himself, or, more likely, no ability outside of my office to accept compromise.

Cooking, recipes, and contests

While each session began with some amount of time playing ball, Ethan and I talked about "issues." He addressed his feelings about teachers, classmates, his sense of "boyness" and "girlness," his relationship to his parents, and sibling rivalry. He railed at their indulging of his younger sister, Tess, who to him was a continuous thorn in his side, spoiled, a terror. He himself was very kind and indulgent toward her in general, but would get to the brink of exploding, and felt helpless about expressing himself to his parents. He still played tricks on her, like flushing her things down the toilet. He resented that his parents let her sleep in his bedroom, and he couldn't bring himself to "kick her out" of his bed when she wanted to cuddle with him. He believed his father, especially, favored Tess, and always took her side in a fracas that she started. (This was unfortunately true, and no amount of parent sessions ameliorated this to my satisfaction).

As we worked, I saw that Ethan began to harness his anxiety about competing with his classmates in his new, challenging school environment, where he felt helplessly incapable of producing the kind of work his classmates had been trained to produce since their kindergarten year, and thus were four years ahead of him in the process of delivering that which made his teachers happy. Although

Ethan had been watching cooking shows for a very long time, and had done a little experimentation at home with cooking, he now discovered a talent for all aspects of cooking. He experimented with prepping and presenting what he considered Michelin-quality meals sophisticated enough to pass muster in a restaurant that might feed a well-heeled crowd: sauces and plating and styling; imagining variations on recipes he watched prepared on television cooking shows and contests; how to make creative use of odd ingredients, including those items that happened to be in his mother's pantry; how to win a taste test before a panel of judges, how to impress a crowd of his parents' guests at a dinner party, and how to shop for unique and interesting ingredients. He was nearly nine years old and a star in his kitchen, but also in the minds of his relatives whom he impressed with his tasty concoctions and elaborate plating. Ethan was also preoccupied with knives and used very sharp cutlery in preparing his meals. His parents argued over whether he should have access to knives in the kitchen, supervised or not; his father absolutely forbade him to use sharp knives, his mother was somewhat more conflicted about taking the privilege away, but Ethan was sufficiently headstrong and cagey that he managed to use knives that were forbidden, preparing clandestine dinners.

In our sessions, Ethan's arrogance began to be enacted in his refusal to use a recipe, or even to follow the instructions offered by a TV show host demonstrating a way of preparing a meat, fish, or vegetable dish. His mother marveled at his ability to create meals with recipes out of his head, that is, unconsciously processing ingredients and measurements and cooking methods, extrapolating from one to another. I could see this extrapolation process in our discussions.

After some months, Ethan wanted me to see his work. He brought in things he had made, but what he truly desired was that I visit his kitchen and observe him prepare dinner for his parents. I agreed. (I had been in his home several times over the years, as home visits are standard for the kind of work I do with children with developmental delays/differences.) He made an incredible meal of chicken and mango sauce with a pureed green vegetable, plated like a professional. He was comfortable around the entire process, just slightly arrogant, only once a flash of humility at not finding the correct frying pan, and having to compromise. Yet an authority, that is, arrogance deserved. It was impressive; I did not taste it, but his mother reported on its excellence. Importantly, I only observed the process of him being a chef, I was not asked to engage in evaluating the final product: Was this a mirror of our work? He and I are a work in process, not able to evaluate or measure the final product.

Ethan and I continued to work on these substantial issues of competitiveness and arrogance superiority/inferiority, mine and his, transference/reality, maternal identification vs. paternal identification, as these issues were manifested in not being able to take criticism from teachers, or to practice at sports, or to accept defeat. Each session – these issues at the forefront – we wrestled with his sense of multi-determined defectiveness, reviewing and reinterpreting his family dynamics through discussing his history as he and I knew it from his toddlerhood. We addressed his identifications, indeed, not only with his mother and father, but with his aunts, uncles, and grandparents, all of whom he "saw" quite clearly, as if discussing case material with a colleague. An astonishing example was his assigning percentages of "masculine" and "feminine" to each of his relatives, and to my mind, nailing them completely! His ability to compromise expanded, to a lesser degree in school, to a greater degree at home.

In this context, I encountered the most memorable example of Ethan's arrogance. We had prepared a few recipes together in my office; my office hallway is equipped with a small refrigerator and tabletop oven, and my playroom has a sink and some counter space. We had collaborated on making various things from Ethan's imagination, like sauces or guacamole, which were successful extrapolations of foods he had learned to prepare. But we had come to blows on whether one could conjure up the ingredients for baked goods, including the exact amounts of such ingredients. I insisted that one needed to know the ratio of dry ingredients, like baking powder, flour, etc. to wet ingredients, like eggs and butter. Ethan had been determined to make an angel food cake for his mother's birthday, without consulting her, and without using a recipe, and had failed. He was humiliated, but still adamant.

Consequently, he announced that he and I were going to have a baking contest: I was to choose the item to bake. I spontaneously said, "Okay, let's bake scones. The prep time is quick, and they bake in fifteen minutes, so we could do this in a session." We each brought our ingredients. Ethan arrived at our session with his mother in tow, helping him carry a large bowl of batter he had put together at home as "the ingredients for my 'scones.'" He explained how he had made his batter, with butter, eggs, sugar, flour, chocolate chips, etc. His mother was browbeating him, berating him, chastising him for his arrogance, his belligerence: "You have made a batter for snickerdoodles," she kept insisting. "Not scones!"

Ethan shooed her out of the office, officiously, and she left as annoyed at me (for indulging him?, for setting him up?) as she was at him. We put our "scones" in the oven and waited for them to bake. Ethan insisted, at first, that his batter was indeed batter for scones, but eventually confessed that he had never heard of scones, but nonetheless was totally sure he could make them, and make them better than I could. Much as I thought I knew Ethan, I could not have imagined that he would have agreed to bake something he had never heard of, that at least he would have googled "scones."

Working through the baking fiasco led to an alteration in Ethan's approach to learning that was consistent with Ethan's interest in magic and keeping things up in the air. He taught himself to do something physical, from scratch, which required a great deal of practice, patience, and persistence, namely to juggle. During our subsequent sessions, Ethan thus devoted a portion of every session to practicing juggling until he was perfect at keeping three balls in the air. Only after he had been perfect at juggling for several months did he reveal his expertise to his parents. (An important part of this exercise was that I cannot juggle three items. Thus, his skill was all his own).

For his tenth birthday, Ethan wanted, as his present, to be allowed to prepare a multi-course dinner for his extended family. And so, he did, successfully. But, unfortunately, Ethan's parents could not comprehend that the underlying neuro-biological wiring of a child like Ethan continues to need tuning and fine-tuning through adolescence and often beyond. The arrogance had been misleading all around: If Ethan had a neurobiological problem, and psychoanalysis was the fix, why had it not been remedied by now? Was I too arrogant to admit failure? And by the same token, ironically, if he were to continue with me, how would he ever learn to cope on his own? Was I reinforcing the arrogant posture through my own arrogant belief in my expertise, thus denying him the actual academic training he needed? They believed he needed a tutor, not an analyst, a complete separation from me.

Discussion

It is not hard to see that in his telling his life story, Ethan is unapologetic about calling attention to himself, and the self-congratulatory tone is stunning. Having been the star of his class in the first two years of primary boys' school, once he was transferred to a top-ranking co-ed school in third grade, he developed a defensive wall of resistance and strengthened his resolve to show those inferior to him – just about everybody, but especially his father – that he was a superior human being, converting his sense of being "defective" into real deficits in spelling and grammar with an arrogant attitude toward corrective criticism. Thus, globally, about his style of presentation, Ethan used his language skills to show off and thus attempt to compete with his classmates successfully, but already he was too arrogant – or, a circular process – to have mastered the pragmatics of essay writing. Turning passive into active, he was enjoying snubbing his teachers' corrections by defensively aggrandizing his defects.

Ethan's historical sense of being damaged from birth is scattered throughout his story. Nearly every time he described doing or feeling something special, or approaching success, his display was followed by a reference to a disaster: I counted them, twelve in all. However, some of these were clearly defined in terms of compromise formation – trying to make the best of an unpleasant situation. For example, the story of making his sister giggle at his chicken dance is followed by "getting a splinter" and being subjected by his babysitter to a random, stray dog. "I made lots of new friends in my preschool," then on a trip to Florida, he was stung by a bee; "I am an expert at Scrabble," followed by his mother (whom he had bragged about beating at Scrabble) "bought me a Halloween costume that was too big, but I forgave her;" "I swam (happy) every day at the beach, an idiotic boat leaked and spoiled the beach." "I had a swim teacher . . . I was going to throw up." "In baseball, I was an important player . . . I had a stuffed neck . . . and forced myself to try." Last but not least, his history emphasizes his parents' outsized inter-est in travel, entertaining, and, especially, the expertise of his mother at hosting large parties and at cooking. He opens and closes a paragraph extolling her ability to entertain twenty people for Thanksgiving.

Ethan's competitive and performance anxieties permeate every anecdote: Ethan links most of his displays of real and imagined damage with experiences of physical or emotional pain/distress/conflict. He describes turning his explicit fear of Melody's school – "I got accepted, I was crushed" – into becoming a chef. He learned a skill on his own terms that combined his new and healthy identifications with his parents – their being great hosts, great cooks, self-employed, deeply caring about other people and their comfort – in other words, into something he could master on his own and display proudly to his whole family.

Losses similarly were met with compromise formations, as though he was responsible for the loss: Tess never got to meet her grandparent as an expression of his loss, the replacement baby who would not be ASD nor be a boy, while aggrandizing the problem; there are too many chocolates just as there are too many children. "My internal rivals were my friends at the end of the year." The greater the experience of potential danger or worry, the greater the aggrandizing reaction formation. For example, he connects his experience of his mother's delivery of Tess ultimately to one in which he is upset and scared by a stray dog being let into the house. His distress at her arrival is not measured in decibels or numbers on a Richter scale, but in terms of the numbers of nannies needed to care for her while also protecting her from his impending explosions – getting three new babysitters who would not cause the commotion that Tess causes! (i.e., who would, reaction formation-wise, protect Tess from the commotion he wants to make).

In summary, one can see Ethan's history schematically as an elongated rope in a tug-of-war with his mother, one with many notches or bumps along the rope, but nonetheless a continuous developmental schema. It is, indeed, an umbilical cord that gets stretched successfully, with degrees of true separation, individuation, and peace, as well as true academic success, but also threatening to snap and destroy her with each of the aggressions he describes – bee stings, vomit, rejections, throwing balls to break the playroom wall, or cooking poison. Arrogance, as a defense against being "born broken," and despite years of work at repairing those "tracks," still failing to meet his overachieving mother's pressure to compete, is reinforced with secret confidences in my office that bespoke a shared arrogance about the value of being smarter than everyone else, regardless of age, size, height, and education. Each of those moments countered the daily feeling Ethan had of assault on his ability to compete successfully with his parents and his sister.

Epilogue

Chapter 10

The realm of humility

Salman Akhtar

Very little has been written on humility in the field of psychoanalysis. PEP-Web (the electronic compendium of analytic literature of over 100 years) lists ten papers with the word "humility" in their titles but most of them focus upon the exhortation for psychoanalysts to exercise modesty and temper their enthusiasm for this or that theoretical persuasion. Only one paper (Weber, 2006) has something to say about the concept of humility itself. In addition to this paper, I have been able to locate a chapter on humility in Paul Marcus's (2013) book, *In Search of the Spiritual: Gabriel Marcel, Psychoanalysis, and the Sacred* as well as a few passing remarks here and there in the psychoanalytic literature.

This lack of attention to humility is puzzling since (i) the clinical enterprise of psychoanalysis is based upon devoted care and non-selfish concern with the Other, (ii) psychoanalytic developmental theory upholds renunciation of omnipotence and working through the smug certainty of the "paranoid position" in favour of the self-effacing modesty of the "depressive position" (Klein, 1940), (iii) contemporary analysts frequently implore their colleagues for "a measure of humility" (Richards, 2003) and to set aside the allure of theoretical "purity," (iv) a vast majority of papers on psychoanalytic technique advocate the attitude of humility, and (v) almost all published obituaries of psychoanalysts extol the deceased's humility. All this suggests that "humility" would be a topic of great interest to psychoanalysts. One expects them to eagerly explore its origins, aims, objects, and relational implications. That this is not true comes as a jolting surprise.

Descriptive characteristics

The English word "humility" is derived from the Old French *umelite* and the Latin, *humilitas*. The former evokes the qualities of modesty and sweetness. The latter is a noun related to the adjective *humilis*, which can be translated as "humble" but also as "well-grounded," or "from the earth"; the word *humus* in Latin means "earth." The dictionary definition of "humility" characterizes it as "the state or quality of being humble ... freedom from pride and arrogance ... a modest estimate of one's worth ... [and, also] an act of submission and courtesy" (Mish, 1998, p. 565). Although the word "humility" appears frequently in a religious context, it is also used outside such context to denote an attitude of modesty and self-restraint from vanity.

Humility seems to enhance self-growth and deepen interpersonal relatedness. The "lay" press is replete with short, simple, and quickly assembled books on the virtues of humility. Most of them come from Christian evangelists. However, there are three books (Whitfield, Whitfield, Park, & Prevatt, 2006; Williams, 2016; Worthington, 2007) that keep matters in the secular realm and offer some meaningful insights about humility. Whitfield et al. (2006) make the dialectical bond between humility and gratitude explicit, note that "[H]umility allows for different interpretations of the same event" (p. 31),[1] and observe that humility anchors the self in its finitude. According to them, renunciation of pride and its relentless demands upon the mind opens up psychic space for recognizing the benefits one is drawing from the goodness of others. They also note that humility permits a re-framing of one's interpretative stance; "not attached to being 'right' or 'wrong', we become more inclusive of others and do not compete with their reality' (p. 31). And finally, Whitfield et al. (2006) underscore that humility facilitates (and is facilitated by) the acceptance of the time-limited nature of our existence. It grounds us in reality. Such salutary portrayal, however, leads them to subsume all sorts of desirable qualities under this rubric. They state that: "There are at least twelve key characteristics of humility. These include (1) openness, (2) an attitude of 'don't know', (3) curiosity, (4) innocence, (5) a child-like nature, (6) a spontaneity, (7) spirituality, (8) tolerance, (9) patience, (10) integrity, (11) detachment and (12) letting go" (p. 15). This seems to be an overextension of the concept of humility and detracts from the other, good ideas contained in their book.

Worthington's (2007) book emphasizes that humility unshackles the ego from self-serving drives and makes it interested in others' pursuits. In this respect, humility resembles altruism. But whereas altruism can exist without "lowering" oneself, humility cannot. According to Worthington, humility rests upon our discovery and acceptance of

> ... something bigger than we are. The bigger – God, humanity, the environment, or the cosmos – differs across people, communities, and cultures. But the constant in the question is this: something is bigger than we are. And, we know it.
>
> (p. 43)

Another feature of humility is that it is noticed more by others than by oneself. Indeed, self-evaluation of humility is always suspect since a truly humble person does not claim to have this "quiet virtue" (p. 17). Worthington goes on to say that maintaining humility over the life span and in varying circumstances is no easy task. However, active avoidance of pride, acceptance of one's limits, keeping one's mortality in mind, and cultivation of nonselfish interests can enhance the capacity for humility.

The third "popular" book on humility is by Pat Williams (2016), the senior vice-president of the NBA's well-known team, Orlando Magic. Williams declares

---

1 This aspect of humility is of great significance to the clinical enterprise of psychoanalysis, as will be highlighted in a later section of this contribution.

humility to be "a modest and realistic view of one's importance" (p. 36) and, citing an anonymous source, adds that "Humility does not mean thinking less of yourself. It just means thinking of yourself less" (p. 36). Williams goes on to emphasize that those who possess humility treat all others as equals and thus earn trust, respect, and loyalty. His book, even though a bit preachy, contains convincing illustrations of humility from the lives of not only great people like Washington, Lincoln, Gandhi, and Mandela, but also from the lives of ordinary individuals. Williams's message is loud and clear: Humility begets respect and that, in turn, can bring actual success. More important, he states that "humility is a choice" (p. 40) and follows this up by suggesting ways to enhance this personality trait: (i) taking time for self-reflection, (ii) inviting a few friends to be brutally honest with one, and (iii) readily acknowledging one's faults and failures. Williams's cognitive-behavioral approach needs to be "softened" by the addition of insights that psychoanalysis has to offer on this matter.

Psychoanalytic literature

Freud's views

Freud used the word "humility" a mere nine times in his entire writing (Guttman, Jones, & Parrish, 1980, p. 262). He valued this character trait and referred to Frau Emmy von N. as "a true lady" (Freud, 1893, p. 104) since she possessed, among other qualities, a great "humility of mind" (p. 103). His other references to humility occur in the context of romantic love, man's awe of nature's majesty, and religion. While declaring that "Traits of humility, of the limitation of narcissism, and of self-injury occur in *every case* of being in love" (1921c, p. 113, emphasis added), Freud regarded the attitude of "humility and the sublime overvaluation of the sexual object characteristic of the male lover" (1920a, p. 154). This was true even when the case he was discussing was that of a woman. Thus, in describing a girl's profound erotic attachment to an older woman, he referred to her "humility [as manifesting] the characteristic type of masculine love" (ibid., p. 160). Such phallocentric bias in theorizing was also evident in his tracing the female hysterics' "humility towards their lovers" (1897, p. 244) to their dimly recalling the encounter with "the height from which the father looks down upon a child" (ibid., p. 244) but never attributing a male lover's humility to a parallel ontogenetic encounter with the mother's height.[2]

A second context in which Freud remarked upon the experience of humility was in man's awe of the mysteries of nature. Talking of the great Leonardo da Vinci, Freud (1910c) stated the following:

> A man who has begun to have an inkling of the grandeur of the universe with all its complexities and its laws readily forgets his own insignificant self. Left

---

2 Another striking example of such bias in Freud's (1924d) thinking is his coining the term "feminine masochism" based upon clinical work with two *male* patients who wished to be beaten.

in admiration and filled with true humility, he all too easily forgets that he himself is a part of those active forces and that in accordance with the scale of his personal strength the way is open for him to try to alter a small portion of the destined course of the world – a world in which the small is still no less wonderful and significant than the great.

(pp. 75–76)

In contrast to such "true humility," Freud traced the "religious sense of humility" (1923b, p. 37) to the individual and collective ego of man realizing that it has fallen far short of its wished-for ideal state. Curiously, the word "humility" does not appear even once in Freud's (1927) *The Future of an Illusion* which posits man's struggle to bear his smallness vis-à-vis nature and mortality to be a major contribution to the origin of religious ideas. While interesting and even somewhat instructive, Freud's observations on "romantic," "true," and "religious" humility were largely made in passing and did not delve into the exact nature of this emotional attitude.

Subsequent contributions

Although a few later psychoanalysts (e.g., Clark, 1932; Feldman, 1953; Kirman, 1998; Marcovitz, 1966; Menninger, 1943) did mention humility in other contexts, only two (Marcus, 2013; Weber, 2006) wrote papers specifically devoted to this topic. Weber acknowledged that "Humility is a loaded word for Americans and escapees from our familiar organized religions" (p. 219) but went on to explore its dynamics in detail. She emphasized that humility necessitates that one renounce "both the arrogance of the superior ego and the wallowing victimization of the sense of inferiority" (p. 221). Unlike the polarities of narcissism and masochism which draw all one's energy back into oneself, humility spreads the psychic energy broadly and connects one to others. It defeats egotism and prepares ground for respect and awe. Weber declared that human beings are connected to each other not because of instinctual needs or via the repetition of early attachments but owing to the fact that humility drives them to seek out the external world. She recommended that we "surrender humbly" (p. 219) to this inner command and declared that

> . . . we are connected to life because life itself is perfect. Each of us, each moment we experience, is momentarily perfect, even when it is perfectly awful. We can know that perfection through our own experience, in fact only through our own experience. Our duty and our joy are to know it as well as we can, to be open to every vast and mysterious moment.

(pp. 218–219)

Representative of the emerging consilience between psychoanalysis and Buddhism (Coltart, 1985; Epstein, 1995; Hoffer, 2015; Rubin, 2005), Weber anchored her proposal in the psychoanalyst Ghent's (1990) dictum that in each individual there exists "a longing for something in the environment to make possible the surrender, in the sense of yielding, of the false self" (p. 109). Weber's faith in the self-evident and absolute truth of each moment is akin to Bion's (1965) concept of "O" though she herself does not make this connection.

Weber's "psychoanalytic spirituality" finds a counterpart in Marcus's (2013) paper on humility even though his views have little to do with Buddhism. Marcus's perspective arises from the contributions of Gabriel Marcel (1889–1973), a French philosopher, playwright, music critic, and leading Christian existentialist, which focused upon the modern individual's struggle in a technologically dehumanizing society. Drawing upon them, Marcus (2013) notes that "Humility always moves against the prison-house of the self-centric, against inordinate narcissism, selfishness, and other such neuroses" (p. 90). For Marcus, a well-cultivated sense of humility in daily life is "the basis of wholesome personal growth and development, enhanced communality, and a modicum of personal happiness" (p. 92). Humility is not an isolated character trait; it pervades one's entire being.

Marcus acknowledges Marcel's insistent linking of humility to faith in a supreme being – God – but struggles himself to retain a secular view of the attitude. He cites philosophers, scientists, and poets ranging from Socrates to T. S. Eliot and from Gandhi to Einstein in support of his proposal that, even without invoking God, humility involves the acknowledgement that one's self is not the center of this universe. Thus, humility revolves around a process of radically "unselving" (Smith, 2005, p. 104) oneself. This profoundly affects the relationship one has to oneself and to others.

Marcus highlights the "self-relation" in humility as (i) mindfulness of one's relatively insignificant place in the larger scheme of things, (ii) awareness of the time-limited nature of one's existence, (iii) lack of preoccupation with oneself, (iv) realistic self-awareness that is devoid of both inferiority and arrogance, (v) capacity to admit to errors, (vi) openness to new ideas, and (vii) freedom from boredom. In relation to others, a humble person shows respect, hospitality, and non-exploitativeness.

> The humble person can relate to others with greater honesty and openness since he is not afraid to show his imperfections to them. He also sees the best in others and knows that he needs other people to live a satisfying, productive, and decent life, as does everyone. He graciously wants to pass on his "glory", his hard-earned insights on how to live a "good life" to others. He is more than willing to give someone a helping hand and, overall, he tends to a service mentality (serving others is almost always to some extent humbling, the humble spirit is always associated with kindness and compassion).
>
> (p. 106)

Weber's (2006) and Marcus's (2013) contributions pretty much exhaust what psychoanalysis has to offer regarding the topic of humility. The existence of a few other passing remarks by others will become evident later in my contribution.

Synthesis and critique

Pooling together the various features attributed to "humility," one finds that the attitude is comprised of (i) *a self-view* of being "nothing special" without masochistic disavowal of one's assets, (ii) *an emotional state* of gratitude and tenderness, (iii) *a cognitive attitude* of openness to learning and considering one's state of knowledge as non-exhaustive, (iv) *a behavioral style* of interacting with others with attention, respect, and politeness, and (v) *an experiential capacity* for surrender and awe. Passed through the filter of classical metapsychology (Freud, 1915c; Rappaport, 1960), the constituents of humility can be reconfigured in the following way.

- *Topographic perspective*: The attitude of humility exists mostly on an unconscious basis, though its behavioral aspects might be preconscious or conscious.
- *Genetic perspective*: Humility is an outgrowth of a combination of the infantile awe of parents, oedipal phase acceptance of generational differences, and latency phase wonder about the world-at-large. Later, adult life developments also contribute to it.
- *Economic perspective*: Humility reflects a psychic state where the instinctualized qualities (e.g., pressure, relief upon discharge, cyclical nature) of libido and aggression are renounced and neutralized energy flows peacefully towards the outer world.
- *Dynamic perspective*: Humility arises from the ego's capacity to achieve a balance between self-deflation and self-inflation, and to maintain ongoing concern for others. There is also a peaceful tolerance of the gap between the ego and the ego ideal.
- *Adaptive perspective*: Humility results in a relational pattern that is disarming, trust-earning, and therefore interpersonally beneficial.

Humility is regarded as a component of dignity by Markovitz (1966); the latter is an elusive concept that has only recently come under psychoanalytic scrutiny (Akhtar, 2015; Levine, 2016). Humility also has a close relationship with awe. And this has dual implications. The *first issue* pertains to the ontogenetic origin of the capacity for humility. The intermingling of humility with awe reflects a reactivation of the nonverbal subjective experience of the supine infantile eye. After all, the human infant spends his first year or so in a supine posture, looking upwards toward the much taller parents. Looking up thus becomes associated with safety and protection (and God comes to reside up in the heavens). Freud (1897) did hint at this root of humility but, in his characteristic phallocentrism, restricted it to the female gender only. The psychoanalyst who has elaborated on this notion more meaningfully is Ostow (2001). He declares that:

> Since awe seems to be a response to major discrepancies of scale, it would seem reasonable to attribute its origin to the earliest experiences of the infant who must be impressed by, and responds to, the large sizes, loud sounds, and

bright lights that he first encounters at the hands of his parents and the world in which they live. It is inconceivable that there is no affective response to the enormous scale of these perceptions, though it would seem impossible to retrieve them . . . I do not know that the awe we experience as adults reproduces literally the affect of this early experience; it may be that the activation of the non-declarative residues of the early experience now yields an affective experience different from that which it originally elicited, but I would suspect that it resembles it in some way.

(pp. 206–207)

To such early infantile experiences, later encounters with oedipal realities[3] and with the latency age requirement to respect school-based hierarchies give further coloration. Awe of parents spreads to that of teachers, principals, and national heroes, strengthening the capacity for humility. All in all, the cadence of humility arises from a safe, bearable, and well-protected sense of smallness that exists in relation to the bigness of others.

The *second issue* raised by the correlation of awe with humility is the essentially hybrid nature of this concept. Like identity (Erikson, 1950) or forgiveness (Akhtar, 2000), the experience of humility is partly intrapsychic and partly interpersonal. And, the latter dimension is not restricted to the human realm; it extends to the nonhuman environment. This stretches our conventional psychoanalytic theory to its limits.[4] No wonder that psychoanalysts, being uneasy with hybrid concepts of this sort, have tended to avoid the topic altogether. The close association between humility and religion has also played a role in their disinterest. With the advent of modern "anthropological psychoanalysis" (Akhtar, 2013a), however, the possibility of thinking about such concepts has expanded.

Sociocultural realm

Two areas especially demand attention when it comes to the sociocultural dimension of humility. The first pertains to religion and the second to the East-West difference.

Humility across religions

As far as the religious variable is concerned, it is almost reflexive to associate humility with Christianity. The glut of "popular" books on this topic written by evangelist Christians lends credence to such an impression. And, it is true that

---

3 In a frequently cited paper, Greenacre (1956) traced the human capacity for awe to the child's feelings about the larger bodies of parents and especially to his or her seeing the father's erect penis.

4 Most psychoanalysts view man's relationship to the known human environment as a displaced and symbolic derivative of his ties to the primary human objects. Only a few (Akhtar, 2003; Bollas, 1992, 2009; Searles, 1960) allow for the possibility that there might be a "direct" relationship between man and "things."

the New Testament of the Bible contains passages that are so often quoted as to become a part of daily speech. Take a look at the following.

- "Blessed are the meek for they shall inherit the earth" (Matthew 5:5).
- "He who exalts himself will be humbled and he who humbles himself will be exalted" (Matthew 23:12).
- "Do nothing out of selfish ambition or vain conceit. Rather, in humility, value others above yourselves" (Philippians 2:3).

Moreover, all Christian saints, especially St Augustine and St Thomas Aquinas, uphold humility as a fundamental virtue. Saint Bernard went on to declare Jesus Christ to be the ultimate definition of humility. More recently, C. S. Lewis (1942) declared pride to be an "anti-God" state and humility to be the true moral stance. All this, and more, has led to a compact of essentialism between humility and Christianity. The fact, however, is that all religions of the world extol the attitude and encourage their followers to adopt it.

Within the other two Abrahamic faiths, Judaism and Islam, there are numerous such "reminders." The Old Testament regards humility as a sign of godly strength and purpose and states that "Moses was a man exceeding meek above all men than dwelt upon earth" (Numbers 12:3). It underscores the relationship between humility, wisdom, and inner peace and explicitly declares that "God opposes the proud but gives grace to the humble" (Proverbs 3:34). The influential writings of Jewish philosophers Martin Buber (1878–1965) and Emmanuel Levinas (1906–1995) have consistently emphasized the moral significance of humility. And, Rabbi Lord Jonathan Sacks, perhaps the most respected Jewish theologian of our times, has written that:

> Humility – true humility – is one of the most expansive and life-enhancing of all virtues. It does not mean under-valuing yourself. It means valuing other people. It signals a certain openness to life's grandeur and the willingness to be surprised, uplifted, by goodness wherever one finds it . . . Humility, then, is more than just a virtue: it is a form of perception, a language in which the "I" is silent so that I can hear the "thou", the unspoken call beneath human speech, the Divine Whisper within all that moves, the voice of others that calls me to redeem its loneliness with the touch of love. Humility is what opens us to the world.
>
> (2017, pp. 1–2)

The youngest of Abrahamic religions, Islam, too, celebrates the virtue of humility. The following three quotations from the Quran should suffice to illustrate this, though more examples can readily be given.

- "The servants of the Most Merciful are those who walk upon the earth in humility, and when the ignorant address them, they say words of peace" (Surah-al-Furqan, 25: 63).

- "Remember your Lord in yourselves with humility and in private without announcing it in the mornings and evenings, and do not be among the heedless (Surah-al-A'raq, 7: 205).
- "Lower to your parents the wing of humility and of mercy and say: My Lord have mercy upon them as they brought me up when I was small" (Surah-al-Isra, 17: 24).

Besides these passages from the Quran, there are multiple sayings of Mohammad that uphold humility and its propitious impact upon human bonds.

- "Verily, Allah has revealed to me that you must be humble towards one another, so that no one wrongs another or boasts to another" (Sunnah, reported by Iyad ibn Haman).
- "There is no human being except that the wisdom of his mind is in the hands of an angel. When he shows humility, the angel is ordered to increase his wisdom. When he shows arrogance, the angel is ordered to decrease his wisdom" (Sunnah, reported by Ibn-Albas).

Eastern religions such as Hinduism, Buddhism, Jainism, Sikhism, and Taoism similarly champion the silent force of humility. Sanskrit, the language of Hindu scriptures, contains many words that convey the essence of humility: *viniti* (kindness), *samniti* (respect of others), *amanitvam* (pridelessness), and *namrata* (modest behavior). And, the great *Bhagavad Gita* (c. second century BCE) explains humility to mean the lack of desire to be honored by others. Outside of religious texts, though emanating from them, Gandhi (1940) emphasized three aspects of humility: (i) it is an internal state and does not refer merely to good manners, (ii) it cannot be cultivated; it is foundational, and (iii) it does not make itself evident to consciousness; a humble person is not aware of his humility. And between the ancient religious texts and the mid-twentieth-century proposals of Gandhi lies a huge corpus of Hindu philosophy and spiritual exegesis that elucidates humility. The three important derivatives of Hinduism, namely Buddhism, Jainism, and Sikhism all consider humility to be a virtue and decry conceit and overconfidence. The Far Eastern religion, Taoism, defines humility by an extended Chinese phrase instead of a single word: "*Bugan wei tianxia xian*," which means "daring not to be at the world's front" (cited in Chen, 1989, p. 209). To be in front is to court death while to stay behind is to allow oneself time to fully ripen and bear the fruit of wisdom. All in all, it can be said that the religions derived both from the Abrahamic faith (Judaism, Christianity, and Islam) and from Eastern belief systems (Hinduism, Buddhism, Jainism, Sikhism, and Taoism) uphold humility as a virtue.

Humility across cultures

If all aspects of human life were regulated by religion, the foregoing statement would imply a uniform prevalence of the character trait of humility across the globe. But since modal personality patterns, to the extent such generalizations are possible, emerge from a large variety of factors which go far beyond religious belief (economy, history, folklore, child-rearing practices, ecology, nationalistic agendas, and so on), it seems reasonable to ask whether the prevalence of humility as a character trait is uniform or variable across cultures? No hard data is available to answer this question. However, there are some studies of leadership styles that do shed light on this matter. The prominent Dutch social psychologist, Geert Hofstede (2001), for instance, has found that some countries (e.g., Russia) have high "power distance" scores (93 on a 1–100 scale), whereas others (e.g., USA) have far lower scores (40 on a 1–100 scale). This means that organizational leaders in Russia prize hierarchy, inequality, and a top-down decision-making approach whereas those in the USA value collaboration, informality, and team-driven decision making. Paradoxically, "subordinates" in Russia display submissiveness and humility whereas "subordinates" in the USA are encouraged to be independent and contribute to problem-solving.

Commenting upon the parallel difference in the world of pedagogy, I have elsewhere observed that:

> In Western countries, especially the United States, the apprentice (be it a young mechanic or a medical student) is expected to ask questions and learn by active engagement with his teachers. Too quick agreement with what the teacher says is viewed with suspicion. The relationship between the teacher and apprentice is based upon mutual respect and cordiality; it strives to stay away from authoritarianism. In the East, typically, the situation is different (Moore, 2009; Roland, 1996). The teacher is authoritarian. His word is not to be questioned. The apprentice is to learn by submission and emulation, not by questioning and challenging the teacher. The relationship between the two is somber and leaves little doubt about the teacher's authority over the student. If such differences are not taken into account, a Western apprentice (say in yoga, martial arts, or Tibetan Buddhism) in the East can come across as disrespectful to his Eastern mentors. And, an Eastern apprentice in the West can appear inhibited and neurotically tongue-tied. Clearly, misunderstanding of this sort can create problems at the work place. Also to be kept in mind is the fact that over time, these differences in the apprenticeship patterns affect what kind of teacher the respective apprentices become. The assertive and questioning apprentice of the West, over the course of time, turns into a teacher who is modest and willing to be challenged. The humble and submissive apprentice of the East, in contrast, becomes a more forceful teacher expecting his word to be taken on surface, and without questions asked.
>
> (Akhtar, 2011, p. 44)

Yet another perspective on the difference vis-à-vis humility between East and West comes from Roland's (1988, 1996) anthropological studies of India and

Japan. Roland proposes that unlike highly individualized Westerners (especially North Americans), Indians and Japanese have a powerful familial and spiritual dimension to their selves. Their "we-self" enhances concern for others and identification with the reputation and honor of their families. Moreover, there is a spiritual flavor to the individuals' existence: This is expressed in India via rituals and meditation and in Japan via esthetics and communion with nature. Roland asserts that the individualized self typical of Americans is less prominent among Indians and Japanese whose narcissistic cathexis is submerged in the twin rivers of connection and compression.

Finally, there is the information forthcoming from culturally sensitive studies of self-enhancement patterns. Heine, Lehman, Markus, and Kitayama (1999) went so far as to suggest the need for self-enhancement is not universal; it manifests only in some cultures and is most marked in the United States. Their claim was vociferously disputed by a number of subsequent studies (for a comprehensive listing of these, see Lee, Leung, and Kim, 2014) which asserted that the difference resided not in the extent of the desire for self-enhancement but in the way people in different cultures went about enhancing their selves. Many such studies found that humility functions as a useful tool for maintaining harmony in collectivist cultures and hence is an important regular of self-esteem (Kim & Cohen, 2010; Lee, Leung, & Kim, 2014). A cross-cultural study of Chinese and American subjects (Cai et al., 2011) found that the former reported increased self-respect when instructed to be as modest as possible while the latter did not. The result suggests that being humble is instrumental for self-enhancement in Eastern cultures but not in Euro-American cultures.

Pooling together all the sociocultural observations mentioned above yields a broad-based notion that the trait of humility might be more marked in non-Western cultures. For the clinician who must draw conclusions from deeper contact with a single individual, this information can serve as a gentle reminder to scan his or her non-Western patients' material with a culturally sensitive lens. And, this brings us back to considering the pertinence of humility in the clinical realm.

Psychopathology

Like any other positive personality attribute, humility is subject to distortion and morbidity. Elsewhere, I (Akhtar, 2012) have delineated the psychopathological syndromes involving generosity, gratitude, and forgiveness. Here, I focus upon the maladaptive variants of humility, including (i) excessive humility, (ii) deficient humility, (iii) false humility, and (iv) compartmentalized humility. Brief comments on each follow.

Excessive humility

There are individuals who are simply too "humble" and are forever ready to help others. They cannot accept compliments. They underestimate their strengths and often verbally indulge in self-depreciation. Between the polarities of pride and self-abnegation, they seem to have tilted too far in the latter direction. Herein lies an important theoretical and clinical point. Klein's (1940) "paranoid" and "depressive" positions are respectively characterized by omnipotence, self-congratulatory certainty, and externalization of all "badness" *and* by modesty, gratitude, and tolerance of ambivalence. This has given rise to the common misunderstanding that the "paranoid" position is always unhealthy and the "depressive" position is always healthy. What is overlooked in this dichotomous vision is that, at times, the opposite is true. Skills of political oratory, trial law, and editorial scrutiny of a manuscript, for instance, benefit by a "paranoid" position. And, the self-flagellation of the melancholic gives evidence to the "depressive position" gone awry. Excessive humility wipes out the psychic traces of healthy narcissism and thus represents a morbid extreme of the "depressive position." However, "excessive humility" is not "false" (see "false humility" below). It does not mask grandiosity or caricature inferiority. It is merely a guilty intensification of humility that resides in the individual. Excessive humility is a collusive concoction of a ferocious superego and a slavish ego.

Deficient humility

This symptom constitutes the "negative twin" of pathological narcissism. Experiencing and expressing humility requires lowering oneself in the given matrix of object relations; the self is accorded less value than the object. Taking such a "risk" is difficult for a pathological narcissist. Continually warding-off this inferiority-laden and morose self-representation (Akhtar, 1989; Kernberg, 1984), such an individual cannot bring himself to say "sorry" or "thank you," both of which acknowledge the higher status of his object. Full of self-concern, the narcissist is empty of remorse and gratitude. He lacks humility. And, so does the antisocial individual who holds the world accountable for his humiliating and deprived childhood.

False humility

Not all that looks like humility is humility. Many mental mechanisms can lead to the appearance of humility while matters at the psychic core are quite different. In fact, the spectrum of such "false humility" is broad. On its benign end resides the air of "affected humility" (Feldman, 1953) that one sometimes encounters in poets and artists. On the malignant end, is the antisocial individuals' crafty façade of humility for extracting favors from others. Superego-driven reaction formation against anal-phase megalomania can give one's character a flavor of undue reticence which is mistaken for humility (Menninger, 1943). In the "shy narcissist" (Akhtar, 2000), the competing pressures of exhibitionism and modesty can also result in false humility.

False humility needs to be distinguished from what Green (1986) has termed "moral narcissism." The falsely humble person wears his self-effacement on his sleeve and desires admiration from onlookers. In contrast, the moral narcissist seeks to destroy his instinctual needs and free himself from all libidinal ties to others. Both of them can appear self-depriving but the former is propelled by object hunger and the latter by an attack against that very hunger.

An entirely different pathway for the evolution of false humility is via the defense called "denial by exaggeration" (Fenichel, 1945). Here, a person correctly estimates his status in a given relationship as low but plays up this inferiority for moralistic and sadomasochistic purposes. Long before the description of this mechanism though, Clark (1932) had noted that "[M]any children are known to disguise their underlying neuroses by a mock humility" (p. 48).

Compartmentalized humility

In certain individuals, the sector of personality that is suffused with genuine politeness and humility shows a "mirror complimentarity" (Bach, 1977) with another sector of personality that is brimming with self-centeredness and vanity. Dramatic examples of this in the lives of renowned individuals (e.g., politicians and socially conscious movie personalities) draw great public attention but "compartmentalized humility" can as easily be found in less illustrious citizens. Regardless of their social stature, those with compartmentalized humility can be seen performing humble acts of religious devotion and public service on the one hand and exercising ruthless control over their subordinates and children on the other. The important point to remember here is that their subjective experience of both extremes is authentic and devoid of fakery. Thus, Gandhi could clean latrines and stay overnight in the poor abodes of India's "untouchables," but could also be "extremely dictatorial when dealing with his closest relatives or followers" (Kapoor, 2017, p. 117); when enraged, he could easily slap his wife. His humility, even though marked and genuine, was certainly compartmentalized.

Technical implications

As we begin to consider the role of humility in clinical work, we are immediately struck by a peculiar contradiction in our profession's attitude towards this matter. On the one hand, there exist numerous – in fact, too numerous to mention here – reminders in the literature on psychoanalytic technique that one ought to sustain an attitude of humility. On the other hand, none of these remarks explains what humility is and how exactly having this attitude might affect clinical technique. Dissatisfied with such unhelpful complacency and having given the matter serious thought, I have concluded that humility plays – or should play – an important role in the way we: (i) select the patients with whom we work, (ii) conduct ourselves vis-à-vis matters of daily life with our patients, (iii) listen to our patients, (iv) speak with our patients, and (v) decide about the longevity of our professional careers as psychoanalysts.

Humility in selecting patients

Before saying anything at all about this matter, it should be acknowledged that not all clinicians have the luxury of selecting who they work with. Young professionals who are just opening a private practice might therefore wince at my idea of "selecting" patients and even consider it a bit arrogant. I acknowledge that, with gaining some experience and after getting more or less established, one does acquire greater choice in what sort of individual one would take into treatment. However, upon closer scrutiny, the matter turns out to be less simple than this.

The widespread, even though unspoken, assumption that any psychoanalyst can help any patient is open to question. No one says this publicly but when analysts refer a patient to someone, they often select the colleague who will be "best" for that particular person.[5] In this choice is embedded the unmentalized belief that other analysts might not do so well by this patient and it will not be too far-fetched to assume that a few others might not be at all suitable for this particular referral. And this should not be surprising. After all, psychoanalysts have their own "pathos" and "ethos" just as does the patient and a reasonable "fit" between such interpersonal concavities and convexities is best for a decent therapeutic alliance to emerge. Of course, such "fit" must not become a nidus for "shared ethnic scotoma" (Shapiro & Pinsker, 1973), "nostalgia collusions" (Akhtar, 1999), and countertransference-based "deaf spots" (Akhtar, 2013b).

Let me put it bluntly. All of us do better work with certain kinds of patients than others. Whether the determining factor is diagnosis, age, race, religion, gender, social class, sociopolitical leanings, or something more elusive remains variable. Some psychoanalysts seem to work better with severely traumatized patients, others do not. Some can retain the same quality of empathy and efficiency with patients of diverse cultural backgrounds, others can not. A few have the knack of working with sociopathic individuals while most others get uneasy and avoid taking such patients into their practices. Some can work with older individuals. Others are better with children and adolescents.

Besides such patient-related variables, there are state and trait variables in psychoanalysts themselves that can and should affect patient selection. Here are a few questions to ponder upon:

- Should an analyst who is undergoing a bitter and contentious divorce take a new analytic patient, especially one with serious marital difficulties?
- Is it appropriate for an analyst over eighty years of age, no matter how physically healthy he or she is, to start a fresh analysis?
- Can a stridently atheistic psychoanalyst treat a deeply religious patient in a meaningful manner?

---

5 The highly respected British psychoanalyst, Nina Coltart (1927–1997) was known for her skill of finding the analyst who would be best suited for the needs of a given patient. This talent earned her the affectionate moniker of "The Matchmaker"!

The point I am trying to make is simply this: We psychoanalysts accept our characterological and situational limitations and exercise utmost humility in taking on patients. We delude ourselves if we hold on to the idea that we can treat anyone who shows up at our doors. The fact is that most of us cannot do so and will do great service to those seeking our counsel by sending them to others who might be better situated to help. A related consideration here is also of differential therapeutics. Being a psychoanalyst should not make one overlook that other treatment modalities (e.g., couples therapy, family therapy, medication, ECT) might, at times, be better for the individual sitting in our offices. Psychoanalysis is not the treatment for all emotional suffering and psychoanalysts are not the only useful mental health professionals.

Humility in our daily conduct with patients

Elsewhere, I have commented upon the need for the analyst to behave in accordance with "good manners" (Akhtar, 2011). I also entered some caveats to his doing so. Here, I wish to extend that discussion to the analyst conducting himself with humility. To be sure, judicious accommodations of the therapeutic frame to the patient's cultural idiom (Akhtar, 1999, 2011), adjustment of fee during periods of a patient's financial difficulties, respecting the patient's academic- or work-related absences, and other sundry "silent sacrifices" (David Sachs, personal communication, April 15, 2001) give evidence to the analyst's humility. However, there is something deeper at stake here.

It is by regarding the patient to be a full human being, capable of moral and, yes, therapeutic, reciprocity, and by discarding the view of the patient as infantile and unwanted, that the analyst shows true humility. Viewing both the patient and himself as "works in progress" and capable of further growth is yet another constituent of the analyst's humility. In elaborating upon such matters, Frank (2004) reminds us that the analyst, having been the beneficiary of a training analysis, carries within himself the "obligation of the cured" (p. 55) and this imparts tenderness and humility to his stance. Griffith (2010) evokes the writings of the Jewish philosopher, Emmanuel Levinas (1906–1995) who proposed that ethical relatedness to the Other is the foundation stone of the psychic self and requires the acceptance of difference. Erasing self-other distinction leads to totalization and sets the stage for domination and control. Commitment to dialogue, in contrast, endorses a relation to the Other while accepting the autonomy of both parties. No partner in a dialogue has all the answers and each can enrich the process between them.

While applicable to all clinical situations, this stance becomes even more important when a cultural chasm exists between the therapist and the patient. Here, a position of "cultural humility" (Tervalon & Murray-Garcia, 1998) is badly needed. It encourages the therapist to be open-minded, accept his ignorance of the patient's ethos, and learn from the patient. For instance, the therapist with cultural humility asks a culturally diverse patient how his or her name is pronounced, rather than making it up himself. It should be noted that the stance of "cultural humility" has the prerequisite of "cultural neutrality" (Akhtar, 1999, pp. 113–116). Cultural neutrality means that the therapist does not assume any particular culture to be inherently superior to another. Holding such a belief is in essence "anti-humanity and in the widest sense, anti-sanity" (Kareem, 1992, p. 21). It is only by sustaining cultural neutrality that the therapist can achieve a state of cultural humility.

Humility in the act and attitude of listening

Listening is in itself an act of humility. One can discern in it the remote echoes of an infant taking in the maternal breast and a near-archetypal identification with receptivity of the maternal vagina to the father's penis. Listening involves creating internal space for someone else. It is essentially an act of surrender and its servile dimension (if the expression can be used without any derogatory implications) becomes more marked when listening is done with "evenly suspended attention" (Freud, 1912e, p. 111). One does not exert personal choice and listens with equal consideration to all that is offered.

Resolute avoidance of listening in only one way (i.e., objective, subjective, empathic, and intersubjective; for elaboration on these models, see Akhtar, 2013b) and from only one theoretical perspective (e.g., Freudian, Kleinian, Winnicottian) is also evidence of an analyst's humility. To listen in only one way and from only a theoretical perspective narrows the analyst's receptive capacities and pushes him towards arrogance. He "knows" what the patient means. In an admittedly exaggerated fashion, I have portrayed the impact of such heuristic arrogance upon the analyst's listening.

> An "ego psychologist" sees only drive-defense sort of compromises in the patient's material. A "Kernbergian" sees idealization as a defense against regression and a "Kohutian" sees it as a resumption of a thwarted developmental need. A "Mahlerian" regards patients' fluctuating levels of intimacy as representing merger-abandonment anxieties while a "relationist" sees a craftily enacted scenario of mutual teasing and seduction in the same oscillation. A "Kleinian" views patients' hatred of the analyst's silence as an envious attack on a withholding breast while a "Winnicottian" views that very outrage as manifestation of hope (that the analyst can "survive" the patient's assault) and therefore of love!
>
> (Akhtar, 2013b, p. 107)

Such listening lacks humility. It declares that one theoretical perspective of psychoanalysis is inherently superior to others and is the preferred model for all sorts of clinical material and all varieties of patients. In contrast is the listening attitude of the analyst who is forever mindful of the "principle of multiple determination" (Waelder, 1936) and of the "four psychologies of psychoanalysis" (Pine, 1988), with their own respective claims upon the hermeneutics of the clinical exchange. The psychoanalyst who can oscillate between various levels of attunement (Killingmo, 1989), maintain allegiance to the existence of multiple determinants of all psychic material, and be comfortable with diverse theoretical models shows humility. Greater "analytic humility" might also be inherent in the current two-person, intersubjective perspective on listening provided it is not carried to an extreme.[6]

Humility in the manner of intervening

It is rare that a working analyst feels suddenly, sharply, and absolutely clear about what is going on between him and his patient, which aspect of it needs to be interpreted, and in what manner and to what extent. Such moments of uncanny clarity do occur (Bion, 1967, 1970; Brottman, 2011) but are infrequent and sporadic. Most of the time, the work of analysis involves patient listening, careful "collection" of data (within a single session or spanning many sessions), clarification, development of "conjectures" (Brenner, 1976) and then making interpretations or reconstructions. Throughout such work, an attitude of tentativeness is maintained. This attitude is mostly private and allows the analyst (on a preconscious or unconscious basis) to mull over the material, cross-check competing hypotheses, sort out countertransference, and "choose" the most suitable form and extent of the intervention to be made. At other times, the tentativeness might be shared with the patient. For instance, the analyst might say something like this: "You know, what you are saying seems like the very complaint that you have voiced, at other times, about your sister, and actually about me as well. What do you think? Does this make sense?" On another occasion, the analyst might "invite" the patient to consider his "still-not-so-clear-about-it" sort of interpretation. Thus, the analyst might say: "Allow me, please, to put a thought in front of you and see what you make of it. I am not sure about this but, behind this reserve of yours, I sense a deep anxiety about loving. Do you have any further thoughts about this?" Ehrenberg's (1995) recommendation of "inviting the patient to engage collaboratively" (p. 215) in the therapeutic exchange reflects this very spirit. At the same time, I am aware that some colleagues regard such manner of talking as "too didactic" and "Freudian pussy-footing" (as a senior Kleinian analyst once referred to it). I, for one, believe that maintaining such humility precludes the sort of certainty that we analysts can rarely possess. It also demonstrates to the patient an open and receptive attitude towards not only our interventions but towards his or her own therapeutic strivings.

A related measure pertains to the analyst's occasionally demystifying the basis for his interventions. The German analyst, Helmut Thomä, has written most cogently on this topic. He suggests that the analyst not only explain, at the outset, why free association is required but, from time to time during the treatment, share with the patient his reasons for making a particular intervention. Thomä states that "It is nothing special for me to offer a patient insight into my psychoanalysis thinking" (cited in Thomä & Kächele, 1994, p. 86). In fact, he feels that decisive

---

6 Kirman (1998) has provided a thorough review of the literature on this matter.

and salutary shifts in the relationship between transference and therapeutic alliance can occur as a result of such disclosure.

Yet another manifestation of humility in the analyst's manner of speaking is his persistent regard for the principles of "over-determination" (Freud with Breuer, 1895d) and "multiple function" (Waelder, 1936). The analyst makes interventions that are inclusive of psychic and external reality, of multiple vectors in psychic reality, and of his and the patient's take on the material under consideration. Moreover, the analyst remains open to correction by the patient, to seek consultation from colleagues when in difficulty, and to apologize to the patient (Goldberg, 1987) if he makes a "hurtful" mistake in his behavior or interventions.

Humility in deciding upon the longevity of our professional careers

A footnote I appended to my elucidation of greed (Akhtar, 2014), including analytic greed, read as follows:

> An analytic colleague and a good friend, Ira Brenner, told me that early on in his career, he marveled at senior analysts who kept working well into their eighties, and sometimes even in their nineties. With greater maturity, he has tempered this idealization and thinks that a combination of love of psychoanalysis, anxiety about aging, and greed for prestige and money drives such professional longevity (personal communication, November 6, 2013). This latter dynamic became especially apparent to me during a recent visit to a North American psychoanalytic institute where younger training analysts confided their dismay at their seniors' (who were far along in their eighties) grabbing all the attractive and well-paying applicants for training analyses.
>
> (p. 65)

This sad state of affairs came even closer to my own experience when an eighty-two-year-old colleague asked me to support his starting a new training analysis since his institute had raised objections to it. And, incredible though it might sound, more recently in a North American psychoanalytic institute, a ninety-two-year-old training analyst expressed his desire to take on a fresh candidate into treatment.

Clearly, such practices betray an alarming degree of arrogance. The denial of aging, increased potential for infirmity, and the proximity with one's own death[7] in such cases is truly disturbing. Even under the rationale and rationalization of continuing good health, continuing to take on new analytic patients beyond a certain age carries not only a kernel of arrogance but also of compromised ethics;

---

7 Upon hearing the subtitle of one of my edited books, *Fear, Denial, and Acceptance of Death*, a prominent analyst said, "Well, I don't accept death." It took me some effort to resist shooting back, "But death accepts you; in fact, it is going to get you."

after all, one is knowingly exposing the new patient to the potential of a devastating loss.

Fortunately, a trend is now evolving where matters of aging and death are deemed topics for serious consideration. Many training institutes are setting age limits after which analysts may not take on new cases in analysis. But this is externally imposed. What about the analyst's own humility in limiting his or her professional career? The now-deceased San Francisco-based analyst, Alan Skolnikoff (1933–2016) has been the only colleague to have told me, when he was seventy-one years old, that he has decided to stop taking new analytic cases upon turning seventy-three and to restrict his practice to teaching, supervision, and finishing ongoing cases. This, to my mind, was an expression of great humility. Skolnikoff died at the age of eighty-three but it is to be noted that he was considering ending his career as an analytic clinician some twelve years before his death. Instead of quibbling over this or that number of years as the upper limit for continuing to practice as an analyst, we – all of us – need to exercise a modicum of humility in making such decisions and not go on and on despite failing bodies and minds.

Concluding remarks

In this contribution, I have delineated the phenomenological terrain, ontogenetic roots, sociocultural dimensions, psychopathological variants, and technical implications of the concept of humility. I have noted that humility comprises modesty, self-effacement, regard for a higher power be it religious or secular, openness to fresh input, and a capacity for awe. Humility arises from infantile respect for parents' psychophysical stature, is strengthened by phallic-oedipal surrender to them, and is deepened by the latency age wonder at the mysteries of the world-at-large. Humility is upheld by all religions as a virtue. However, the purported East-West difference in the trait is less clear. What *is* clear is that humility exists in both normal and pathological (e.g., excessive, deficient, false, and compartmentalized) forms. The conduct of psychotherapy and psychoanalysis is affected by the analyst's humility in multiple ways outlined in the immediately preceding section of this chapter.

Two issues still remain to be addressed. One pertains to gender and the other to the unfolding of the human life span. Let us take up the first issue. Are men more humble than women? Or, vice versa? And, if a difference does exist, what might be its explanation? Averse to generalizations, psychoanalytic literature has no answers to these questions. Turning to general psychology research, we find two interesting studies. The first, asking 213 American, 229 British, and 114 Japanese students to assess their own IQ levels and those of their parents and siblings (Furnham, Hosoe, & Tang, 2001) revealed that, regardless of the country of origin, male students consistently noted their own, their fathers', and their brothers' IQs higher than those of their mothers and their sisters. This suggested a lack of humility in them as compared to their female counterparts who demonstrated no such bias in their assessments. A second study involving 202 Swedish students (Kajonius & Dåderman, 2014) found that the "honesty-humility" trait was strongly correlated with liberal values and was endorsed at a higher level by women (M=12.8, SD=3.4) than men (M=12.0, SD=3.7). Meager as research is in this area, it does suggest that on a "gross" level, at least, men are less humble than women.[8]

The second unaddressed realm pertains to life span. It involves the question whether humility is a trait that is discernible early on or, like Erikson's (1950) "generativity," makes its appearance only with mature adulthood? Little information is available to answer this question with certainty. However, it seems reasonable to assume that while the ingredients of humility (e.g., wonder, awe, gratitude) originate in childhood, its fully consolidated experience does not emerge till mid- to late adulthood. It is only after experiencing a sustained sense of commonality with fellow human beings, the puncture of omnipotence in the process of child-rearing, and repeated encounter with limits and failures, that humility sets in. Aging and infirmity also affect one's value system and mobilize a reassessment of one's place in this world; this enhances the capacity for humility. The acknowledgement and acceptance of one's approaching mortality acts as an even stronger stimulus for realizing the small space that one ultimately has occupied in this world. If one can bear this realization, one becomes truly humble. If not, one regresses into defensive omnipotence and conceit.

Talking of infirmity and old age and their relationship to the arrogance-humility dialectic brings to mind the following joke told to me by my friend, the noted historian, Norman Itzkowitz (personal communication, April 21, 2003).

A highly-respected teacher of Torah, Rabbi Goldstein, had turned ninety-three and was now quite frail. One day, while instructing three students who sat in great awe of him, the Rabbi fell asleep. Not daring to disturb him, the students spoke to each other in hushed whispers. One said: "I respect Rabbi Goldstein for his immense knowledge of the Torah." The second student said: "I agree with you but respect him more for how he imparts that knowledge to others." The third expressed his agreement with both of them and added that he respects the Rabbi even more for his living a life that is true to the Scriptures. At this time, Rabbi Goldstein opened one of his eyes, looked with bemused dismay at his three protégés, and said: "And, not a word about my humility?"

---

8 It is worth noting that colloquial references to arrogance often invoke that most-prized part of the male anatomy: the penis. Thus, an arrogant person is called "cocky," "dick-head," "prick," and so on.

References

Akhtar, S. (1988). Hypomanic personality disorder. *Integrative Psychiatry*, *6*: 37–52.

Akhtar, S. (1989). Narcissistic personality disorder. *Psychiatric Clinics of North America*, *12*: 505–529.

Akhtar, S. (1990). Paranoid personality disorder: a synthesis of developmental, dynamic, and descriptive features. *American Journal of Psychotherapy*, *44*: 5–25.

Akhtar, S. (1992). *Broken Structures: Severe Personality Disorders and Their Treatment*. Northvale, NJ: Jason Aronson.

Akhtar, S. (1998). From simplicity through contradiction to paradox: the evolving psychic reality of the borderline patient in treatment. *International Journal of Psychoanalysis*, *79*: 241–252.

Akhtar, S. (1999). *Immigration and Identity: Turmoil, Treatment, and Transformation*. Northvale, NJ: Jason Aronson.

Akhtar, S. (2000). The shy narcissist. In: J. Sandler, R. Michels, & P. Fonagy (Eds.), *Changing Ideas in a Changing World: Essays in Honor of Arnold Cooper* (pp. 111–119). London: Karnac.

Akhtar, S. (2002). Forgiveness: origins, dynamics, psychopathology, and clinical relevance. *Psychoanalytic Quarterly*, *71*: 175–212.

Akhtar, S. (2003). Things: developmental, psychopathological, and technical aspects of inanimate objects. *Canadian Journal of Psychoanalysis*, *11*: 1–44.

Akhtar, S. (2007). From unmentalized xenophobia to Messianic sadism: some reflections on the phenomenology of prejudice. In: H. Parens, A. Mahfouz, S. Twemlow, and D. Scharff (Eds.), *The Future of Prejudice: Psychoanalysis and the Prevention of Prejudice* (pp. 7–21). Lanham, MD: Jason Aronson.

Akhtar, S. (2009a). *Comprehensive Dictionary of Psychoanalysis*. London: Karnac.

Akhtar, S. (2009b). Narcissism. In: *Comprehensive Dictionary of Psychoanalysis* (p. 179). London: Karnac.

Akhtar, S. (2011). *Immigration and Acculturation: Mourning, Adaptation, and the Next Generation*. Lanham, MD: Jason Aronson.

Akhtar, S. (2012). *Good Stuff: Generosity, Resilience, Humility, Gratitude, Forgiveness, and Sacrifice*. Lanham, MD: Jason Aronson.

Akhtar, S. (2013a). Psychoanalysis and culture: Freud, Erikson, and beyond. In: A. Gerlach, M.-T. Hooke, & S. Varvin (Eds.), *Psychoanalysis in Asia: China, India, Japan, South Korea, and Taiwan* (pp. 19–42). London: Karnac.

Akhtar, S. (2013b). *Psychoanalytic Listening: Methods, Limits, and Innovations*. London: Karnac.

Akhtar, S. (2014). Meanings, manifestations, and management of greed. In: S. Akhtar (Ed.), *Sources of Suffering: Fear, Greed, Guilt, Deception, Betrayal, and Revenge* (pp. 131–158). London: Karnac.

Akhtar, S. (2015). Some psychoanalytic reflections on the concept of dignity. *American Journal of Psychoanalysis, 75*: 244–266.

Alhanati, S. (2006). Arrogance. In: R. Skelton (Ed.), *The Edinburgh International Encyclopedia of Psychoanalysis*. Edinburgh, UK: Edinburgh University Press.

Altman, L. (1977). Some vicissitudes of love. *Journal of the American Psychoanalytic Association, 25*: 35–52.

Anderson, C., Bryon, S., Moore, D. A., & Kennedy, J. A. (2012). A status-enhancement account of overconfidence. *Journal of Personality and Social Psychology, 103*: 718–735.

Aristotle (c. 350 BC). *Nicomachean Ethics*. R. C. Bartlett & S. D. Collins (Trans.). Chicago, IL: University of Chicago Press, 2011.

Aristotle (c. 335 BC). *Poetics*. Ann Arbor, MI: University of Michigan Press, 1970.

Arlow, J. (1980). The revenge motive in the primal scene. *Journal of the American Psychoanalytic Association, 28*: 519–541.

Aron, L., & Starr, K. (2013). *A Psychotherapy for the People: Toward a Progressive Psychoanalysis*. New York: Routledge.

Arvanitakis, K. I. (1998). Some thoughts on the essence of the tragic. *International Journal of Psychoanalysis, 79*: 955–964.

Auchincloss, E. L., & Samberg, E. (Eds.) (2012). Narcissism. In: *Psychoanalytic Terms & Concepts* (pp. 162–165). New Haven, CT: Yale University Press.

Bach, S. (1977). On the narcissistic state of consciousness. *International Journal of Psychoanalysis, 58*: 209–233.

Backwell, P. R. Y., Christy, J. H., Telford, S. R., Jennions, M. D., & Passmore, N. I. (2000). Dishonest signaling in a fiddler crab. *Procedures of the Royal Society of London, 297*: 719–724.

Banker, A. (2006). *Prince at War: Part Three of the Ramayana Series*. New Delhi: Viking.

Barber, B. M., & Odean, T. (2001). Boys will be boys: gender, overconfidence, and common stock investment. *Quarterly Journal of Economics, 116*: 261–292.

Becker, T. (1974). On latency. *Psychoanalytic Study of the Child, 29*: 3–11.

Beckett, S. (1946). *First Love and Other Novellas*. London: Penguin, 2000.

Ben-Ze'ev, A. (1993). The virtue of modesty. *American Philosophical Quarterly, 30*: 235–246.

Bible, The. *King James Version*.

Bion, W. R. (1958). On arrogance. *International Journal of Psychoanalysis, 39*: 144–146.

Bion, W. R. (1959). Attacks on linking. *International Journal of Psychoanalysis, 40*: 308–315.

Bion, W.R. (1965). *Transformations*. London: Karnac Books, 1984.

Bion, W. R. (1967a). *Second Thoughts*. London: Heinemann.

Bion, W. R. (1967b). On arrogance. In: *Second Thoughts: Selected Papers on Psychoanalysis*. Northvale, NJ: Jason Aronson, 1993.

Bion, W. R. (1970). *Attention and Interpretation*. London: Karnac, 1984.

Bion, W. R. (1992). *Cogitations*. London: Karnac.

Blackman, J. (1987). Character traits underlying self-neglect and their connection with heart disease. *Journal of the Louisiana State Medical Society, 139*: 31–34.

Blackman, J. (2003a). *101 Defenses: How the Mind Shields Itself.* New York: Routledge.

Blackman, J. (2003b). Dynamic supervision concerning a patient's request for medication. *Psychoanalytic Quarterly, 72*: 469–475.

Blackman, J. (2011). Defense mechanisms in the 21st century. *Synergy*, *16*: 1–7.

Blackman, J. (2013). *The Therapist's Answer Book: Solutions to 101 Tricky Problems in Psychotherapy*. New York: Routledge.

Blake, W. (1794). Tyger. In: *Songs of Innocence and of Experience: Shewing the Two Contrary States of the Human Soul* (p. 23). New York: CreateSpace Independent Publishing Platform, 2011.

Blatt, S. (1974). Levels of object representation in anaclitic and introjective depression. *Psychoanalytic Study of the Child*, *29*: 107–157.

Blos, P. (1965). *On Adolescence: A Psychoanalytic Interpretation*. New York: Free Press.

Blum, H. (2010). Adolescent trauma and the Oedipus complex. *Psychoanalytic Inquiry*, *30*: 548–556.

Boesky, D. (1983). Resistance and character theory: a reconsideration of the concept of character resistance. *Journal of the American Psychoanalytic Association*, *31S*: 227–246.

Bollas, C. (1992). *Being a Character: Psychoanalysis and Self-Experience*. New York: Hill & Wang.

Bollas, C. (2009). *The Evocative Object World*. London: Routledge.

Bowlby, J. (1969). *Attachment and Loss, Vol. 1*. New York: Basic Books.

Bowlby, J. (1973*). Attachment and Loss, Vol. 2*. New York: Basic Books.

Bowlby, J. (1980). *Attachment and Loss, Vol. 3*. New York: Basic Books.

Brenner, C. (1955). *An Elementary Textbook of Psychoanalysis*. New York: Random House, 1974.

Brenner, C. (1975). Alterations in defenses during psychoanalysis. In: B. D. Fine & H. F. Waldhorn (Eds.), *Monograph VI of the Series of the Kris Study Group of the New York Psychoanalytic Institute* (pp. 1–22). New York: International Universities Press.

Brenner, C. (1976). *Psychoanalytic Technique and Psychic Conflict*. New York: International Universities Press.

Brenner, C. (1982). *The Mind in Conflict*. New York: International Universities Press.

Brenner, C. (2006). *Psychoanalysis: Mind and Meaning*. New York: Psychoanalytic Quarterly Press.

Briskin, A. (2009). *The Power of Collective Wisdom*. Frankfurt, Germany: Berrett-Koehler.

Britton, R. (2013). Commentary on three papers by Wilfred R. Bion. *Psychoanalytic Quarterly*, *82*: 311–321.

Britton, R., & Steiner, J. (1994). Interpretation: selected fact or overvalued idea? *International Journal of Psychoanalysis*, *75*: 1069–1078.

Bromberg, P. M. (1983). The mirror and the mask – on narcissism and psychoanalytic growth. *Contemporary Psychoanalysis*, *19*: 359–387.

Bromberg, P. M. (2011). *The Shadow of the Tsunami and the Growth of the Relational Mind*. New York: Routledge.

Brottman, M. (2011). *Phantoms of the Clinic: From Thought-Transference to Projective Identification*. London: Karnac.

Broucek, F. J. (1982). Shame and its relationship to early narcissistic developments. *International Journal of Psychoanalysis*, *63*: 369–378.

Bursten, B. (1986). Some narcissistic personality types. In: A. P. Morrison (Ed.), *Essential Papers on Narcissism*. New York: New York University Press.

Buss, D. (1989). Sex differences in human mate preferences: Evolutionary hypotheses tested in 37 cultures, *Behavioral and Brain Sciences*, *12*: 1–49.

Buss, D. (2004). *Evolutionary Psychology: The New Science of the Mind (2nd edn.)*. Boston, MA: Pearson Education.

Byrnes, J. P., Miller, D. C., & Schafer, W. D. (1999). Gender differences in risk taking: a meta-analysis. *Psychological Bulletin, 125*(3): 367–383.

Cai, H., Sedikides, C., Gaertner, L., Wang, C., Carvallos, M., Xu, Y., O'Mara, E., & Jackson, L. (2011). Tactical self-enhancement in China: is modesty at the service of self-enhancement in East Asian cultures? *Social Psychological and Personality Science, 2*: 59–64.

Cao, L., Blackman, J., & Guan, E. (2016). Societal change and language change in China: language-switching during multilingual dynamic psychotherapy. *Psychoanalytic Psychology*. Prepublication internet version.

Casement, A. (1991). *Learning from the Patient*. New York: Guilford.

Casement, P. (2002). *Learning from Our Mistakes: Beyond Dogma in Psychoanalysis and Psychotherapy*. New York: Guilford.

Celenza, A. (2007). *Sexual Boundary Violations: Therapeutic, Supervisory, and Academic Contexts*. Lanham, MD: Jason Aronson.

Celenza, A., & Gabbard, G. O. (2003). Analysts who commit sexual boundary violations: a lost cause? *Journal of the American Psychoanalytic Association, 51*: 617–636.

Chamorro-Premuzic, T. (2013). Why do so many incompetent men become leaders? *Harvard Business Review*, August 22. Retrieved from https://hbr.org/2013/08/why-do-so-many-incompetent-men, September 9, 2017.

Charness, G., Rustichini, A., & van de Ven, J. (2013). Self-confidence and strategic behavior. CESifo Working Paper, No. 4517. https://www.cesifo-group.de. Accessed March 13, 2017.

Chasseguet-Smirgel, J. (1984). *Creativity and Perversion*. New York: W. W. Norton.

Chen, E. M. (1989). *The Te Tao Ching: A New Translation with Commentary*. New York: Paragon House.

Chessick, R. (1989). The two-woman phenomenon revisited. *Journal of the American Academy of Psychoanalysis, 17*: 293–304.

Clark, L. P. (1932). Can child analysis prevent neuroses and psychoses in later life? *Psychoanalytic Review, 19*: 46–55.

Cleckley, H. (1941). *The Mask of Sanity: An Attempt to Reinterpret the So-called Psychopathic Personality*. St Louis, MO: C. V. Mosby.

Coen, S. (1981). Sexualization as a predominant mode of defense. *Journal of the American Psychoanalytic Association, 29*: 893–920.

Coltart, N. (1985). The practice of psychoanalysis and Buddhism. In: *Slouching Towards Bethlehem . . . and Further Psychoanalytic Explorations* (pp. 164–175). New York: Other Press.

Coltart, N. (1996). Buddhism and psychoanalysis revisited. In: *The Baby and the Bathwater* (pp. 125–139). London: Karnac.

Coltrera, J. (1979). Truth from genetic illusion: the transference and the fate of the infantile neurosis. *Journal of the American Psychoanalytic Association, 27S*: 289–313.

Cooper, S. H. (2010). Self-criticism and unconscious grandiosity: transference-countertransference dimensions. *International Journal of Psychoanalysis, 91*: 1115–1136.

Cooper, S. H. (2011). *A Disturbance in the Field: Essays in Transference-Countertransference Engagement*. New York: Routledge.

Cooper, S. H. (2016). *The Analyst's Experience of the Depressive Position: the Melancholic Errand of Psychoanalysis*. New York: Routledge.

Cosmides, L., & Tooby, J. (1992). Cognitive adaptations for social exchanges. In: J. Barkow, L. Cosmides, & J. Tooby (Eds.), *The Adapted Mind* (pp. 601–624). New York: Oxford University Press.

Cosmides, L., & Tooby, J. (2013). Evolutionary psychology: new perspectives on cognition and motivation. *Annual Review of Psychology, 64*: 201–229.

Cunningham, M., Druen, P., & Barbee, A. (1997). Angels, mentors, and friends: trade-offs among evolutionary, social, and individual variables in physical appearance. In: J. A. Simpson & D. T. Kendrick (Eds.), *Evolutionary Social Psychology* (pp. 109–140). Hillsdale, NJ: Lawrence Erlbaum.

Cushman, P. (2005). Between arrogance and a dead-end: psychoanalysis and the Heidegger-Foucault dilemma. *Contemporary Psychoanalysis, 41*: 399–417.

Darwin. C. R (1845). *Journal of Researches into the Natural History and Geology of the Various Countries Visited during the Voyage of* H.M.S. Beagle *Round the World, under the Command of Capt. FitzRoy, R.N., 2nd Edition*. London: John Murray.

Davies, M. W., Nandy, A., & Sardar, Z. (1993). *Barbaric Others: A Manifesto on Western Racism*. London: Pluto.

Dawkins, R. (1986). *The Blind Watchmaker*. New York: W. W. Norton.

Dawkins, R. (1989). *The Selfish Gene*. Oxford: Oxford University Press.

Dawkins, R. (1998). *Unweaving the Rainbow: Science, Delusion and the Appetite for Wonder*. New York: Houghton Mifflin.

Dawkins, R. (2000). Foreword in J. M. Smith, *The Theory of Evolution*. Cambridge: Cambridge University Press.

De Beauvoir, S. (1949). *The Second Sex*. New York: Vintage, 2009.

De Sade, le Marquis (1791). *The Complete Justine, Philosophy in the Bedroom, and Other Writings*. New York: Grove, 1990.

Dean, T., & Lane, C. (2001). Homosexuality and psychoanalysis: an introduction. In: T. Dean & C. Lane (Eds.), *Homosexuality and Psychoanalysis* (pp. 3–43). Chicago, IL: University of Chicago Press.

Dennett, D. (2009). Darwin's strange inversion of reasoning In: J. C. Avise & F. J. Ayala (Eds.), *The Light of Evolution, Volume III: Two Centuries of Darwin* (pp. 343–414). Washington, DC: National Academies Press.

Diagnostic and Statistical Manual of Mental Disorders, 4th Edition (2006). Washington, DC: American Psychiatric Publishing.

Dillon, R. S. (2004). Kant on arrogance and self-respect. In: C. Calhoun (Ed.), *Setting the Moral Compass: Essays by Women Philosophers (Studies in Feminist Philosophy)* (pp. 191–216). New York: Oxford University Press.

Dillon, R. S. (2017). On arrogance. Lehigh University, Department of Philosophy website, *philosophy.cas2.lehigh.edu/content/robin-dillon-arrogance*. Retrieved May 30, 2017.

Doi, T. (1962). Amae: a key concept for understanding Japanese personality structure. In: R. J. Smith & R. K. Beardsley (Eds.), *Japanese Culture: Its Development and Characteristics* (pp. 121–129). Chicago, IL: Aldine.

Dorpat, T. (1999). Inauthentic communication and the false self. *Psychoanalytic Review, 86*: 209–222.

Ehrenberg, D. (1995). Self-disclosure: therapeutic tool or indulgence? *Contemporary Psychoanalysis, 31*: 213–228.

Ellison, R. (1952). *Invisible Man*. New York: Signet.

Epstein, M. (1995). Thoughts without a thinker – Buddhism and psychoanalysis. *Psychoanalytic Review, 92*: 291–406.

Erikson, E. (1950). *Childhood and Society*. New York: W.W. Norton.

Fairbairn, W. R. D. (1940). Schizoid factors in the personality. In: *An Object Relations Theory of Personality* (pp. 3–27). New York: Basic Books, 1952.

Feldman, A. B. (1953). The confessions of William Shakespeare. *American Imago*, *10*: 113–166.

Fenichel, O. (1945). *The Psychoanalytic Theory of Neurosis*. New York: W. W. Norton.

Ferenczi, S. (1913). Stages in the development of the sense of reality. In: E. Jones (Trans.), *Contributions to Psychoanalysis* (pp. 213–239). New York: Basic Books, 1950.

Fieg, J.P., & Mortlock, E. (1989). *A Common Core: Thais and Americans*. Yarmouth, ME: Intercultural Press Inc.

Foucault, M. (1985). *The History of Sexuality: Volume 2, The Use of Pleasure*. New York: Pantheon.

Foucault, M. (1986). *The History of Sexuality: Volume 3, The Care of the Self*. New York: Pantheon.

Fraiberg, S. (1959). *The Magic Years*. New York: Simon & Schuster.

Frank, A.W. (2004). *The Renewal of Generosity: Illness, Medicine, and How to Live*. Chicago, IL: University of Chicago Press.

Freeman, D. (1997). Emotional refueling in development, mythology, and cosmology: the Japanese separation-individuation experience. In: S. Akhtar & S. Kramer (Eds.), *The Colors of Childhood* (pp. 17–60). New York: Jason Aronson.

Freud, S. (1917). A difficulty in the path of psychoanalysis. *Standard Edition* 17: 137–144.

Freud, A. (1936). *The Ego and the Mechanisms of Defence*. Madison, CT: International Universities Press, 1970.

Freud, S. (1893). Case 2 – Frau Emmy von N. In: *Studies on Hysteria. S. E.*, *2*: 48–105. London: Hogarth.

Freud, S. (1895d). Studies on hysteria. *S. E.*, *2*: 1–323. London: Hogarth.

Freud, S. (1897). Extracts from the Fliess Papers: Letter 57. *S. E.*, *1*: 242–244. London: Hogarth.

Freud, S. (1905d). Three essays on the theory of sexuality. *S. E.*, *7*: 135–243. London: Hogarth.

Freud, S. (1910a). Five lectures on psycho-analysis. *S. E.*, *11*: 9–55. London: Hogarth.

Freud, S. (1910c). Leonardo da Vinci and a memory of his childhood. *S. E.*, *11*: 63–138. London: Hogarth.

Freud, S. (1912e). Recommendations to physicians practising psycho-analysis. *S. E.*, *12*. London: Hogarth.

Freud, S. (1912–13). Totem and taboo. *S. E.*, *13*: 1–161. London: Hogarth.

Freud, S. (1914c). On narcissism: an introduction. *S. E.*, *14*: 69–102. London: Hogarth.

Freud, S. (1915c). Instincts and their vicissitudes. *S. E.*, *14*: 117–140. London: Hogarth.

Freud, S. (1916). Introductory lectures on psycho-analysis. *S. E.*, *15*: 3–239. London: Hogarth.

Freud, S. (1917). Introductory lectures on psycho-analysis. *S. E.*, *16*: 243–463. London: Hogarth.

Freud, S. (1920a). The psychogenesis of a case of female homosexuality. *S. E.*, *18*: 145–172. London: Hogarth.

Freud, S. (1921c). *S. E.*, *18*: 65–144. London: Hogarth.

Freud, S. (1923b). The ego and the Id. *S. E.*, *19*: 1–66. London: Hogarth.

Freud, S. (1924d). The dissolution of the Oedipus complex. *S. E.*, *19*: 171–188. London: Hogarth.

Freud, S. (1926d). Inhibitions, symptoms and anxiety. *S. E.*, *20*: 75–175. London: Hogarth.

Freud, S. (1927c). The future of an illusion. *S. E.*, *21*. London: Hogarth.

Freud, S. (1930a). Civilization and its discontents. *S. E.*, *21*: 64–145. London: Hogarth.

Freud, S. (1939a). Moses and monotheism. *S. E.*, *23*: 7–137. London: Hogarth.

Freud, S. (1940a). An outline of psycho-analysis. *S. E., 23*. London: Hogarth.

Friedman, M., & Rosenman, R. (1959). Association of specific overt behavior pattern with blood and cardiovascular findings. *Journal of the American Medical Association, 169*: 1286–1296.

Friedman, T. L. (2017). Where did "We the people" go? *The New York Times*, June 21. www.nytimes.com/2017/06/21/opinion/. Accessed July 21, 2017.

Furey, R. J. (1986). *So I'm Not Perfect: A Psychology of Humility*. New York: Alba House.

Furnham, A., Hosoe, T., & Tang, T. (2001). Male hubris and female humility? A cross-cultural study of ratings of self, parental and sibling multiple intelligence in America, Britain and Japan. *Intelligence, 30*: 101–115.

Gandhi, M. K. (1940). *An Autobiography: The Story of My Experiments with Truth*. M. Desai (Trans.). Boston, MA: Beacon, 1957.

Gandhi, M. K. (1925). *My Experiments with Truth*. Navajivan, India: Ahemdabad.

Ghalib, A. U. K. (1841). *Diwan-e-Ghalib*. New Delhi: Maktaba Jamia, 1965.

Ghent, E. (1990). Masochism, submission, surrender: masochism as a perversion of surrender. *Contemporary Psychoanalysis, 26*: 108–136.

Gibbs. A., Grey, J., & Wood, L. (1922). *Running Wild*. New York: Good Old Timers, Columbia Music.

Gneezy, U., Leonard, K. L., & List, J. L. (2009). Gender differences in competition: evidence from a matrilineal and patriarchal society. *Econometrica, 77*: 1637–1664.

Goldberg, A. (1987). The place of apology in psychoanalysis and psychotherapy. *International Review of Psycho-Analysis, 14*: 409–422.

Goldberg, A. (2012). *The Analysis of Failure: An Investigation of Failed Cases in Psychoanalysis and Psychotherapy*. New York: Routledge.

Goldman, R. P. (1978). Fathers, sons and gurus: Oedipal conflict in the Sanskrit epics. *Journal of Indian Philosophy, 6*: 325–392.

Green, A. (1986). Moral narcissism. In: *On Private Madness* (pp. 115–141). New Haven, CT: International Universities Press.

Greenacre, P. (1956). Experience of awe in childhood. *Psychoanalytic Study of the Child, 11*: 9–30.

Greenson, R. (1965). The working alliance and the transference neurosis. *Psychoanalytic Quarterly, 34*: 155–181.

Griffith, J.L. (2010). *Religion that Heals, Religion that Harms*. New York: Gilford Press.

Griffiths, R. T. H. (1895). *The Ramayana of Valmiki*. Benares, India: E. J. Lazarus.

Grijalva, E., Newman, D. A, Tay, L., Donnellan, M. B., Harms, P. D., Robins, R. W., & Yan, T. (2015). Gender differences in narcissism: a meta-analytic review. *Psychological Bulletin, 141*: 261–310.

Grosskurth, P. (1991). *The Secret Ring: Freud's Inner Circle and the Politics of Psychoanalysis*. Boston, MA: Da Capo.

Grotstein, J. S. (1997). Integrating one-person and two-person psychologies: autochthony and alterity in counterpoint. *Psychoanalytic Quarterly, 66*: 403–430.

Grotstein, J. S. (2007). *An Intense Beam of Darkness: Wilfred Bion's Legacy to Psychoanalysis*. London: Karnac.

Guttman, S. A., Jones, R. L., & Parrish, S. M. (Eds.) (1980). *The Concordance to the Standard Edition of the Complete Psychological Works of Sigmund Freud*. Boston, MA: G. K. Hall.

Hareli, S., & Weiner, B. (2000). Accounts for success as determinants of perceived arrogance and modesty. *Motivation and Emotion, 24*: 215–236.

Haynal, A. (1988). *The Technique at Issue: Controversies in Psychoanalysis from Freud and Ferenczi to Michael Balint*. E. Holder (Trans.). London: Karnac.

Hedges, L. (1983). *Listening Perspectives in Psychotherapy*. Northvale, NJ: Jason Aronson.

Heidegger, M. (1953a). *Introduction to Metaphysics*. R. Manheim (Trans.). New Haven, CT: Yale University Press, 2014.

Heidegger, M. (1953b). *Being and Time*. J. Stambaugh (Trans.). Albany, NY: State University of New York Press, 2010.

Heidegger, M. (1954). *What Is Called Thinking?*. J. G. Gray (Trans.). New York: Harper & Row, 1968.

Heine, S., Lehman, D. R., Markus, H. R., & Kitayama, S. (1999). Is there a universal need for positive self-regard? *Psychological Review, 106*: 766–794.

Herzog, J. M. (2004). Father hunger and narcissistic deformation. *Psychoanalytic Quarterly, 73*: 893–914.

Hitchens, C. (2007). *God Is Not Great: How Religion Poisons Everything*. New York: Twelve.

Hoffer, A. (Ed.) (2015). *Freud and the Buddha: The Couch and the Cushion*. London: Karnac.

Hofstede, G. (1984). *Culture's Consequences: International Differences in Work-Related Values (Cross Cultural Research and Methodology)*. Thousand Oaks, CA: Sage.

Hofstede, G. (2001). *Culture's Consequences: Comparing Values, Behaviors, Institutions and Organizations across Nations, 2nd Edition*. Thousand Oaks, CA: Sage.

Hofstede, G., & Hofstede, G. J. (2010). *Cultures and Organizations: Software of the Mind*. New York: McGraw-Hill.

Homer (c. 500 BC). To Aphrodite. In: *Homeric Hymns*. Houston, TX: University of Houston Press. http://www.uh.edu/~cldue/texts/aphrodite.html. Translated and revised by G. Nagy, 2001. Accessed October 9, 2017.

Horney, K. (1945). *Our Inner Conflicts*. New York: W. W. Norton.

Horney, K. (1947). Maturity and the individual. *American Journal of Psychoanalysis, 7*: 85–87.

Horney, K. (1950). *Neurosis and Human Growth*. New York: W. W. Norton.

Hotchkiss, S. (2002). *Why Is it Always About You?: The Seven Deadly Sins of Narcissism*. New York: Free Press.

Howland, J., Hingson, R., Mangione, T. W., Bell, N., & Bak, S. (1996). Why are most drowning victims men? Sex differences in aquatic skills and behavior. *American Journal of Public Health, 86*: 93–96.

Huang, J., & Kisgen, D. J. (2013). Gender and corporate finance: are male executives overconfident relative to female executives? *Journal of Financial Economics, 108*: 822–839.

Ivimey, M. (1945). The meaning of transference. *International Journal of Psychoanalysis, 5*: 3–15.

Johnson, A., & Szurek, S. (1952). The genesis of antisocial acting out in children and adults. *Psychoanalytic Quarterly, 21*: 323–343.

Johnson, D. D. P., & Fowler, J. H. (2011). The evolution of overconfidence. *Nature, 477*: 317–320.

Jones, J. (1980). *On Aristotle and Greek Tragedy*. Palo Alto, CA: Stanford University Press.

Joseph, B. (1988). The patient who's difficult to reach. In: *Psychic Equilibrium and Psychic Change: Selected Papers of Betty Joseph* (pp. 75–87). London: Routledge, 1989.

Kajonius, P. J., & Dåderman, A. M. (2014). Exploring the relationship between honesty-humility, the big five, and liberal values in Swedish students. *Europe's Journal of Psychology*, *10*: 104–117.

Kakar, S. (2007). *Indian Identity.* New Delhi: Penguin.

Kant, I. (1797). *The Metaphysics of Morals.* Cambridge: Cambridge University Press, 1996.

Kapoor, P. (2017). *Gandhi: An Illustrated Biography.* New York: Black Dog and Leventhal.

Kareem, J. (1992). The Nafsiyat Intercultural Therapy Centre: ideas and experience in intercultural therapy. In: J. Kareem & R. Littlewood (Eds.), *Intercultural Therapy: Themes, Interpretations, and Practice* (pp. 14–37). London: Blackwell Scientific.

Keats, J. (1899). *The Complete Works and Letters of John Keats, Cambridge Edition.* Boston, MA: Houghton Mifflin, 1974.

Kennedy, J. A., Anderson, C., & Moore, D. A. (2013). When overconfidence is revealed to others: Testing the status-enhancement theory of overconfidence. *Organizational Behavior and Human Decision Processes*, *122*(2): 266–279.

Kernberg, O. F. (1975). *Borderline Conditions and Pathological Narcissism.* New York: Jason Aronson.

Kernberg, O. F. (1984). *Severe Personality Disorders: Psychotherapeutic Strategies.* New Haven, CT: Yale University Press.

Kernberg, O. F. (1992). *Aggression in Personality Disorders and Perversions.* New Haven, CT: Yale University Press.

Kernberg, O. F. (1994). Abnormal narcissism in middle-age. In: *Internal World and External Reality* (pp. 121–134). Northvale, NJ: Jason Aronson.

Kernberg, O. F. (2007). The almost untreatable narcissistic patient. *Journal of the American Psychoanalytic Association*, *55*: 503–539.

Kernberg, O. F., & Michels, R. (2016). Thoughts on the present and future of psychoanalytic education. *Journal of the American Psychoanalytic Association*, *64*: 385–407.

Khan, M. M. R. (1963). The concept of cumulative trauma. *Psychoanalytic Study of the Child*, *18*: 286–306.

Killingmo, B. (1989). Conflict and deficit: implications for technique. *International Journal of Psychoanalysis*, *70*: 65–79.

Kim, Y. H., & Cohen, D. (2010). Information, perspective, and judgements about the self in "face" and "dignity" cultures. *Personality and Social Psychology Bulletin*, *36*: 537–550.

Kirman, J. H. (1998). One-person or two-person psychology? *Modern Psychoanalysis*, *23*: 3–22.

Kirsch, J. (2004). *God against the Gods: The History of the War between Monotheism and Polytheism.* New York: Penguin Compass.

Klein, M. (1940). Mourning and its relation to manic depressive states. In: *Love, Guilt and Reparation and Other Works – 1921–1945* (pp. 344–369). New York: Free Press, 1975.

Klein, M. (1957). Envy and gratitude. In: *Envy and Gratitude and Other Works – 1946–1963* (pp. 176–235). New York: Free Press, 1975.

Klein, M. (1963). Some reflections on The Oresteia. In: *Envy and Gratitude and Other Works – 1946–1963* (pp. 275–299). London: Hogarth, 1975.

Kohut, H. (1971). *The Analysis of the Self: A Systematic Approach to the Psychoanalytic Treatment of Narcissistic Personality Disorders.* Chicago, IL: University of Chicago Press, 2013.

Kristof, N. D. (1996). For rural Japanese, death does not break family ties: dead but not gone. *The New York Times*, September 29, p. 1.

Kudoh, T., & Matsumoto, D. (1985). Cross-cultural examination of the semantic dimensions of body postures. *Personality and Social Psychology*, *48*: 1440–1446.

Lailvaux, S. P., Reaney, L. T., & Backwell, P. R. Y. (2008). Dishonest signaling of fighting ability and multiple performance traits in the fiddler crab *uca mjoebergi. Functional Ecology, 23*: 359–366.

Lamba, S., & Nityananda, V. (2014). Self-deceived individuals are better at deceiving others. *PLoS ONE, 9*(8): e104562.

Langs, R. (1978). The adaptational-interactional dimension of countertransference. *Contemporary Psychoanalysis, 14*: 502–533.

Lasch, C. (1979). *The Culture of Narcissism: American Life in an Age of Diminishing Expectations.* New York: W. W. Norton, 1991.

Leary, K. (2007). On the face of it – difference and sameness in psychoanalysis. *Contemporary Psychoanalysis, 43*: 469–473.

Lee, H. I., Leung, A. K., & Kim, Y. H. (2014). Unpacking East-West differences in the extent of self-enhancement from the perspective of face versus dignity culture. *Social and Personality Psychology Compass, 8*: 314–327.

Lee, R. B. (2012). *The Dobe Ju/'Hoansi.* Boston, MA: Cengage Learning.

Lewis, C. S. (1942). *The Screwtape Letters.* New York: HarperCollins.

Levin, S. (1969). A common type of marital incompatibility. *Journal of the American Psychoanalytic Association, 17*: 421–436.

Levine, S. (2016). *Dignity Matters.* London: Karnac Books.

Llosa, M. V. (2015). *Notes on the Death of Culture.* New York: Farrar, Straus & Giroux.

Lunbeck, E. (2014). *The Americanization of Narcissism.* Cambridge, MA: Harvard University Press.

Mahler, M. S. (1968). *On Human Symbiosis and the Vicissitudes of Individuation.* New York: International Universities Press.

Mahler, M.S., Pine, F., & Bergman, A. (1975). *The Psychological Birth of the Human Infant.* New York: Basic Books.

Marcovitz, E. (1966). Dignity. In: *Bemoaning the Dream: Collected Papers of Eli Marcovitz, M.D.* (pp. 120–130). Philadelphia, PA: Philadelphia Association of Psychoanalysis.

Marcus, I. (2004). *Why Men Have Affairs: Understanding the Hidden Motives of Infidelity.* New Orleans, LA: Bon Temps.

Marcus, I., & Frances, J. (1975). *Masturbation from Infancy to Senescence.* New York: International Universities Press.

Marcus, P. (2013). On the quiet virtue of humility. In: *In Search of the Spiritual: Gabriel Marcel, Psychoanalysis, and the Sacred* (pp. 89–110). London: Karnac.

Maslow, A. (1943). *A Theory of Human Motivation.* Washington, DC: Midwest Journal Press, 2016.

McWilliams, N. (2011). *Psychoanalytic Diagnosis, 2nd Edition.* New York: Guilford.

Menninger, W. C. (1943). Characterologic and symptomatic expressions related to the anal phase of psychosexual development. *Psychoanalytic Quarterly, 12*: 161–193.

Merriam-Webster Dictionary Online. www.merriam-webster.com/dictionary. Accessed February 20, 2017.

Menon, R. (2003). *The Ramayana: A Modern Translation.* Noida, India: HarperCollins, 2016.

Millon, T., Millon, C., Meagher, S. E., Grossman, S. E., & Ramnath, R. (2000). *Personality Disorders in Modern Life.* Hoboken, NJ: John Wiley & Sons.

Mish, F. (1987). *Webster's Ninth New Collegiate Dictionary*. Springfield, MA: Meriam-Webster Inc Publishers.

Mish, F. C. (Ed.) (1998). *Merriam-Webster's Collegiate Dictionary (10th Edition)*. Springfield, MA: Merriam-Webster.

Mitchell, A. (1984). Individuality and hubris in mythology: the struggle to be human. *American Journal of Psychoanalysis, 44*: 399–412.

Moore, M. (2009). *Wa*: harmony and sustenance of the self in Japanese life. In: S. Akhtar (Ed.), *Freud and the Far East: Psychoanalytic Perspectives on the People and Culture of China, Japan, and Korea* (pp. 79–88). Lanham, MD: Jason Aronson.

Murphy, S. C., von Hippel, W., Dubbs, S. L., Angilletta Jr., M. J., Wilson, R. S., Trivers, R., & Barlow, F. K. (2015). The role of overconfidence and romantic desirability and competition. *Personality and Social Psychology Bulletin, 41*: 1036–1052.

Niederle, M., & Vesterlund, L. (2007). Do women shy away from competition? Do men compete too much? *Quarterly Journal of Economics, 122*: 1067–1101.

Novick, K.K., & Novick, J. (2014). Psychoanalysis and child rearing. *Psychoanalytic Inquiry, 34*: 440–451.

Nunberg, H. G. (1979). Narcissistic personality disorder: diagnosis. *Weekly Psychiatry Update Series 3*: Lesson 17.

Ogden, T. H. (1995). Analysing forms of aliveness and deadness of the transference-countertransference. *International Journal of Psychoanalysis, 76*: 695–709.

Ogden, T. H. (2008). *Rediscovering Psychoanalysis: Thinking and Dreaming, Learning and Forgetting*. New York: Routledge.

Olden, C. (1941). About the fascinating effect of the narcissistic personality. *American Imago, 2*: 347–355.

Ostow, M. (2001). Three archaic contributions to the religious instinct: awe, mysticism, and apocalypse. In: S. Akhtar & H. Parens (Eds.), *Does God Help: Developmental and Clinical Aspects of Religious Belief* (pp. 197–233). Northvale, NJ: Jason Aronson.

Ou, A. Y., Waldman, D. A., & Peterson, S. J. (2015). Do humble CEOs matter? An examination of CEO humility and firm outcomes. *Journal of Management*, September 21.

Owen, D., & Davidson, J. (2009). Hubris syndrome: an acquired personality disorder? A study of US presidents and UK prime ministers over the last 100 years. *Brain, 132*: 1396–1406.

Oxford Dictionary. Oxford: Oxford University Press. https://en.oxforddictionaries.com. Accessed October 9, 2017.

Paret, I. H., & Shapiro, V. B. (1998). The splintered holding environment and the vulnerable ego: a case study. *Psychoanalytic Study of the Child, 53*: 300–324.

Patricola, Miss, and the Virginians (1922). *Runnin' Wild*. RCA Victor, under the direction of R. Gorman. https://www.youtube.com/watch?v=9aM2pzCr6xI. Accessed August 15, 2017.

Parsons, M. (2000). *The Dove that Returns, the Dove that Vanishes: Paradox and Creativity in Psychoanalysis*. London: Routledge.

Pavlidis, I., Eberhardt, N. L., & Levine, J. A. (2002). Seeing through the face of deception: thermal imaging offers a promising hands-off approach to mass security screening. *Nature, 415*: 35.

Phillips, A. (2002). *Equals*. New York: Basic Books.

Pine, F. (1988). The four psychologies of psychoanalysis and their place in clinical work. *Journal of the American Psychoanalytic Association, 36*: 571–596.

Plato (c. 380 BC). *The Republic*. London: Penguin, 1987.

Poland, W. S. (2013). The analyst's approach and the patient's psychic growth. *Psychoanalytic Quarterly*, *82*: 829–847.

Pullman, P. (2010). *The Good Man Jesus and the Scoundrel Christ*. New Delhi: Penguin.

Pulver, S. E. (1970). Narcissism – the term and the concept. *Journal of the American Psychoanalytic Association*, *18*: 319–341.

Ramanujan, A. K. (1999). *The Collected Essays of A. K. Ramanujan*. New Delhi: Oxford University Press.

Rand, A. (1957). *Atlas Shrugged*. New York: Random House.

Rappaport, D. (1960). The structure of psychoanalytic theory. *Psychological Issues*, *6*: 39–72.

Rappaport, E. A. (1956). The management of an erotized transference. *Psychoanalytic Quarterly*, *25*: 515–529.

Reaney, L. T., Milner, R. N. C., Detto, T., & Backwell, P. R. Y. (2008). The effects of claw regeneration on territory ownership and mating success in the fiddler crab *uca mjoebergi*. *Animal Behavior*, *75*: 1473–1478.

Reich, W. (1933). *Character Analysis*. V. R. Carfagno (Trans.). New York: Farrar, Straus and Giroux, 1972.

Richards, A. (2003). Psychoanalytic discourse at the turn of our century: a plea for a measure of humility. *Journal of the American Psychoanalytic Association*, *51S*: 73–89.

Roland, A. (1988). *In Search of Self in India and Japan*. Princeton, NJ: Princeton University Press.

Roland, A. (1996). *Cultural Pluralism and Psychoanalysis: The Asian and North-American Experience*. New York: Routledge.

Roland, A. (2011). *Journeys to Foreign Selves: Asians and Asian Americans in a Global Era*. New Delhi: Oxford University Press.

Rosenman, R., Brand, R., Sholtz, R., & Friedman, M. (1976). Multivariate prediction of coronary heart disease during 8.5 year follow-up in the Western Collaborative Group Study. *American Journal of Cardiology*, *37*: 903–910.

Rostbøll, C. F. (2009). Autonomy, respect, and, arrogance in the Danish cartoon controversy. *Political Theory*, *3*: 623–648.

Rubin, J. (2005). Psychoanalytic and Buddhist history and theory. In: S. Akhtar (Ed.), *Freud Along the Ganges: Psychoanalytic Reflections on the People and Culture of India* (pp. 335–358). New York: Other Press.

Russell, R. (2000). *The Famous Ghalib*. New Delhi, India: Roli.

Sacks, J. (2017). On humility. *www.chabad.org/library-article*. Accessed on June 23, 2017.

Sartre, J.-P. (1946). *No Exit and Three Other Plays*. New York: Vintage International, 1989.

Schechter, R. A. (1997). The influence of Jewish culture on psychotherapy. In: P. Elovitz & C. Kahn (Eds.), *Immigrant Experiences: Personal Narratives and Psychological Analysis* (pp. 185–194). Cranbury, NJ: Associated University Press.

Schlenker, B. R., & Leary, M. R. (1982). Audiences' reactions to self-enhancing, self-denigrating, and accurate self-presentations. *Journal of Experimental and Social Psychology*, *18*: 89–104.

Schlesinger, H. (1995). The process of interpretation and the moment of change. *Journal of the American Psychoanalytic Association*, *43*: 663–688.

Schmitt, D. P., & Buss, D. M. (1996). Strategic self-promotion and competitor derogation: sex and context effects on the perceived effectiveness of mate attraction tactics. *Interpersonal Relations and Group Process*, *70*: 1185–1204.

Schwardmann, P., & van der Weele, J. (2016). Deception and self-deception. Tinbergen Institute Discussion Paper, University of Amsterdam, the Netherlands.

Searles, H. F. (1960). *The Non-Human Environment in Normal Development and in Schizophrenia*. New York: International Universities Press.

Sen, M. L. (1976). *The Ramayana of Valmiki*. New Delhi: Munshiram Manoharlal, 1997.

Shah, A. (2015). The cultural faces of shame. In: S. Akhtar (Ed.), *Shame: Developmental, Cultural and Clinical Realms* (pp. 49–70). London: Karnac.

Shah, A. (2017). Regret on screen and regret as a screen. In: S. Akhtar & S. Siassi (Eds.), *Regret: Developmental, Cultural and Clinical Realms* (pp. 109–135). London: Karnac.

Shakespeare, W. (1606). *King Lear*. San Francisco, CA: Ignatius, 2008.

Shapiro, D. (1965). *Neurotic Styles*. New York: Basic Books.

Shashtri, H. P. (1959). *The Ramayana of Valmiki*. London: Shanti Sadan, 1992.

Shorter, E. (1997). *A History of Psychiatry: From the Era of the Asylum to the Age of Prozac*. New York: Wiley & Sons.

Shorter Oxford English Dictionary (2008). www.mobisystems.com. Accessed August 16, 2017.

Simons, R. C. (2003). The lawsuit revisited. *Journal of the American Psychoanalytic Association, 51S*: 247–271.

Singh, D., & Young, R. (1995). Body weight, waist-to-hip ratio, breasts, and hips: role in judgments of female attractiveness and desirability for relationships. *Ethology and Sociobiology, 16*: 483–507.

Slade, A. (1998). Representation, symbolization, and affect regulation in the concomitant treatment of a mother and child: attachment theory and child psychotherapy. *Psychoanalytic Dialogues, 8*: 797–830.

Smith, M. B. (2005). *Toward the Outside: Concepts and Themes in Emmanuel Levinas*. Pittsburgh, PA: Duquesne University Press.

Some Like It Hot (1959). "Running Wild" scene with Marilyn Monroe. https://www. youtube.com/watch?v=5At3UCMQSiw. Accessed July 8, 2017.

Steiner, J. (2011). *Seeing and Being Seen: Emerging from a Psychic Retreat*. New York: Routledge.

Stern, D. B. (1985). *The Interpersonal World of the Infant*. New York: Basic Books.

Stern, D. B. (2015). *Relational Freedom: Emergent Properties of the Interpersonal Field*. New York: Routledge.

Stinson, F. S., Dawson, D. A., Goldstein, R. B., Chou, S. P., Huang, B., Smith, S. M., Ruan, W. J., Pulay, A. J., Saha, T. D., & Grat, B. F. (2008). Prevalence, correlates, disability, and comorbidity of DSM-IV neurotic: results of the wave to national epidemiological survey on alcohol and related conditions. *Journal of Clinical Psychiatry, 69*: 1033–1045.

Streeter, L. A., Krauss, R. M., Geller, V., Olson, C., & Apple, W. (1977). Pitch changes during attempted deception. *Journal of Personality and Social Psychology, 35*: 345–350.

Sulloway, F. (2006). Why Darwin rejected intelligent design. In: J. Brockman (Ed.), *Intelligent Thought: Science versus the Intelligent Design Movement* (pp. 107–125). New York: Vintage.

Sulloway, F. (2009). Why Darwin rejected intelligent design. *Journal of Biosciences, 34*: 173–183.

Target, M., & Fonagy, P. (1996). Playing with reality, II: the development of psychic reality from a theoretical perspective. *International Journal of Psychoanalysis, 77*: 459–479.

Tennyson, A. (1859). Tithonus. In: S. Ricker (Ed.), *Selected Poems*. New York: Penguin Books, 2007.

Tervalon, M., & Murray-Garcia, J. (1998). Cultural humility versus cultural competence: a critical distinction in defining physician training outcomes in multicultural education. *Journal of Health Care for the Poor and the Underserved, 9*: 117–125.

Thoma, H., & Kachele, H. (1994). *Psychoanalytic Practice, Volume 2: Clinical Studies*. Northvale, NJ: Jason Aronson.

Thomas, A., & Chess, S. (1984). Genesis and evolution of behavioral disorders: from infancy to early adult life. *American Journal of Psychiatry, 141*: 1–9.

Thoreau, H. D. (1854). *Walden, or Life in the Woods*. New York: CreateSpace Independent Publishing Platform, 2015.

Tice, D. M., Butler, J. L., Muraven, M. B., & Stillwell, A. M. (1995). When modesty prevails: differential favorability of self-presentation to friends and strangers. *Journal of Personality and Social Psychology, 69*: 1120–1138.

Ticho, E. (1972). The development of superego autonomy. *Psychoanalytic Review, 59*: 217–233.

Tooby, J. (2002). Review of "The Power of Place: Volume II of a Biography", by Janet Browne. *New York Times Review of Books*, October 6.

Trivers, R. (1972). Parental investment and sexual selection. In: B. Campbell (Ed.), *Sexual Selection and the Descent of Man, 1871–1971* (pp. 136–179). Chicago, IL: Aldine.

Trivers, R. (2011). *Folly of Fools: The Logic of Deceit and Self-Deception in Human Life*. New York: Basic Books.

Tsugawa, Y., Jena, A. B., Figueroa, J. F., Orav, E. J., Blumenthal, D. M., & Jha, A. K. (2016). Comparison of hospital mortality and readmission rates for Medicare patients treated by male vs. female physicians. *JAMA Internal Medicine, 177*: 206–213.

Tucker, S. R. (2016). *Pride and Humility: A New Interdisciplinary Analysis*. London: Palgrave Macmillan.

Twenge, J. M., & Campbell, W. K. (2009). *The Narcissism Epidemic: Living in the Age of Entitlement*. New York: Free Press.

Vaknin, S. (2014). *Narcissistic Personality Disorder (NPD): The Facts*. Skopje, Macedonia: Narcissus.

Van Tongeren, D. R., & Myers, D. G. (2017). A social psychological perspective on humility. In: E. L. Worthington Jr., D. E. Davis, & J. N. Hook (Eds.), *Handbook of Humility: Theory, Research, and Applications* (pp. 214–237). New York: Routledge.

Viorst, M. (2016). *Zionism: The Birth and Transformation of an Ideal*. New York: Thomas Dunne.

Vocal Majority (1994). *Running Wild*. Pittsburgh SPEBSQSA competition. https://www.youtube.com/watch?v=IyTylK-WTjI. Accessed July 8, 2017.

Volkan, V. (1981). *Linking Objects and Linking Phenomena*. New York: International Universities Press.

Volkan, V. (2010). *Psychoanalytic Technique Expanded: A Textbook on Psychoanalytic Treatment*. London: Open Access.

Waelder, R. (1936). The principle of multiple function: observations on multiple determination. *Psychoanalytic Quarterly, 41*: 283–290.

Walter, C. (2013). *Last Ape Standing: The Seven-Million-Year Story of How and Why We Survived*. New York: Walker.

Weber, S. L. (2006). Doubt, arrogance, and humility. *Contemporary Psychoanalysis, 42*: 213–223.

Wegner, D. M. (2009). How to think, say, or do precisely the worst thing for any occasion, *Science, 325*: 48–50.

Weiss, S. (1987). The two-woman phenomenon. *Psychoanalytic Quarterly, 56*: 271–286.

Werman, D. (1979). Methodological problem in the psychoanalytic interpretation of literature: a review of studies on Sophocles' Antigone. *Journal of the American Psychoanalytic Association, 27*: 451–478.

Whitfield, C. L., Whitfield, B. H., Park, R., & Prevatt, J. (2006). *The Power of Humility*. Deerfield Beach, FL: Health Communications.

Whitman, W. (1855). The song of myself. In: *Leaves of Grass* (pp. 1–8). Brooklyn, NY: The Rome Brothers.

Willett, C. (2001). *The Soul of Justice: Social Bonds and Racial Hubris*. New York: Cornell University Press.

Williams, P. (2016). *Humility: The Secret Ingredient of Success*. Uhrichsville, OH: Shiloh Run.

Winnicott, D. W. (1949). Hate in the counter-transference. *International Journal of Psychoanalysis, 30*: 69–74.

Winnicott, D. W. (1956). The antisocial tendency. In: *Collected Papers: Through Paediatrics to Psychoanalysis* (pp. 306–316). New York: Basic Books, 1958.

Winnicott, D. W. (1960). The theory of the parent-infant relationship. *International Journal of Psychoanalysis, 41*: 585–595.

Winnicott, D. W. (1965). A clinical study of the effect of a failure of the average expectable environment on a child's mental functioning. *International Journal of Psychoanalysis, 46*: 81–87.

Worthington, Jr., E. L. (2007). *Humility: The Quiet Virtue*. Philadelphia, PA: Templeton Foundation.

Worthington, Jr., E. L., Davis, D. E., & Hook, J. N. (Eds.) (2017). *Handbook of Humility: Theory, Research, and Applications*. New York: Routledge.

Wosinska, W., Dabul, A. J., Whetstone-Dion, R., & Cialdini, R. B. (1996). Self-presentational responses to success in the organization: the costs and benefits of modesty. *Basic and Applied Social Psychology, 18*: 229–242.

Wright, E. (1992). *Feminism and Psychoanalysis. A Critical Dictionary*. Oxford: Blackwell.

Wurmser, L. (2015). Primary shame, mortal wound and tragic circularity: some new reflections on shame and shame conflicts. *International Journal of Psychoanalysis, 96*: 1615–1634.

Zetzel, E. (1956). Current concepts of transference. *International Journal of Psychoanalysis, 37*: 369–375.

Zhang, H., Ou, A. Y., Tsuic, A. S., & Wang, H. (2017). CEO humility, narcissism and firm innovation: a paradox perspective on CEO traits. *Leadership Quarterly, 28*: 585–604.

Zimmer, C. (2008). You want a piece of this? (Please please please don't take a piece of this!). *The Loom*. http://blogs.discovermagazine.com/loom/2008/. Accessed March 31, 2017.

Zimmer, C. (2013). Arrogance and surprise in psychoanalytic process. *Psychoanalytic Quarterly, 82*: 393–412.

Zingrone, W. (2016). *The Arrogance of Religious Thought: Information Kills Religion*. Raleigh, NC: Lulu.

Index

For Product Safety Concerns and Information please contact our EU
representative GPSR@taylorandfrancis.com
Taylor & Francis Verlag GmbH, Kaufingerstraße 24, 80331 München, Germany

www.ingramcontent.com/pod-product-compliance
Lightning Source LLC
Chambersburg PA
CBHW070331270326
41926CB00017B/3835

9 7 8 1 7 8 2 2 0 6 6 6 8